*¡ Growing
DAILY...!*

Somethg new...

———————————Celebrate Mid-Life———————————

——Celebrate Mid-Life——

Jungian Archetypes
and
Mid-Life Spirituality

Janice Brewi and Anne Brennan

CROSSROAD • NEW YORK

1989

The Crossroad Publishing Company
370 Lexington Avenue, New York, N.Y. 10017

Printed in the United States of America

Library of Congress Cataloging in Publication Data

Brewi, Janice.
  Celebrate mid-life.

  Bibliography: p.
  1. Middle age—Psychological aspects.   2. Archetype
(Psychology)   I. Brennan, Anne.   II. Title.
BF724.6.B75   1988   155.6   87-20178
ISBN 0-8245-0853-X
ISBN 0-8245-0953-6 (pbk)

ACKNOWLEDGMENTS

Grateful acknowledgment is made to Pantheon Books, a division
of Random House, Inc., for permission to reprint excerpts from
Memories, Dreams, Reflections by C. G. Jung, recorded and edited by
Aniela Jaffe and translated by Richard and Clara Winston.
Copyright © 1961, 1962, 1963 by Random House, Inc.

To our mid-life sisters and brothers

Kathy, Michael, Patsy, John, Kay, Jim,
Elaine, Maureen, Tom, Eileen, and Kevin

Claire, Michael, Grace Mary, Bill, Rita,
Edward, Barbara, and Donald

Contents

Introduction

Mid-life crisis is not a luxury of the affluent; it is an inevitable part of everyone's life. Just like all the other developmental stages of the life cycle, mid-life erupts in us unbidden. Just as the child leaves the womb and the young adult leaves childhood, the adult is thrust into a mid-life crisis-transition. Like any aspect of human development the experience can be nurtured and celebrated or denied and aborted. In the stage pattern of the life cycle, mid-life is as archetypal as gestation, the "terrible twos," the adolescent crisis-transition, or dying.

This book, *Celebrate Mid-Life*, celebrates the mid-life experience as an essential element of the human journey and a gift to the flowering of the human personality. *Celebrate Mid-Life* also celebrates the first decade of Mid-Life Directions, a ministry of workshops, seminars, and retreats that we began in 1978 and have expanded in our training programs for Mid-Life Directions Consultants.

The four parts of this book flow out of the ongoing experience we have had with almost twenty thousand people in our programs. Four archetypal experiences—mid-life itself, the Shadow, the Child, and Wisdom—are described in these pages. They are fleshed out here in the stories (disguised to protect privacy) of some of those thousands of people.

These four archetypal experiences are foundational to a mid-life transition and to the period of mid-life itself. This archetypal perspective on human psychological development is the contribution of Carl Gustav Jung (1875–1961). Jung has been called the father of adult developmental psychology. His psychology is largely a second-half-of-life psychology. We have found that the terms he uses to discuss mid-life experiences resonate strongly in mid-life adults. Used in conjunction with the long tradition of Western spirituality, his psychology not only sheds light on the experiences of mid-life people but touches psychic depths within them, moving them to new hope, enthusiasm, and direction for living mid-life to the full.

This archetypal perspective on the human life cycle itself is a major thesis of this book. It supports the theory of broad predictable life stages or phases with their physical, psychological, and spiritual dimensions without locking anyone into how these inner developmental changes will be fleshed out in cultural contexts, life styles, or behaviors. These stages are only relatively chronological. In this framework, mid-life is an experience of new birth to be celebrated. The mid-life crisis then is: Will I or will I not allow these new areas of myself to creatively emerge moving me toward my individuation, spiritual maturity, and unique contribution to the human race?

A primary task of mid-life adults is to come to terms with their Shadows. "Shadow personality" is the term we use for dormant aspects of the personality. Unfamiliar, unknown, sometimes threatening, sometimes exhilarating experiences of oneself surprise the mid-life person. A whole other side of one's personality begins to be felt. To close off or deny these experiences is to become stuck, rigid, one-sided, closed. It is to die at forty and not get buried until ninety. To embrace these experiences too enthusiastically, however, is to throw off and demolish all that has been built in the first half of life. It is to regress, vainly trying to hold on to youth. Integration and individuation require bearing the tension until these apparently irreconcilable opposites come together in one.

One's inner Child and inbuilt Wisdom are keys to transforming mid-life Shadow experiences into the fullness of life. The Child leads the adult into newness without allowing one's beginnings to get lost. The Child keeps wonder and awe and risk alive in the face of the mid-life loss of naiveté and the threat of cynicism as one ages.

Wisdom is the fruit of living. It integrates within us the joys, sorrows, glories, mediocrity, and even the evil of a lifetime. Yet Wisdom is there at the beginning. It is the spark of God that each of us is and is becoming. It goes before and breaks through and consumes into life all the dyings of a lifetime.

Wisdom within leads us into our own futures, our own whole-ness.

Each person's spirituality is unique to the person since each lives out the image of God that she or he is. Yet, that spirituality is contextualized in different life stages. What is appropriate spirituality and rich pasture in youth may become at mid-life a lie and a poison. Recognizing the archetypal dimensions of human life, our commonalities help each of us to nurture and support growth into the uniqueness that is our own.

Jung saw other important archetypes emerging in us at mid-life: animus (the masculine in woman) and anima (the feminine in man). In this book, we have subsumed this polarity somewhat in the discussion of the Shadow, the Child, and Wisdom. The whole question is an enormous and conflictual one at this time in our culture and would require a larger study than this small work. We hope in the future to address it.

This book is addressed to people in Mid-life who are strug-gling to understand, name, and grow through a new experi-ence of themselves as they live into and out what must be called "the second half of life." In 1900 the average life expectancy for people in the United States and in Japan was the early forties. Now that average life expectancy is close to eighty. The first world has seen a dramatic doubling of the life cycle. The fact that at the same time, many people on the earth are denied basic necessities and consequently a "second half of life" under-lines the terrible inequalities and injustices on our planet and raises significant questions about the human quality of life of those who have been given this gift of years. Ideally, perhaps the fullness of years should mean the fullness of life and love. Thus, such spiritual growth and riches could have significant impact on these larger world questions, not only of human justice but of the survival of the planet. To these ends it seems, not only individually but socially and culturally crucial that serious consideration be given to the meaning and spiritual growth questions raised by this significant development of human life expectancy.

It is the hated and despised parts of ourselves, our Shadows, that we project on our enemies. It is national Shadows that get projected on international enemies. Jung once warned that whether or not there would be a nuclear holocaust was profoundly dependent on how many people in the second half of their lives were creatively able to bear and integrate this tension of opposites within themselves. The Child within will lead us to this growth in wisdom, age, and grace that could save our earth.

Although the parts of this book were written by the person named, the layers of authoring preceding the writing were shared by both.

We are profoundly grateful to those who led to the production of this book: our families, community, and friends. We are grateful to the places and the individuals who have sponsored our programs as well as the women and men in every Mid-Life Directions program and our Mid-Life Directions Consultants. In a special way we are grateful to Dr. Roy Fairchild of San Francisco Theological Seminary for his valued advice and to Dr. Joanmarie Smith, C.S.J., who saw this manuscript through all its stages. We are grateful to Crossroad who supported our frontier ministry to mid-life adults by publishing *Mid-Life: Psychological and Spiritual Perspectives* in 1982. That book elaborates the psychological and theological underpinnings of our ministry, of our book *Mid-Life Directions: Praying and Playing Sources of New Dynamism* (Paulist, 1985), and of this present book.

PART I

The Wonder of the Life Cycle:
The Life Cycle As Archetypal

by Janice Brewi

1

Emergence of Mid-Life: Mid-Life as Archetypal

Alice came into the meeting room on the first night of the mid-life workshop and walked right up to talk to me. She had arrived with her husband and they made an elegant couple. "I don't know why we came," Alice said,

> I said to John on the way in, why are we doing this anyway? What can we get out of this kind of weekend workshop? Our life together has been so great that anything good that can happen to us after this is just going to be icing on the cake.

I was glad to know that there was such a happily married couple in the group. As I looked at Alice I suspected that she was in her early forties at most (later I found out she was forty-four and that they had just celebrated their twenty-fifth wedding anniversary). I quickly did some arithmetic and realized that if she lived to be ninety, it would mean forty-five years of icing! Without knowing it, Alice had made a terribly negative remark about her present and her future.

What Alice really meant was that the real living is over, all the "real stuff" is finished, all the important things have been done, anything good that can happen to them after this will be just a little trimming, "just icing on the cake." And in their case, what was all that real living? They had found each other, had created a life together, worked hard at everything, remained faithful, and grew—all of it no small accomplishment. They had had a family right away (as did many couples who married when they did), gave their time and energy to raise their children, and now those young adults were moving out, somewhat normal and well prepared. They had been successful in their parenting. Together Alice and John had built his career. Because of John's creativity, ingenuity, and steadfastness—and because of Alice's support, encouragement, and sacrifice—they had made it socially and economically, he professionally. "All the real living has been accomplished." Is it possible that this young forty-four-year-old woman is finished? That all her real living, creativity, growing, and generativity has been accomplished? Does the "icing" Alice anticipates represent an unconscious fear that there is nothing left to do, to become?

In a real sense she is stuck at this moment. She is identifying herself with all that she has accomplished in her forty-four years. She is equating herself with what she has come to know about herself, with her hard-found and hard-earned identity. Alice and John are comparatively successful at this moment. Their choice of vocation, relationship, commitment, profession, parenthood, social setting, moral standards, religious affiliation, economic standards, and much more have all created and defined their joint life in the last twenty-five years. Is there anything else for this man and woman? What could happen to Alice and John in the months ahead to make them aware that there is so much more to each of them then they can ever realize, that far from ending their lives they are just beginning, that there will come a time when they will celebrate mid-life?

Many adults have this woman's tendency to identify with and to hold on to the image of who they have become in youth. That image is connected to one's primary relationships, physical appearance, roles, careers, social and cultural setting, and so on. Indeed, who is one without them? Yet questions remain deep within: Who am I really? Who have I been in the process of becoming in these forty years?

The Season of Discontent

Roger came to a mid-life workshop for the second time. He came searching, he said, for answers, but didn't know what his questions were. He didn't know what he was searching for. On this occasion, participants had been asked to bring to the workshop a symbol of themselves, something that represented themselves at this time in life. "Ten, perhaps even five, years ago,"

Roger began, "I was close to my wife, my children, and my God. Right now I don't feel close to any of them." Roger went on,

> I don't want to brag, but I own three homes. The one here, a chalet in a ski resort, and a summer home. I can give my family anything they want. I am the vice-president of my corporation. But somehow I have this strange feeling: I know I am not close to God any longer, or to my wife and children. I could not find anything to represent me, so I just brought along this little bottle of men's cologne.

Roger passed the bottle and it moved from one person's hand to the next. He knew he didn't feel close to anyone, but did he suspect that the cologne symbolized how much he wanted to draw people to himself? Because he had been energetic, creative, and successful he could give his family anything that money could buy. But now there was another whole side of him to be developed. Roger was successful in what he had set out to do; but future growth was going to call forth other dimensions of himself. The perfume represented that relational side from which he was estranged; it was very much like a cartoon I found with one fifty-year-old saying to another, "I've learned a lot in the past thirty-five years. Unfortunately it's all about petroleum."

Not all adults find difficulty in letting go of "their petroleum," of their familiar images of themselves and their set ways. But some personalities have the opposite problem. In contacting new dimensions, images, and experiences of themselves, they become completely alienated from their past, see nothing good in it, and lose all sense of continuity.

Ellen had been divorced after twenty years of marriage. Ellen and her first husband had both been chemistry teachers in two different colleges in a large city. Ellen and Hank were compatible and there had never been any significant difficulties. They had two children. With the first child Ellen had taken a year's leave of absence. They planned their second child around Hank's sabbatical. Friends and family admired both of them. No one could explain what happened.

During their marriage Ellen went for some career counseling. She wanted to discern whether she should give up her tenure and take a position she had been offered in a chemical corporation. What started out as a small issue turned into months of counseling.

Ellen was attracted to the counselor from the start. She looked forward to the session every week and found it gave her life. He was very different from other men she had encountered. Soon the sessions moved from the office to different spots around the city, and increased to two or three times a week. In these rendezvous Ellen was contacting a whole side of herself that she had never known. Without any warning, Ellen filed for divorce from Hank thirteen months later and gave him custody of the children. She became the career counselor's third wife, for five years. He then left her to marry again.

There is a common thread in the lives of Alice, Roger, and Ellen. All three are having common mid-life experiences. Alice and Roger are at early stages of the mid-life experience. Both have reached a certain level of fulfillment and lack awareness and imagination about the possibilities in the years ahead. They had had a script for the past twenty-five years telling each of them what to do next: basic education, graduate school, careers, romance, marriage, home, children, social life, and so much more. What should the next twenty-five years be about?

Alice is happy with all of it and imagining that her contentment will remain. The agonizing question What am I, what are we, to do next? has not yet made its way into her heart. Alice is in touch with a pseudowholeness. Perhaps the thought of beginning again, of being in a new position, of having the future so open, is too threatening to her.

Roger is at a different stage. Already he senses that something is wrong. It is this feeling that he is paying attention to. In a sense he is asking, What is this telling me, where is this leading me? Roger feels there is something missing in all his primary relationships and this is opening him to whole other areas of potential in himself. He is asking, What have I neglected? How can I change? What should I change? He had no desire to pour himself into another career: work, job, career, had lost their all-consuming attraction. Something deeper but unknown was calling.

Ellen had gone to a career counselor for what she thought was a simple discernment about career. But underneath a career question was a fear of joyless routine in being Ellen: Hank's wife, chemistry teacher, mother of two, forever and ever. Ellen was frightened of this new experience of not being happy, content, confident, and thoroughly reliable. It was all so new and unexpected. She didn't suspect it was telling her that it was time to explore other ways of being Ellen. How to be Ellen in continuity with her past, her genuine relationships, and to ✓ still become *new* was unimaginable to her.

Being swept into a romance and a new experience of herself gave Ellen a sense of being saved from the dark feelings she had begun to experience so suddenly. Only this new Ellen gave her a feeling of aliveness and safety. Ellen chose that newness and alienated herself from whole parts of herself; Hank, with whom she had always had a basically good relationship, and her children, Amy and Joe.

Yet the contacting of new dimensions of self does not have to lead to such a shipwreck. It can lead to growth and development for oneself and others. It can and should be the opportunity to become a richer, deeper self.

Thomas Merton and the Pattern of Mid-Life

Thomas Merton entered a Trappist monastery in Kentucky at the age of twenty-six, on December 10, 1941. In 1948 his world-famous autobiography, *The Seven Storey Mountain,* was published. Only five years after that publication, we find signs in his thirty-eighth year of the early mid-life experience of changing self-image in his book *The Sign of Jonas.*

> It is sometime in June. At a rough guess, I think it is June 13 which may or may not be the feast of St. Anthony of Padua. In any case every day is the same for me because I have become very different from what I used to be. The man who began this journal is dead, just as the man who finished *The Seven Storey Mountain* when this journal began was also dead, and what is more the man who was the central figure in *The Seven Storey Mountain* was dead over and over. And now that all these men are dead, it is sufficient for me to say so on paper and I think I will have ended up by forgetting them. Because writing down what *The Seven Storey Mountain* was about was sufficient to get it off my mind for good. Last week

> I corrected the proofs of the French translation of the book and it seemed completely alien. I might as well have been a proofreader working for a publisher and going over the galleys of somebody else's book. Consequently, *The Seven Storey Mountain* is the work of a man I never even heard of. And this journal is getting to be the production of somebody to whom I have never had the dishonor of an introduction. (328)

At another time Merton declared that he was embarrassed by *The Seven Storey Mountain,* in a sense disowning the young, thoroughly modern, enthusiastic, reformed, idealistic monk whose ego strength enabled him to leave everything for solitude and God. For Merton, being for God demanded being continually true to himself and the revelation going on in him. It had been that quality of response that brought him to the Monastery of Our Lady of Gethsemani in the first place. In his forties he was coming to realize that following God, being for God, demanded a different kind of involvement in the pain and suffering of this moment in history. He was being called to be, among other things, a living critique and an effective example of nonviolent protest on many levels, and to find a way to be a monk in the midst of activity and so-called worldliness. In fact it was the profound religious experience of "worldliness" that first shattered that early self-image of Father Louis, as Merton was called in Gethsemani. On March 19, 1958, almost two months after his forty-third birthday, he wrote in his personal journal of an experience he had on a rare occasion of being outside the monastery. We hear echoes here of another level of mid-life awakening:

> Yesterday, in Louisville, at the corner of Fourth and Walnut, I suddenly realized that I loved all the people and that none of them were, or could be, totally alien to me. As if waking from a dream—the dream of my separateness, of my "special" vocation to be different. My vocation does not really make me different from the rest of men [and women] or just one in a special category, except artificially, juridically. I am still a member of the human race—and what more glorious destiny is there for man [or woman], since the Word was made flesh and became, too, a member of the human race. (Mott:311)

Both *The Sign of Jonas* and the "vision at Louisville" are testaments to Merton's expanding consciousness. The vision at Louisville changed Merton's life. It was for him an epiphany that became a turning point. Because of that religious experience Merton underwent a major mutation in his images of himself as a monk, of his God, and of humanity itself. Religious experiences are those moments in a person's life that are memorable, that become the sources of decisions, and that help a person to know more about who they really are. At forty-three, this mid-lifer was discovering anew who he really was. This inner and outer event was evoking in him the archetypal experience of mid-life.

A little more than a year after the "vision at Louisville" Merton continued his mid-life saga and in his personal journal recorded his total disillusionment that would pave the way for further new dimensions. Under the date June 11, 1959, he writes,

> What I find intolerable and degrading is having to submit, in practice, to Don James' idea of himself and of Gethsemani and to have to spend my life contributing to the maintenance of this illusion. The illusion of the great, gay, joyous, peppy, optimistic, Jesus loving, one hundred percent American Trappist monastery. Is it possible to be here and not to be plunged into the midst of this falsity? (Mott:330)

The movement in Thomas Merton's soul depicted here in his writings reverberates in the psyche of all mid-lifers. A twenty-year-old reader of Merton, whether in 1953 or today, can no more identify nor comprehend the full significance, angst, and poignancy of what this thirty-eight to forty-four-year-old was experiencing than a four-year-old boy can understand the sexual awakening of his fourteen-year-old brother. It is only when the archetypal experience arises in us that we are able to understand and say, "Oh, that is what they meant."

As they approach mid-life many people have the experience of disorientation and its accompanying crisis in feelings of

> lethargy, apathy, monotony, indifference, frigidity, uncertainty, listlessness, dawdling over tasks, loss of interest in

things that were once of vital concern; going through the
motions, boredom—these are familiar constellations of crisis
feelings. (Brewi and Brennan:35)

Another structural characteristic of this early phase of mid-
life is

regret, anger, self-doubt, doubt about all relationships and
commitments, religious doubt, anxiety, threat; feeling imprisoned, trapped, desperate, hopeless, tortured, hemmed in,
restless, dissatisfied, morose, melancholy, nauseous, despair-
ing and fearful. (Brewi and Brennan:39)

Moments of disillusionment, dark nights of the soul as well as
new awakenings, expanded horizons, liminal periods, and turning points are all ingredients of the mid-life crisis-transition
time. Being stuck, feeling that "anything good that can happen
to us after this is just icing on the cake," is going to turn into
restlessness, boredom, and discontent before it matures hope-
fully into new dimensions of self and inner and outer transformation. "It is from need and distress that new forms of life take
their rise, and not from mere wishes or from the requirements
of our ideals" (Jung, *Modern Man in Search of a Soul:*217).

The last decade of his life, before his early death, was filled
with personal and spiritual growth and original contributions
to the world for which he will long be remembered. Because he
was faithful to the revelation going on in him, he became not
only a unique personality, an individual, but he became a paradigmatic person of our twentieth and twenty-first centuries—
despite the fact that he called himself a "fourteenth-century
man" (Mott:362). Bridging the gap from youth into mid-life
can do that for us. As we become integrated, we can integrate
the centuries within ourselves.

Once one makes the psychic mid-life transition oneself, once
one begins the arduous adventure of individuation, one has the
possibility of becoming a "mana personality" for others. A mana
personality is someone who puts us in contact with our own
living spirit, our own psychic depths. A mana personality is
someone who releases our inner potential, putting us in contact
with our own uniqueness and truth and empowering us to be
true to Self and a leaven to others. The universal popularity of

Merton shows that he resonated in others. Indeed, he was a fourteenth- as well as a twenty-first century person. That is what each of us is called to be as we mature.

The archetypal patterns found in our depths, as they were found in the depths of those people in the centuries before us, can give us the psychic energy to live creative lives now. They have the power, when operative, to move us in the process of becoming whole and eventually to a creative influence on the culture, causing it to become its true Self in this new moment of time.

The Second Journey

A beautiful ninety-year-old woman told us this: "I don't know I am old unless I look into the mirror. Then I say, 'You old fool. Look at yourself. You are an old woman.'" This same woman had left her homeland, France, and moved to Ireland only eight years prior to our conversation. Her exodus from France at eighty-two placed her in a new cultural setting and forced her to engage the English language in a way she never had before. One could sense that this woman was still in the process of growing and becoming. Her style of life and patterns of being and relating were radically different from what they had been thirty, twenty, or ten years earlier. We were the beneficiaries of her individuation process. We were being nourished by the self that she was. "I do not know that I am old unless I look into the mirror," she said. "The soul is always young, you know."

Aging should put us in contact with such realities. In the second half of life, aging becomes a call back to wholeness, to the One, to union. Meister Eckhart was aware of that:

> The soul is as young as it was when it was created. Old age concerns only the soul's use of the bodily sense . . . My soul is as young as it was when it was created. Yes, and much younger! I tell you, it would not surprise me if it were younger tomorrow than it is today! (Fox, 1980:107)

This is what the mid-life experience is all about. It is time to begin the process of reclaiming one's soul. It is time to let the inner man or woman take over the steering wheel of our becoming. It is time to begin the "second journey" (O'Collins, 1978), the second half of life.

Does one make a conscious choice for this? "Oh, I'm bored now. It is time to get involved in a new me and go on my second journey." Or, "I'm fifty. My mid-life experience is long overdue. I hear it usually occurs between your thirty-fifth and forty-fifth years. I'd better start having it now." No, it is not a deliberate, conscious choice I make. It does not depend on *will*. It is a phenomenon that produces itself. It is an experience that happens to me. The mid-life experience consists of psychic, emotional, and spiritual movements that go on in us, usually couched in some outer or inner life event. Some typical catalytic events are: one's first child going off to college; one's youngest child marrying; the birth of a first grandchild; retirement; being "let go," promoted, or demoted; the death of a loved one; the climacteric; the first serious illness; loss of beauty, strength, or vigour; an unwanted pregnancy; a failure, disappointment, financial loss; illness of a spouse, infidelity of a spouse, or one's own infidelity. Almost any event or combination of events can be the catalyst for the surfacing of the initial mid-life crisis.

One does not choose the mid-life experience any more than the twenty-month-old chooses to join the ranks of the "terrible twos." A new stage of physical or psychological growth arises in us, chooses us, as it were. The time is now.

Recently, I saw a beautiful two-year-old. The two-year-old experience is one of shattering the "participation mystique." She is discovering her own ego in the making. *Me* and *no* are the words she uses to claim her own identity and separate herself from the giants in her world, Mom and Dad. This particular youngster was jaunting ahead of her parents around the shore of a lake. The loving young couple behind her let her tramp off independently a few feet ahead of them. Periodically, they called out, "Don't get your shoes wet. Stay away from that water." She never did put her feet into the water but each time she heard their command she called out in defiance, "no, no." This classic two-year-old is having an archetypal experience just as the thirty-five- and fifty-five-year-olds evolving into mid-life are having an archetypal experience. It is an awakening, an outbreak that arises from within because the time is ripe. Now is the hour. In a sense the self is choosing or executing the next phase in development. All future growth or decline is dependent on this encounter, on grasping and entertaining this call.

Archetype is a term that Jung employed in speaking about the built-in patterns of human becoming, relating, behaving, or just plain being. He recognized the archetypes as constitutive of humanity (Jung, *Symbols of Transformation:*313).

The inner psychic archetypes are, Jung discovered, the very qualities that make us human, that distinguish human life from all other life. From the moment of our conception we are the recipients of this psychic dimension, the collective history of the human race, the patterns of physical, psychological, and spiritual growth.

We are a human pattern. Mid-life is a human pattern. As we reach the end of youth the psyche prepares itself to move out of the way of acting, being, and relating that characterized youth and readies itself to move into a new phase of development and self-knowledge and thus to social, cultural generativity in a new key.

Inner Life: The Unconscious Personality

The mid-life call to the inner life is as real as the two-year-old's call to ego discovery and development.

The inner life has always given depth, character, and richness of personality in childhood and youth. It is not a total stranger to the mid-life person. The inner Self was in existence from the start of life, in fact: it engineered the early ego development. Now that one is mature enough to recognize the inner Self, one can make way for its new demands for growth and wholeness by giving attention to the unconscious side. While this unconscious side of oneself is mostly unknown to each of us, it is not unknown to the history of humanity. Marie-Louise Von Franz, a colleague of Jung, realized that people are bewildered and stunned when introduced to the fact that aside from all that they know about themselves (the conscious side or ego) they have another side to the personality that they do not know (the unconscious). She assures us that it is no stranger to humanity.

> But what, in fact, is this unconscious. . . ? Actually, it is just a modern technical expression for an inner experience which is

as old as mankind, the experience which occurs when something alien and unknown overwhelms us from within, when
the working of inner forces suddenly changes our lives, when
we have dreams or inspiration or hunches which we know we
have not "made up" but which come to us from a psychic
"outside" and push their way into consciousness. In earlier
times these effects of unconscious processes were ascribed to a
divine fluid (mana) or to a god or demon or "spirit." Such
names gave expression to the feelings of an objective, alien an
autonomous presence, as well as to a sense of something
overwhelming to which the conscious ego has to submit. (Von
Franz, 1975:7)

Jung devoted his life to the observation and the study of the
human psyche. He came to understand the unconscious as
personal and more than personal. He observed in the human
person an objective psyche, not coming from our personal
history, but a given in each of us. Jung came to realize that our
very humanity is rooted in this objective psyche.

In a true sense then, we are all brothers and sisters sharing
this one and the same objective reality of the human psyche. Is
this so strange? We each share the same human physical form
with its evolutionary marks and vestiges from the archaic ages.
These bodies of ours function and grow in remarkably similar
fashions. Should it be so very different for our psyche and its
development? Here, too, is something given from archaic ages.
As we have a common anatomy of inner and outer parts but
each our own unique body, so too, we have common psychic
structures with common psychic equipment, though each his or
her own unique personality and mysterious spirit. We are, each
of us, an embodied spirit with built-in psychic patterns. Just as a
bird has an inner clock and instructor telling her when and how
to break out of her egg, to leave her first nest, to mate, to go
about building a new nest, to teach her young to fly, we have
dormant within us the broad motif of each new stage of development. Mid-life is such a motif. Of course, the origin of
these archetypes, as of the psyche, is part of the deepest mystery of life.

"All that is outside, also is inside," we could say with Goethe.
But this "inside," which modern rationalism is so eager to

derive from "outside," has an a priori structure of its own that antedates all conscious experience. It is quite impossible to conceive how "experience" in the widest sense, or, for that matter, anything psychic, could originate exclusively in the outside world. The psyche is part of the inmost mystery of life, and it has its own peculiar structure and form like every other organism. Whether this psychic structure and its elements, the archetypes, ever "originate" at all is a metaphysical question therefore unanswerable. The structure is something given, the precondition that is found to be present in every case. (Jung, *The Archetypes and the Collective Unconscious:*101)

Not all psychologies hold to this fundamental built-in pattern of human growth and development. Yet the studies of many are at present confirming and complementing Jung's work. In 1958, Dr. John Bowlby published a now famous paper, "The Nature of the Child's Tie to His Mother," in which he suggested

that infants become attached to their mothers, and mothers to their infants, not so much through learning as by instinct. Mothers and infants had no need to learn to love one another: they were innately programmed to do so from birth. The formation of mother-infant attachment bonds is a direct expression of the genetic heritage of our species. (Stevens:3)

Of course, it hardly needs to be said that this instinct to mother-love still needs to be educated and that the mother archetype, as all other archetypes can, and does often, go awry.

2

The Unconscious Elements
of the Human Psyche

The objective psyche, or the collective unconscious, is with us
from the beginning of life and remains with us throughout
life. The child does not enter the world at birth with a blank
psyche but with an inherited, transpersonal psyche. This
psyche, according to Jung,

> does not derive from personal experience and achievement
> but is inborn. This deeper layer I call the "collective" because
> this part of the unconscious is not individual but universal; in
> contrast to the personal psyche, it has contents and modes of
> behaviour that are more or less the same everywhere and in
> all individuals. (Jung, *The Integration of the Personality*:53)

We cannot designate a special place for the psyche as it is
beyond space and time. Yet we often use words like *within,
center, depths,* and *interior,* to situate the psyche, especially the
unconscious aspects of one's psyche, whether personal or collective.

> It would be entirely erroneous, however, to imagine con-
> sciousness as a kind of Here and the unconscious as a sort of
> There, because the psyche is in fact a conscious-unconscious
> whole, an "all-embracing One . . ." Conscious and uncon-
> scious, as a kind of two-in-one, are the substrate of psychic
> processes in which now the unconscious predominates, as in
> dreams, or again the conscious, as in the waking state. The
> phenomenon of archaic identity, which is the feeling of being
> one with the environment and which is also the basis of all
> communication between human beings, is ultimately rooted

16

in the existence of the collective unconscious. (Von Franz, 1972:124–25)

Aside from this objective psyche there is another personal aspect to the psyche which Jung called the personal unconscious. Unlike the collective unconscious the personal unconscious is unique to each of us. During life in the mother's womb the personal unconscious is assimilating the history of those nine months, and after birth it continues to assimilate the history of moments and years. One's personal unconscious consists of all the moments of personal existence of which we are unaware, of which we are not conscious: this could be because the prenatal or neonatal child is not conscious of anything because consciousness or ego has not yet become a reality. But throughout life one encounters situations, has negative or positive emotions, and responds and reacts to events and circumstances of which one never becomes conscious. All this is a most intimate part of one's history that has never been made conscious. Situations, events, emotions, and so on, that were conscious at one time but are unconscious now, are also recorded in the personal unconscious. This could be because we have forgotten them with time or repressed or suppressed them because of the pain or confusion such recollections would cause. That this part of one's history is unconscious is no reason to think it is not operative in one's personality. Our personality is always the result of conscious and unconscious forces. This means that I can never totally explain myself to myself or others. I can only do that to a degree. I can only tell what I am conscious of. A person's choices regarding careers, relationships, partners, marriage, styles of life, attitudes, or religious affiliations could come from an unconscious motivation arising from the personal or collective unconscious.

Personal Experiences of the Unconscious

A few years ago I found myself holding my left arm behind by back, resting it, as it were, in the cleft of my back. I remember being startled and thinking, "My goodness, I'm holding my arm just as my father held his." My father had Parkinson's disease for the last thirty years of his life. He held his arm that way to prevent tremors. After that experience I became conscious that I was often doing the same thing, usually when lecturing or teaching. As far as I know it was a new gesture on my part. I do not recall this ever being characteristic of me, nor do the people who know me well. It was and continues to be an unconscious, spontaneous act on my part that goes back to those thirty years. Again and again I ask whether there is much more of my father in me than I can ever know? What is the significance of this unconscious act? How can I understand myself better at this moment by understanding the history that this gesture points to? Why did I start to hold my arm this way after all these years? My father is dead more than twenty years. In those years I was never really mindful of him until this experience. I now have a sense of his presence as I remain open to the mystery of what it means. It is very possible that my own conscious life is in need of something dormant in my personal unconscious.

There is a story in my family about my grandmother. Her husband died, leaving her with six children, the eldest of whom was my father, a fourteen-year-old. One day, shortly after my grandfather was buried, my grandmother was sitting in a chair staring out the window. Michael, the fourteen-year-old, came to her and said, "Mama, are you just going to sit here like this? Don't you know that the children are hungry?" The pleading of her son snapped her out of herself, she often said, and she went about all the things a woman had to do to bring up her family. Grandma had to deliberately suppress her loss and "get on with it," as we say. But sometime, somewhere, the grieving had to be done. All our losses, all our sorrows, need to be tended eventually, if not at the time of their occurrence.

Rosemary had been divorced after twelve years of marriage. It all happened quickly. She never suspected he was seeing other women. He had been more than a good provider and had also managed all their financial matters on his own. She used to say, "He left behind four children, the three boys and me." Left with her home and the boys, in a state of shock, she had to "pull herself together" for the sake of the boys:

> I look back now, ten years later, and I say, "Rosemary, you did some job. You raised three great boys." They are all off now in colleges doing very well. Right now, I just want to sit down

and cry. I want to cry over my marriage, my desertion, my loss and loneliness. I couldn't do it back then.

What will Rosemary find as she looks back at her marriage? Isn't it a waste of time to dwell on the past? People have a disease with looking back, re-collecting, remembering the difficult things. Yet, it is important to keep in mind that the past is present, consciously or unconsciously. We allow this personal unconscious story of ours to come to consciousness so that we can own it, take it on as our history, make peace with it, learn from it, and move beyond it.

Joyful, Sorrowful, and Glorious Mysteries of Life

At mid-life our history is at a transitional moment. We are moving out of the child-youth half of life into the second half of life made up of the mid-life and mature years. At this turning point we ask, Who is turning? To understand that question and its answer we must turn to the joyful, sorrowful, and glorious events of our life, conscious and unconscious.

The liturgical year of the church calls Christians to reflect annually on the joyful, sorrowful, and glorious mysteries of the life of Christ. Because those joyful, sorrowful, and glorious events in his life incorporated the ongoing growth, becoming, development, and maturing of Jesus of Nazareth, they can never be fully appreciated or assimilated. They are mysterious in every way. As one ages and reflects on these mysteries, they become more mysterious even as one is more nurtured by them. The mysteries of one's personal life are the same. They are in the grain of our being and have created us and continue to do so. To understand that is to evoke faith, hope, and love in the past, in life itself. Sometimes one needs a professional helper to engage in this life review. It could take months or years to allow the days of one's life to come together. The mid-life person must give time to this story in reflection, prayer, journal writing, and intimate conversation with a friend, spiritual guide, or professional helper.

Our stories may come to us at strange times: in dreams; at family gatherings, weddings, or funerals; while viewing old pictures and albums; at times of meditation, prayer, or solitude.

Ann was in her thirties, tall, attractive, energetic, and always proper. I recall her sharing with another woman her own experience of growing up with an addicted mother. Her sharing companion in this little group encouraged her to talk. Crying had never been natural to Ann but she began to cry softly as she shared the effect her mother's addiction had on her as a child. Of course she had no idea how it was still affecting and motivating her at this moment. Then the other woman began to talk. She understood because she was the daughter of an alcoholic mother. "I can't believe you," she said. "Didn't you ever say to your mother, even if not to her face, You, bitch. You robbed me of my childhood." Ann was shocked as she came and shared with me the exchange. I knew even as she told me that she sensed it was something that would be good to do, even if so very out of character for her.

Anger and grief over the tragedies of one's personal life are necessary if we are truly to know our sorrowful mysteries. Anger and grief allow us to work through the events and move on in our story. One often discovers that one's greatest gift or cherished dreams come from a sorrowful event in one's life.

Margaret put together the parts of her story when she was able to understand the gift she had been given by a stern, unbending, uncompromising nun forty years ago, when she was sixteen. For forty years she carried deep resentment and animosity for the principal who dismissed her from school because she had not kept up her tuition payments. Margaret attended a high school for young girls who were interested in entering the religious congregation of the sisters staffing the school. All during her sophomore year she grew in her suspicion that she really didn't want to do that with her life. Meanwhile, there were difficulties at home and unpaid tuition bills. She had received some notices about payment but felt things were so bad at home she could not give them to her parents. Finally, to her shock one Friday she was called to the principal's office and Sister Hilda told her to find another school during the upcoming summer vacation. She was no longer welcome at her present school.

All these years Margaret harbored bad feelings for the humiliation she had received and the cold, uncharitable way she had been treated. As she looked back on this event now, she realized that she did not have the courage to go to the sisters and tell them she was going to leave because she no longer wanted to be a sister herself. "Perhaps I would have stayed on and graduated and even entered the community," she said in horror, "if I had not been thrown out." There was relief in her voice and even laughter in her eyes. "Imagine, if Sister had not asked me to leave perhaps I never would have had the courage not to enter! Perhaps, I never would have had my six wonderful children." Margaret was grateful and elated at the result of contacting this part of her story. She was healed of a wound long overdo in the healing. She was also put in touch with a psychological truth:

> "The psychological rule says that when an inner situation is not made conscious, it happens outside, as fate. That is to say, when the individual remains undivided and does not become conscious of his inner opposite, the world must perforce act out the conflict and be torn into opposite halves." (Jung, *Aion:*71)

Margaret had discovered that the evil done against her had turned into a blessing. She had been saved from years, if not a lifetime, of being out of place, misplaced. No doubt her abrupt dismissal from school was a cruel blow to the child. Still, the paradox was the fact that the evil done against her was later acknowledged as a blessing in disguise. Paradox is at the heart of life (Jung, *Aion:*70). The cross of Jesus was a paradox. In the second half of life we learn that all of life is a paradox, especially the mysteries of our life.

I remember sitting in a living room with a group of people. We were sharing evening prayer. Following the prayer one women said,

> Tomorrow, I'll be sixty. It's my birthday, you know. I have the feeling that this is going to be a wonderful year. Something new is going to happen. I have no idea what it will be, just this feeling of great expectations.

I marveled at someone on the eve of her sixtieth being so optimistic! I was even more surprised because I knew this woman's life had had more than a normal share of sorrows.

Born a Jew in Europe, she had seen her mother and sisters

taken off by the Nazis. She knew they lost their lives in Auschwitz. After the war, she spent ten years in a communist prison. When she was released, she had to live alone and worked in a factory. During this time she was always under surveillance and suspicion. Finally, she endured the sorrow and humiliation of the fact that her homeland allowed someone to buy her freedom. This ransom brought her to the United States and made her, in a sense, a political exile. Why wasn't this beautiful woman dried up with bitterness? Why hadn't she lost her faith, hope, and love for life? How can she be expecting something good to happen when her life has been filled with tragic happenings? What joy, relief, transcendent moments, and hope sustained this woman amid the tragedies that she lived through?

The Vatican art collections contain a very beautiful painting called *The Rest on the Flight into Egypt,* by the sixteenth-century Italian Federigo Barocci. The flight into Egypt was a sorrow in the life of Jesus, Mary, and Joseph. "Rise, take the child and his mother, flee to Egypt, and stay there until I tell you. Herod is going to search for the child to destroy him" (Mt. 2:13). Yet Barocci depicts the Holy Family picnicking under a cherry tree during their escape. Under the tree, Mary sits on a rock, taking some water from a stream in the rocks. Joseph stands behind her: one hand is raised to pull down a branch of the tree and with his other hand he offers the child some cherries. The child's face is bathed in light and one can see his bright smiling glee. Darkness and light dance around the picture. Some places are so dark one can hardly make out the figures, and in other spots, Mary, the child, the evening sky are diffused in light. We live through and in and beyond our sorrows when we get in touch with the light in us and beyond us. Sometimes we end up being grateful for the darkness because without it we would never have come into contact with the light.

When one is able to integrate one's sorrows one is able to have faith, hope, and love for the present and the future. One is also able to relate to other people at times of sorrow. Being in touch with the sorrowful mysteries of one's personal life, one can be present to others in their sorrowful moments. One can be with others in pain and grief, sorrow and disappointment. One can be satisfied to be present without having answers or being able to plumb the mystery of the event. One can allow people to grieve and not rush the process of grieving. If someone cannot be with others in pain and sorrow they have most likely not reconciled their own pains and sorrows. There comes a time when one cannot minister to others unless one has ministered to one's own wounds and hurts. One cannot tolerate the tragic sobs of another unless one has experienced darkness turning into light, sorrow into joy.

No Lonely Pilgrim

The mid-life transition calls for a change in orientation from the conscious personality or the ego to the Self or larger personality. This new phase of development takes place in the unconscious. As one comes to the midpoint in life there is a natural movement toward wholeness. One's own unconscious story, dormant in the psychic layers of the personal unconscious, are the first to be claimed. The mid-life person is called to be open to the mystery of one's own becoming in all the years one has already lived. This unknown story invites one to one's own depths and mysteries. One becomes conscious of the mystery one is to oneself. *"Be still and know that I am God."*

The mystery that one is to oneself need not be a threat. Our biblical tradition tells us that our most intimate story and all the details of our past, present, and future are known by the One who called us into being. No one is a lonely pilgrim or a solitary wanderer in life. Each of us has been conceived in direct relationship to God. Deep within the psyche of each of us is the sense of a personal relationship with the source of our life, God. One could call on this God to re-create for us and put us in touch with the time of our becoming, conception, the time of birth and all the moments of our personal history. One could do so in the faith that in and through this "clay of the ground" the Lord God reenacted the creation of the first humans. "The Lord God formed man [and woman] out of the clay of the ground and blew into his nostrils the breath of life, and so man [and woman] became living being" (Gn. 2:7).

As one gets in touch with one's conscious and unconscious life story, one is preparing the way for increased self-knowledge, self-appropriation, and self-acceptance.

✓ Truly you have formed my inmost being; you knit me in my
mother's womb. I give you thanks that I am fearfully, wonder-
fully made; wonderful are your works. My soul also you knew
full well; nor was my frame unknown to you. When I was
made in secret, when I was fashioned in the depths of the
earth. Your eyes have seen my actions; in your book they are
all written; my days were limited before one of them existed.
How weighty are your designs, O God; how vast the sum of
them! Were I to recount them, they would outnumber the
sands; did I reach the end of them, I should still be with you.
(Ps. 139:13–18)

It is the nonpersonal dimension of the psyche that all humans
share in common. This collective unconscious has been operative in the person long before mid-life. Yet at mid-life the
activation of the collective unconscious, this other dimension of
psychic depths, is essential. The eruption of mid-life itself is a
witness to the collective unconscious and its archetypes. One
has come to the point in life when one can no longer continue
to be simply the person one became in youth. The areas of one's
personal and collective unconscious need in the course of time
to be brought to consciousness and integrated into the larger
✓ picture of who one is. The Self that one is called to become in
the mid-life years demands that one's dormant personal history
come to life in faith, hope, and love and that one becomes open
to the archetypal patterns of humanity as sources of renewal
and life.

Joseph B. Wheelwright, a founding member of the Society of
Jungian Analysts of Northern California and co-author of the
Gray-Wheelwright test of psychological types, was a student of
Jung's. In a recent interview he discussed Jung's intense interest
and concern with the archetypal dimension of the psyche.

During most of the time that I worked with Jung, he was
principally interested in the collective unconscious. Well, I
had a lot of personal stuff. I had had hundreds of hours of
analysis in London with Anna Rosenbaum and Peter Baynes,
and I had had a good many hours with Toni Wolf. As Jung
had said to me once, "Don't mention the word 'Mother' to me!
I've been listening to that for forty years. You go to Toni Wolf.
She's a bottomless pit and you can talk about your mummy

with her. But if you get some kind of collective unconscious stuff, archetypes, well then, we can talk about that, can't we?" (Serbin:159)

Jung saw this archetypal dimension of the psyche as the source of growth and development in the second half of life. The conscious personality developed during childhood and youth is no longer the center of the stage. One's monarchical ego is unthroned as the journey toward wholeness is embarked upon. No longer is the ego the center of psychic life. Like a Copernican revolution the individual finds that a shift has occurred: the Self is the center and psychic life revolves around it (Jung, *The Integration of the Personality*:4). The Self becomes the source of energy, the motivating force, the energizer, the healer, the reason for being, the integrating force bringing the conscious and unconscious into a wholeness. This is a wholeness never achieved, always in process. One is becoming what one is, all during the second half of life and, from a faith perspective, beyond it.

3

The Life Cycle
as Archetypal

Archetypes are built-in universal patterns, or "patterns of instinctual behaviors" (Jung, *The Archetypes and the Collective Unconscious:*44). They are the creative matrix of the psyche:

> The archetypes make up the actual content of the collective unconscious; their number is relatively limited, for it corresponds to the number of typical and fundamental experiences incurred by man since primordial time. (Jacobi, 1973:47)

There is an account of a five-year-old boy who was kidnapped by a man who kept the boy and raised him. Seven years later, when the boy was twelve, the man came home with another five-year-old boy. It was like history repeating itself. The twelve-year-old remembered the fear and terror that had been his seven years earlier. He agonized for the little five-year-old. That night when the man was sleeping he took the five-year-old and ran off. He had one desire: to find help for the five-year-old and let him be returned to his family. The newspapers reported the story and the reunion, not only of the five-year-old but also of the twelve-year-old with his parents. What happened to this boy after seven years?

He grew. He grew from childhood into youth. Being a young man, standing on his own two feet, being psychically independent of the caretaker (even if he was a kidnapper) all erupted in him simultaneously. This growing up was on target for a twelve-year-old. It was stimulated by the feeling of solidarity he had for the five-year-old. The little boy could be saved from the harrowing experience of being abducted from a loving home and family if someone would save him. Our twelve-year-old did not reason this out or intellectualize the events. He acted out the pattern of the independent youth, as Jesus did at age twelve.

> Each year his parents went to Jerusalem for the feast of Passover, and when he was twelve years old, they went up according to festival custom. After they had completed its days, as they were returning, the boy Jesus remained behind in Jerusalem, but his parents did not know it. Thinking that he was in the caravan, they journeyed for a day and looked for him among their relatives and acquaintances, but not finding him, they returned to Jerusalem to look for him. After three days they found him in the temple, sitting in the midst of the teachers, listening to them and asking them questions, and all who heard him were astounded at his understanding and his answers. When his parents saw him, they were astonished, and his mother said to him, "Son, why have you done this to us? Your father and I have been looking for you with great anxiety." And he said to them, "Why were you looking for me? Did you not know that I must be in my Father's house?" But they did not understand what he said to them. (Lk. 2:41–50)

Both twelve-year-olds experienced psychic independence through the assistance of an outer event. The outer event provoked—as it were, crystallized—the moment of maturing. Or, the inner psychic event of moving out of childhood was realized in the context of outer circumstances. The boy Jesus did not leave childhood and enter youth that day. This, too, is a process. But the process had begun. Today, we grace it with the name adolescent transition. That time where one is allowed to have one foot in childhood and one foot in youth. The transitional time allows one to move out of one stage and into another. In this case the twelve-year-olds were moving into youth but both needed, as all do, the freedom to be sometimes in childhood and sometimes in adolescence as they prepared for a final entrance into a new stage of growth. Luke's narrative ends by saying: "He went down with them then, and came to Nazareth, and was obedient to them" (Lk. 2:51a).

Raymond Brown, a biblical scholar, points out to us that this

Lucan story is a "chronological transition between the infancy and ministry and it supplies a transition between revelation about Jesus by others (angels, Simeon) and revelations that Jesus himself will proclaim; for in 2:41–52 Jesus speaks for the first time" (1977:481). It is symbolic of a new birth, the birth of a youth.

Jesus' parents were "astonished." All adults are astonished at the birth of an infant, and at the birth of a boy or girl becoming a young adult. Puberty, the emergence of a new stage of sexual maturation, usually accompanies this change in the psyche. Childhood was in a sense a kind of womb where the child could grow, protected by caring adults. When children leave their mother's womb they are thrust into a new womb. As in their mother's womb, there is no choice about this new womb. As our mother's womb contained us, now this new womb will contain us. As one grows in one's mother's womb, participating in the mother's life, so one will now grow in the new womb of childhood.

Birth and Death as Archetypal

Growth in the womb is archetypal. There are patterns of becoming built into the psyche of the little fetus. One progresses in those nine months week by week in a precision that will never again be matched in one's life. Birth, too, is archetypal. The time comes when being in the womb will no longer do. One must emerge, separate from the mother. It is the human pattern. But even here we are given a transitional time. We spend the first nine months of life still participating in the mother. We suck our food from her breast, nestled against her warm and loving flesh. Our eyes and ears seek her out continuously as our first natural and primitive prayer, looking for the Other.

> . . . there are also archetypal modes of action and reaction and archetypal processes, such as the development of the ego or the progress from one phase of age and experience to another; there are archetypal attitudes, ideas, ways of assimilating experience, which, set in motion under certain circumstances, emerge from their hitherto unconscious state and become visible, as it were. . . .

Actually all typical, universally human manifestations of life, whether biological, psycho-biological, or spiritual ideational in character, rest on an archetypal foundation. (Jacobi, 1973:41)

All these early stages of growth are normative for the person and set the patterns for life. One's first birth demanded that one die to life in the womb. When all the growing that could be accomplished in the womb was completed, when the time in the womb was fulfilled, the unborn child had to die to that way of life in order to be born and continue the process of growth. Indeed, the unborn child had to die to that way of life in order to live. No longer could the child be contained in the womb, or nourished through the umbilical cord. For each of us the first birth demands a death. The human navel is a sacramental sign of life's first lesson about paradox. Death brings life. Beginnings come from endings. All throughout infancy and childhood this pattern continues until the second great death, the death to childhood.

Psychic Birth, and with it the conscious distinction of the ego from the parents, takes place in the normal course of things at the age of puberty with the eruption of sexual life. (Jung, *Modern Man in Search of a Soul*:99)

Dying to childhood allows one to enter a new stage of growth. When all the growing in childhood is accomplished, when childhood has reached its fulfillment, to continue to grow and to live one must die to childhood. Childhood will no longer nourish growth. One must separate oneself from the environment given to oneself in childhood and choose one's environment. What do I want to do with my life? What kind of person do I want to become? What kind of people do I like to be with? What kind of work do I want to be involved in? Vocational and career choices mark the transition into youth, creating a new nourishing environment.

All during childhood and youth the environment of the person is the primary factor in personality development. The people in our life and the lives of the primary people surrounding us, the neighborhood we settled in, our chosen vocation and careers, and the culture at large effect and nourish the ongoing development of personality. The environment is primary in childhood and in youth, the only difference is that in youth we choose our own environment.

Not only are the stages of life archetypal but the human response of others to someone in one or another stage of life is archetypal. Riding on a train recently, I saw a beautiful black woman with her baby. She was camped out in a large seat with her little king's belongings for a twelve-hour ride. Almost everyone who passed stopped to speak to the baby or the mother. The baby was everyone's baby—babies have that way about them. This little fellow was truly seductive. He would never be without. His needs would be amply met because he invited care, concern, attention, and love. A common chord was touched in almost every passenger in the face of the situation of the mother and infant. This common chord was the archetypal layer, in particular the mother archetype.

> A mother with her child evokes the image not of an individual woman with her individual child but of an archetype common to all mankind. From time immemorial men [or women] have been deeply stirred by this fact and looked upon it as suprapersonal. (Neumann, 1973:23)

Normally, every man and woman on the train would have responded in a caring and loving way if something had happened to the mother and the child was left alone. We each have within us the human pattern of mothering, of caring for the needy without looking for reward. The reward is the caring itself.

Our human life cycle is made up of births and deaths. Even as our first birth means death to life in the womb and our second birth as a youth, following the adolescent transition, means death to childhood, so does our birth in the mid-life period mean death to our youth. Death to our youth can seem like a tragic thing in our youth-oriented culture. But as one reaches the end of youth, perhaps sometime between the ages of thirty-five and forty-five, the things of youth no longer nourish one as they did before. Very often without knowing why, and apparently for no reason, a person reaches the season of discontent. This very discontent is a sign that new pasture is needed. It is a sign of a call to a new way of life, a new orientation. It is a call to a new fork in the journey. It is foreshadowing a "change of life" that is both psychological and spiritual. Merton reflects this stage of life.

> As you say, I represent my own life. But not as I ought to. I have still too much reflected the kind of person others may have assumed I ought to be, I am reaching a happy and dangerous age when I want to smash that image above all. But that is not the kind of thing that is likely to be viewed with favor. Nor do I have any idea of what way the road will take. (Mott: 355)

Mid-Life as Integral to the Human Journey

Mid-life stories are not the exclusive product of our times; developmental psychology did not manufacture the life cycle. Jung did not imagine into being the mid-life crisis, the mid-life transition, or the mid-life period—these have always been integral to the human journey. The Italian poet Dante was thirty-five in the year 1300. That is the date he assigns to the journey he embarked upon and that he describes in *The Divine Comedy* (Luke, 1975:9).

> Midway this way of life we're bound upon,
> I wake to find myself in a dark wood,
> Where the right road was wholly lost and gone.
> (Translation by Dorothy Sayers, in Luke, 1975:9)

Within the past decade numerous books on mid-life have flooded the market. Perhaps this is because more and more people are living into and through the mid-life period and so there is a greater demand for such books. But there is also a greater need, because of that demand, to plumb the depths of this mid-life experience that is integral to the life cycle.

At the present time, eighty-year-olds are the fastest growing age group in America. There are many out there wanting to know the meaning and the purpose of life after youth. We have become more holistic in everything, or want to be. People want to have healthy bodies and healthy psyches all throughout life, especially in the second half, where we may imagine both breaking down.

Helen Luke tells us that the dictionary defines psyche as "soul, spirit, mind." As used by Jung she tells us "it includes all the nonphysical realities of the human being" (Luke, 1975:162). This psyche of ours includes conscious (ego) and unconscious aspects. The psyche includes the personal as well as the collective unconscious. It is at mid-life that a person begins to feel an acute need to tend, pay attention to, respect, and honor her or his own other neglected side. This other half of us is what the second half of life is all about.

Many authors of "mid-life" books refer to Dante and his mid-life journey (Bianchi, 1982, and Studzinski). His classic poem of 1300 depicts the same mid-life experience of crisis and transition that is described by the developmental psychologists of our century. Whether in Dante's poem or a modern book on mid-life we read about a common built-in universal pattern or archetype of mid-life.

> The archetype we are dealing with in considering the experience of a deep-going psychological transformation at midlife is the same that operates in all other transitional periods of life. It is reflected in images of the edge, of boundary lines and border lines, thresholds, in-between spaces and times. (Stein, 1983: 111)

Murray Stein also makes reference to Dante (1983:23) and he describes mid-life as "a time when persons often come unhinged and lose their footing in a secure social and psychological world" (1983:23).

What is this crisis, this "falling apart," leading to? What is the meaning of "losing one's way" or the "dark night of the soul"? Because this mid-life experience is an expected human phenomenon we know it must have special significance. This significance lies in the fact that the development of the ego in the first half of life is not the journey's end, it is only a beginning. The person is on the threshold of a third birth. All the growing that can be done in youth is over. New growth, new development, demands leaving youth and entering a new stage of development.

The consciousness developed in the first half of life is pre-parative for the inner journey, the becoming of the Self and an expansion of consciousness. We have no script for this second journey. We are in a "dark wood" and cannot imagine the Self we are in the process of becoming. Nor can we imagine how the dark, murky waters of the unconscious have any good to offer.

This is the third major birth that one encounters in the life cycle. It is a dying and a rising. Mid-life is a transpersonal moment in the person's life as essential as the first and last transpersonal moments in the life cycle, being born and dying. The mid-life experience is the result of the human psyche entering a new phase of its development. The psychic process of becoming a unique individual self is being readied for the next stage of its development. This process, which Jung called individuation,

> is a spontaneous, natural process within the psyche; it is potentially present in every man [and woman], although most men are unaware of it. Unless it is inhibited, obstructed, or distorted by some specific disturbance, it is a process of matu-ration or unfolding, the psychic parallel to the physical pro-cess of growth and aging. (Jacobi, 1973:107)

The mid-life transition is not only a movement from youth to mid-life. It is a withdrawal of psychic energy from the tasks, goals, and values of the whole first half of life in the same way that the adolescent experience was a withdrawal from the tasks, goals, and values of childhood.

Just as the first stage of life, childhood, has its own unique purpose and predictable stages as one moves through the pro-cess of continual becoming toward the goal of childhood, so, too, does adult life. Adult life has its predictable stages: youth, mid-life, and the mature years. Youth is the completion of the ego development that began in childhood. In the beginning each of us is in a womb of unconscious. There is neither ego nor personal unconscious. But as one moves through those first precious moments and months of life one's personal unconscious is being formed and one is in the initial, preparatory stages of ego development. The formation of an ego from this unconscious of ours is an archetypal experience. It is the first stage in the becoming of a Self that each of us is in the process of becoming.

> Any discussion . . . of the child personality must start from the assumption that the unconscious comes first and that consciousness follows. The total personality and its directing center, the Self, exist before the ego takes form and develops into the center of consciousness; the laws governing the development of the ego and consciousness are dependent on the unconscious and/or the total personality, which is represented by the Self. (Neumann, 1973:9)

The ego and the Self are related and interdependent. The Self, that unique "image of God" and mystery that each of us is called to be, is present in nucleus from the very start of life. The Self engineers the ego development of the first half of life, including its first birth from the mother's womb and its second birth or psychic birth at puberty.

Celebrate Mid-Life and the Mature Years

All of life is developmental. Mid-life and the mature years are as developmental as childhood and youth.

> There is much still to be done, and many more developmental crises to endure, not only after the fifth year, but also after the thirty-fifth, after the fiftieth, even after the seventy-fifth . . . We are beginning to realize that in all of life we are in psychological process and therefore subject to internal flux and change. (Stein, 1983:3)

Erik Erikson, who has dedicated his life to the study of the life cycle, tells us that just to "speak of life as a cycle . . . already implies some kind of completion" (1982: 9). The mid-life years bring us to an experience of the other side of the personality. They summon us to the inner journey, to the venture of integrating the unconscious elements of the psyche with the conscious. This venture and journey toward integration and wholeness should go on all during the second half of life and be completed in and through the process of dying, the process of death, our fourth and final birth. This fourth death becomes a fourth birth, a birth into eternal life. One's final death is also an archetypal experience. It is the natural evolution of the life cycle, the cycle of growth. In and through these four archetypal death-birth experiences, the human person continues to grow and become the unique individual that each of us is called to be. Death is a goal, because life itself is a goal.

As one moves through the second half of life one moves closer to death. Yet, there is much growing and integrating to be about in these decades. The mature years are the later years in this second journey. Some call these years old age, elderhood, the third age, the fourth season, or the fourth stage.

These mature years are essential to the fullness of life, to the completion of life's journey. In Jung's essay "The Stages of Life" he reminds us:

> A human being would certainly not grow to be seventy or eighty years old if this longevity had no meaning for the species to which he [or she] belongs. (*Modern Man in Search of a Soul:*109)

The vitality and health of persons in the mature years depends on their success in making a mid-life transition. Has this person moving into the last years, the last decade or two of life been more inner oriented? Has she made friends with her shadow? Has she owned her own story in childhood and youth? Has she made peace with the past, mourning all that there is to mourn? Has she forgiven herself for her failures, for her sins against others, and for the evil done to her? Has she discerned her own inner depths and learned to be present to the inner self? Has she been baptized by the Spirit and come to know that God is truly pleased with her? Has she remained committed to this earth of ours and in prayer and action continued to heal its wounds? Is she aware of the culture she is part of and its struggles to become the Kingdom of God? Is she able to rest and know peace even in turmoil? Is prayer of quiet and contemplation a large part of her day? Does she look for opportunities to relate to others, to give and to receive? Does she handle her losses and diminishments as well as a veteran handicapped person? Is the spirit more important than the body to her? Still, does she know how to give her body the care and attention it needs? Has she long ago given up all competition? Has she related to the child within and developed a spirituality of play? Has she learned to be poor in spirit? Did she celebrate mid-life? Is she celebrating the mature years?

The more a person moving into old age has done the work of mid-life the more she is able to continue the second journey. The mature years are the Spirit years, the Pentecost time, and they depend on and build on the conversion of mid-life.

> Whoever carries over into the afternoon the law of the morn-ing—that is, the aims of nature—must pay for so doing with damage to his [or her] soul. . . ." (Jung, *Modern Man in Search of a Soul:*109)

Old age comes to each of us.

> This is old age, and a limitation. Yet there is so much that fills me: plants, animals, clouds, day and night, and the eternal in man [or woman]. The more uncertain I have felt about my-self, the more there has grown up in me a feeling of kinship with all things. In fact it seems to me as if that alienation which so long separated me from the world has become transferred into my own inner world, and has revealed to me an unex-pected unfamiliarity with myself. (Jung, *Memories, Dreams, Reflections:*359)

Today we have a pressing need both to observe and to rethink the roles of old age (Erickson, 1982:62), for old age is truly archetypal. The winter years are to be as growth-filled as the spring, summer, and fall. Each season has its purpose, goal, and reason for being. Winter has its joys and sorrows and the old person must drink fully of both. As with all the other stages the mere fact of accumulating chronological years does not mean that one is in fact in the corresponding psychological and spir-itual phase of development. If one did not die to youth and suffer the pain of letting go and moving on into the second half of life back there in the midpoint (ages thirty-five to fifty-five), one must go through that travail now. The afternoon and evening of life are a call to conversion, a third birth, and one cannot have faith, hope, and love for the mature years or one's final death without moving through the psychic and spiritual phase of development. "To speak of the morning and spring, of the evening and autumn of life is not mere sentimental jargon" (Jung, *Modern Man in Search of a Soul:*107).

John XXIII and the Evening of Life

The journal writings of octogenarians can shed light on the realities and the possibilities of the evening time of life. Angelo Giuseppi Roncalli was born and baptized November 25, 1881, in Bergamo, Italy. Known to all of us as John XXIII, Pope John managed to turn the Roman Catholic church around during the years of his papacy (1958–1963). These were the seventy-seventh to the eighty-second years of his life.

The following excerpts are from Pope John's retreat notes of August 1961, when he was preparing for his eightieth birthday and recollecting his election to the papacy.

> When on 28 October 1958 the Cardinals of the Holy Roman Church chose me to assume the supreme responsibility of ruling the universal flock of Jesus Christ, at seventy-seven years of age, everyone was convinced that I would be a provisional and transitional Pope. Yet, here I am, already on the eve of the fourth year of my pontificate, with an immense programme of work in front of me to be carried out before the eyes of the whole world, which is watching and waiting. As for myself, I feel like St. Martin, who "neither feared to die"; nor "refused to live."(303)

And later again in prayer John reflects on the great graces he had been given.

> To have been able to accept as simple and capable of being immediately put into effect certain ideas which were not in the least complex in themselves, indeed perfectly simple, but far reaching in their effects and full of responsibilities for the future. I was immediately successful in this, which goes to show that one must accept the good inspirations that come from the Lord, simply and confidently.

> Without forethought, I put forward, in one of my first talks with my Secretary of State, on 20 January 1959, the idea of an

Ecumenical Council, a Diocesan Synod and the revision of the Code of Canon Law, all this being quite contrary to any previous supposition or idea of my own on this subject.

I was the first to be surprised at my proposal which was entirely my own idea.

And indeed, after this everything seemed to turn out so naturally in its immediate and continued development.

After three years of preparation, certainly laborious but also joyful and serene, we are now on the slope of the sacred mountain.

May the Lord give us strength to bring everything to a successful conclusion! (325–26)

How did this simple man during his late seventies and early eighties manage to be so creative, to turn the papacy and the church around. He brought together people of all religions at a time when "the one true Roman Catholic church" was still proclaimed and believed. He challenged the elitist position of the church and proclaimed that we needed to open the windows and let fresh air in. He welcomed Jews into the Vatican, invited the other churches to send representatives to the council, and left his Vatican home to visit the prisons. All this was a work of reconciliation. All this opened the church to the mystery of paradox about God, other religions, the human community, and all Christian churches. Only someone who has dealt with mystery and paradox in himself and in his own life would be able to achieve what he achieved. Only someone without competition, with a genuine sense of his own true Self and a commitment to the values he had come to discern anew, and who was "obedient to awareness" would have been able to do what he did in his mature years.

As one reads *Journal of a Soul,* one is struck by both the ordinariness and the greatness of this peasant priest who was so simple and yet so learned. He, like all of us, was shocked at the aging process in himself, as we discover in these Holy Week notes of 1945, when he was in his sixty-third year.

I must not disguise from myself the truth, I am definitely approaching old age. My mind resents this and almost rebels, for I still feel so young, eager, agile, and alert. But one look at my mirror disillusions me. This is the season of maturity; I must do more and better; reflecting that perhaps the time still granted me for living is brief, and that I am drawing near to the gates of eternity. This thought caused Hezekiah to turn to the wall and weep. I do not weep.

No, I do not weep, and I do not even desire to live my life over again, so as to do better. I entrust to the Lord's mercy whatever I have done, badly or less than well, and I look to the future, brief or long as it may be here below, because I want to make it holy and a source of holiness to others. (264)

John, like all of us, felt the losses and sorrows of old age even while he knew the joys of that same season, the winter of life.

These last notes of his come from his seventy-sixth year, the year before his election, a new birth and a new spring in the midst of old age.

Give me more light as evening falls. O Lord, we are now in the evening of our life. I am in my seventy-sixth year. Life is a great gift from our heavenly Father. Three-quarters of my contemporaries have passed over to the far shore. So I too must always be ready for the great moment. The thought of death does not alarm me. Now one of my five brothers also has gone before me . . . my beloved Giovanni. Ah, what a good life and a fine death! My health is excellent and still robust, but I cannot count on it. I want to hold myself ready to reply *adsum* at any, even the most unexpected moment.

Old age, likewise a great gift of the Lord's, must be for me a source of tranquil inner joy, and a reason for trusting day by day in the Lord himself, to whom I am now turned as a child turns to his father's open arms. (291)

Unknown to Cardinal Roncalli at the time he wrote this, on retreat in Venice in June 1957, he had only six more years to live. The last five years of his life would be spent as Pope John XXIII.

Death came to John XXIII, as it comes to each of us. Our biological clock marks our time, our fate. This last great archetypal moment comes to us as life came, a call from God.

Confucius spoke of life and death. As far back as 500 B.C.

Confucius identified six steps in the life cycle. A century earlier the Greek poet and lawmaker Solon divided the life cycle into ten stages (Levinson, et. al.:324).

Poetry, too, has always been a vehicle to speak of the mystery of aging. Walt Whitman was born on Long Island in 1819 and died in Camden, New Jersey, in 1891. A year before his death, he wrote "My Seventy-first Year."

> After surmounting three-score and ten,
> With all their chances, changes, losses, sorrows,
> My parents' deaths, the vagaries of my life, the many
>   tearing passions of me, the war of '63 and '64,
> As some old broken soldier, after a long, hot, wearying
>   march, or haply after battle,
> To-day at twilight, hobbling, answering company
>   roll-call,
>   Here, with vital voice,
> Reporting yet, saluting yet the officer over all.
>
> (553)

4

Jesus and the Archetypes

Can we presume that Jesus shared this life cycle with us? Can we assume that Jesus also grew and progressed steadily in wisdom, age, and grace before God and humanity because he shared with us the archetypal nature of the unconscious (Lk. 2:52)? I believe we can, since the Scriptures tell us that "we do not have a high priest who is unable to sympathize with our weaknesses, but one who has similarly been tested in every way, yet without sin" (Heb. 4:15). If this is true then Jesus' experience of his birth was archetypal, as ours was. "While they were there, the time came for her to have her child, and she gave birth to her firstborn son" (Lk. 2:6–7).

Although the Gospels are not a biography of Jesus and do not give us a strict historical or chronological account of his life, they do tell us his story. The Gospels are not a psychological analysis of Jesus but they do proclaim his mind-set, his point of view. He is "the way, and the truth and the life" (Jn. 14:6a). The Christian turns to prayer and to the Scriptures to become acquainted with her savior and to discern how she is to put on the mind of Christ (Phil. 2:5; 1 Cor. 2:16b).

As one prays Jesus' story in reading the Gospels one can be bewildered over the fact that one knows so little of his life. There is almost total silence about his youth: except for one short story about the twelve-year-old in the temple and his "second" or "psychic birth," and then a great silence for about eighteen years. Traditionally, we have called these the "hidden years."

We do know something about the "hidden years," however. Matthew's Gospel tells us Jesus was the son of a carpenter, and Mark says that Jesus was himself a carpenter. We know, then,

41

that Jesus was a worker. He did not belong to the upper class but to the class made up of small farmers and independent craftsmen (Dodd:119). We know he was educated and learned, a man very familiar with the Scriptures and this tells us something about those "hidden years." We know he was a man who was observant of nature, people, and circumstances. We also know that people were surprised at his teaching and his work. Because of this we can presume that such behavior on the part of Jesus was a new manifestation and that Jesus did nothing during the "hidden years" to prepare people for his new way of being and activity.

the "good news" is...

Jesus at Mid-life

Until he was nearly thirty, Jesus lived an ordinary life. After his own experience of baptism, Jesus begins his unique ministry of proclaiming the "good news" of God's reign in words and actions. He calls disciples to "follow him." In Matthew, Mark, and Luke, the story of the baptism is immediately followed by the story of the temptations. Can we not say that both of these events in the life of Jesus mark the midpoint of his life and the archetypal experience of mid-life? What happened to Jesus in the hidden years that brought him to the third birth? What experiences were culminated and launched with the baptism and the temptations? Luke tells us, "When Jesus began his ministry he was about thirty years of age" (Lk. 3:23). This little bit of biography is sandwiched between the stories of his baptism and his temptations.

After these events Jesus began the public ministry that led directly to his crucifixion, death, and resurrection, his fourth death and birth. Jung tells us that the mid-life experience is a spiritual crisis calling for a religious experience (*Modern Man in Search of a Soul:* 229). Jesus, too, must have had a spiritual crisis moving him from the hidden years to his public ministry. Jesus is identifying himself with all humanity when he asks John to baptize him. Obviously, Jesus has identified with all of humanity from the time of his birth into childhood and youth. The hidden years tell us how he identified with us by living an ordinary life. Whatever movements occurred in him, as they occur in all of us, brought Jesus to this heightened identification with the crowds and the call for repentance. Yet, when he goes about his ministry, he is certainly not another John the Baptist. Jesus is unique and original in his approach to sinners, to the law, to the poor, to women, and to prayer. Jesus reveals his own unique relationship to God and calls us to share that new consciousness. Jesus speaks with an authority that is unheard of before him. As he is no stranger to earthly things, he shows he is no stranger to heavenly things.

In the baptism Jesus is affirmed by the Father. Deep within his own depths, at the culmination of thirty years, Jesus hears, "You are my beloved Son; with you I am well pleased" (Mk 1:11). At the midpoint of our lives each of us needs to be affirmed. This affirmation must come from deep within our psyche, our own depths. It must be an affirmation of our being regardless of our works. I must come to know about myself, that I am good and I am God's loved one.

Surely Jesus had been proclaimed good and loved by his outer environment many times. Mary, Joseph, and numerous others had affirmed him from birth. The Hebrew Scriptures had affirmed him. In prayer now, at the baptism in the Jordan, the Father affirms Jesus as he is inaugurated into a new way of life, a new work, a new way of being, a second journey.

Following this deep and intense religious experience Jesus goes into the desert to pray. He encounters there, in his own depths, all the possibilities for sin. He comes to a new radical self-knowledge. The three temptations reveal three hidden possibilities to Jesus. A temptation is only a temptation when it touches real possibilities. Each possibility is in direct contrast to the ego ideal of Jesus. He does not fall into sin. Jesus does not equate himself with his temptations, these newly discovered possibilities. He does not collapse his ego and identify with these unconscious elements. He banishes Satan (Lk. 4:13).

It was the Spirit, present at the baptism, who led Jesus into the desert (Mk. 1:10, 12). It is the Spirit who leads and directs us also through this third birth. Both the baptism experience and the desert experience become foundational in the life journey of Jesus of Nazareth. He comes to understand and relate to himself, to all people, and to the Father in a whole new way through these experiences.

Jesus had experienced in the desert his own potential for evil but he did not equate himself with it. Therefore Jesus never equated any person with their sin or evil, realized or not. He did not condemn the sinner. He called each person to wholeness. He called sinners to be his chosen disciples. For Jesus, as for each of us, transformation came in and through the religious experience of "I am loved" and the experience of the shadow side of the personality. The archetypal experience of mid-life demanded of Jesus a change of life. We see that change of life operative in the drastic distinction between the hidden life and the public ministry. We see that the change of life brought him into the second half of his life. Here there was a new orientation. No longer was the outer environment to be the primary influence on his development. Inner experience, personal revelation, his own psychic depths, his own unique calling and vocation, the true Self that he was at his conception and birth—and now that Self, the Son of God, our brother and savior—was directing this new dimension. With Jesus, as with each of us, ego development went on in childhood and youth. Jesus grew under the influence of the womb of Mary, the womb of childhood—whatever its specifics were: Bethlehem, Nazareth, the carpenter shop, Jewish culture, the synagogue and temple, Hebrew Scriptures, first-century Palestine. The outer environment continued, after the twelve years of childhood, to guide and direct him. In mid-life, Jesus reached the time of becoming more his own true Self. This was the time for creativity and generativity. Mary, Joseph, and the culture, under the influence of the Spirit, had birthed him and now he had a gift to give in return: his own true self that he was becoming. He had to share, to make known, his revelation. This demanded new structures for him. He could not put the new wine into old skins.

Matthew, Mark, and Luke give an account of the story of Jesus' mother and brethren arriving at the scene where he is teaching. Mary and the brethren want to see and talk to him. The crowds pass the word on to Jesus and Jesus uses this occasion to make known his change of life, his new orientation, commitment, vocation. "Who are my mother and my brothers? And looking around at those seated in the circle he said, "Here are my mother and my brothers. For whoever does the will of God is my brother and sister and mother" (Mk 3:33–35).

Clearly, Jesus did not negate the relationship of son of Mary that had so identified the first half of his life. But the new meaning, new values, and new goals in his life transformed his relationships and shifted Mary to a new place. Yet, deep love, filial piety, devotion, and duty on the part of Jesus remained regarding Mary. She who was the handmaid of God, who birthed and mothered him, remains important and essential. In the midst of crisis and conflict—his own dark night of the soul, the dissolution of his own dreams, and his agonizing death—he is concerned with her future and welfare (Jn. 19:25–27). Jesus is here concerned also with John, the Beloved Disciple. In this time of crisis John's faith can be nourished by Mary: the archetype of mother is still operative in Mary despite Jesus' death.

Even Jesus' death was archetypal. Like so many people he appears to have suspected that his life was in danger and that his time was near. At the same time, he was taken by surprise and confounded. Mark's Gospel, the earliest account, reports Jesus crying out, "My God, my God, why have you forsaken me?" (Mk. 15:34). And yet there was a sense that Jesus gave his life willingly. In Luke's tradition Jesus continues his ministry of preaching, teaching, and saving even on the cross. He does not respond to the challenge, "If you are the King of the Jews, save yourself" (Lk. 23:37). But he does respond to the "good thief" in their last hour. "Amen, I say to you, today you will be with me in Paradise" (Lk. 23:43). At the moment of death itself, Jesus gives his life to the Father. "Father, into your hands I commend my spirit" (Lk. 23:46). This sense of cooperating with the final events of his life is found in Luke again: "Was it not necessary that the Messiah should suffer these things and enter into his glory?" (Lk. 24:26). This is not just postresurrection, not just an understanding of the past events in the light of the new reality. It is the attitude of Jesus himself regarding his fate, his purpose; from the start of his ministry, he was being led by the Spirit. His work, his ministry, was a response to the Spirit deep within himself awakened by numerous inner and outer events.

Finally, as his hour drew near, Jesus had to discern in prayer whether he was to surrender his life in the course of the present events. In the garden, Jesus comes to a new abandonment to the Spirit. "Father, if you are willing, take this cup away from me; still, not my will but yours be done" (Lk. 22:42). Once again, following this test, this life decision, Jesus senses the peace that comes from a true discernment, the operation of the Self, the move toward wholeness, the surrender to God's will, to one's own fate or call: "And to strengthen him an angel from heaven appeared to him. He was in such agony and he prayed so fervently that his sweat became like drops of blood falling on the ground." (Lk. 22:43–44)

Eight Archetypes and Jesus

All of life is archetypal. Jesus therefore had within himself all the patterns of being, relating, growing, and ministering that all people have. Among the numerous archetypes operative in us, eight are typical to some degree. Each were obviously operative in Jesus. We see them operative in his style of relating, being, growing, and ministering. They are the archetypes of mother, companion, solitary, visionary, eternal youth, hero, father, and sage. All men and women have these archetypes as part of their human psychic equipment. Culturally, mother, companion, solitary, and visionary may be seen as feminine archetypes (Wolff). The style of being an eternal youth, hero, father, and sage may be seen as masculine archetypes (Whitmont:181). Yet all are possibilities for both men and women. In mid-life when a man is called to integrate his feminine side and a woman her masculine side these archetypes may become the source of new growth and creativity. Jesus was obviously at ease with his feminine side; we do not see Jesus projecting on women. He is at ease with them, befriends them, and invites them to accompany him. Jesus can mother as well as he can father.

MOTHER

Every human, male or female, begins life in the womb of a mother and is dependent upon that woman for life itself. *Mothering* is actively being concerned for life. Mothering is the willingness to give oneself to the needy or undeveloped. The mother archetype awakens in persons when they discover they have something to give that another needs for physical, emotional, psychological, or spiritual life. The archetype of mother is genuinely operative when one responds to the needy and looks for no reward except the reward of giving and receiving on the part of the needy. This is not a reciprocal relationship of peers. This is a relationship between the haves and the have-nots. The mother archetype is at work when someone responds with care for the sick, elderly, unlearned, or any needy human or a needy cause. The mother pattern can be involved in movements for social justice, women's rights, world ecology, ecumenism, gay rights, or even caring for a poorly tended garden, an abandoned puppy, or a wounded bird.

The public ministry of Jesus is filled with signs of the mother archetype operative in him. Jesus was at times truly maternal and nurturing.

> Come to me, all you who labor and are burdened, and I will give you rest. (Mt. 11:28)

> Jerusalem, Jerusalem, you who kill the prophets and stone those sent to you, how many times I yearned to gather your children together, as a hen gathers her young under her wings, but you were unwilling! (Mt. 23:37)

> In those days when there again was a great crowd without anything to eat, he summoned the disciples and said, "My heart is moved with pity for the crowd, because they have been with me now for three days and have nothing to eat. If I send them away hungry to their homes, they will collapse on the way, and some of them have come a great distance. (Mk. 8:1–3)

> And people were bringing children to him that he might touch them, but the disciples rebuked them. When Jesus saw this he became indignant and said to them, "Let the children come to me; do not prevent them. . . ." Then he embraced them and blessed them, placing his hands on them. (Mk. 10:13–14, 16)

COMPANION

The Book of Exodus tells us that the Lord spoke to "Moses face to face, just as a man speaks with a friend." The archetype of companioning is about intimacy and friendship. The pattern or art of companioning involves mutuality and the gift or miracle of genuine friendship. Mutuality means that both parties have something to give the other as well as to receive from the other. Companioning involves a rhythm of giving and receiving. Some people have one or two true friends in a lifetime, while others are able to companion many people. True friends can be found among people of the opposite sex as well as of the same sex. We find among the many people associated with Jesus those who companioned him in mutual friendship.

> So the sisters sent word to him saying, "Master, the one you love is ill." . . . Now Jesus loved Martha and her sister and Lazarus. (Jn. 11:3, 5)

> Then Jesus came with them to a place called Gethsemane, and he said to his disciples, "Sit here while I go over there and pray." He took along Peter and the two sons of Zebedee, and began to feel sorrow and distress. Then he said to them, "My soul is sorrowful even to death. Remain here and keep watch with me." (Mt. 26:36–38)

> One of his disciples, the one whom Jesus loved, was reclining at Jesus' side. (Jn. 13:23)

> Do you not believe that I am in the Father and the Father is in me? The words that I speak to you I do not speak on my own. The Father who dwells in me is doing his works. (Jn. 14:10)

SOLITARY

In each of us there is an archetype or pattern of being a solitary. If this is the archetype that primarily dominates someone, then that person's solitary life style is usually centered around service in the scientific, medical, or religious fields. The solitary is a person noted for her personal independence. She acts independently of others and is highly motivated and dedicated. Because she is to some degree self-contained, she can appear not to need others. At times in everyone's life the pattern of being a solitary is acted out. At these moments we are for the time self-contained, independent, highly motivated, and courageous.

> From that time on, Jesus began to show his disciples that he must go to Jerusalem and suffer greatly from the elders, . . . and be killed. . . . Then Peter took him aside and began to

rebuke him, "God forbid, Lord! No such thing shall ever happen to you." He turned and said to Peter, "Get behind me, Satan! You are an obstacle to me. You are thinking not as God does, but as human beings do." (Mt. 16:21–23)

Then he made his disciples get into the boat and precede him to the other side toward Bethsaida, while he dismissed the crowd. And when he had taken leave of them, he went off to the mountain to pray. (Mk. 6:45–46)

Filled with the holy spirit, Jesus . . . was led by the Spirit into the desert for forty days. (Lk. 4:1)

The Spirit of the Lord is upon me, because he has anointed me to bring glad tidings to the poor. He has sent me to proclaim liberty to captives and recovery of sight to the blind, to let the oppressed go free. (Lk. 4:18)

VISIONARY

To love someone is "to summon..."

The visionary is in touch with the future. All our prophets are visionaries. The visionary is aware of what is dormant or emerging in the culture or in the church and calls it forth. The visionary archetype is operative when one is in touch with the unconscious possibilities in another and calls them forth. The visionary can put us in contact with both unconscious motivation and the future results of a situation. In every way, Jesus was a genuine visionary.

Moving on from there, he went into their synagogue. And behold, there was a man there who had a withered hand. They questioned him, "Is it lawful to cure on the sabbath?" so that they might accuse him. He said to them, "Which one of you who has a sheep that falls into a pit on the sabbath will not take hold of it and lift it out? How much more valuable a person is than a sheep. So it is lawful to do good on the sabbath." (Mt. 12:9–12)

[H]e said to Simon, "Put out into deep water and lower your nets for a catch." Simon said in reply, "Master, we have worked hard all night and have caught nothing, but at your command I will lower the nets." When they had done this, they caught a great number of fish and their nets were tearing. . . . When Simon Peter saw this, he fell at the knees of

Jesus and said, "Depart from me, Lord, for I am a sinful man." . . . Jesus said to Simon, "Do not be afraid; from now on you will be catching men." (Lk. 5:4–6, 8, 10)

"Lord, I am prepared to go to prison and to die with you." But he replied, "I tell you, Peter, before the cock crows this day, you will deny three times that you know me." (Lk. 22:33–34)

Jesus said to her, "Mary!" She turned and said to him in Hebrew, "Rabbouni," which means Teacher. Jesus said to her, "Stop holding on to me, for I have not yet ascended to the Father. But go to my brothers and tell them, 'I am going to my Father and your Father, to my God and your God.'" Mary of Magdala went and announced to the disciples, "I have seen the Lord," and what he told her. (Jn. 20:16–18)

ETERNAL YOUTH

When one encounters someone who is enthusiastic, engaged in many activities, tireless and busy, with a gift for getting others involved in all these projects, one is in the presence of the eternal youth. The eternal youth is engaging and friendly and has a way of spreading her enthusiasm and winning people over to her many causes. She can be engaged in many things at one time, moving from one activity to another. Almost every friend of the eternal youth participates in a project, cause, activity, or interest of hers. The eternal youth is never afraid to ask for help, enlist someone to join in or help out, or receive help from others. The eternal youth is witnessed in Jesus throughout his public ministry. Without this quality or archetypal dimension he could not have achieved so much in so short a time or engaged so many people in his saving actions.

[A] woman came up to him with an alabaster jar of costly perfumed oil and poured it on his head while he was reclining at table. When the disciples saw this, they were indignant and said, "Why this waste? It could have been sold for much, and the money given to the poor." Since Jesus knew this, he said to them, "Why do you make trouble for the woman? She has done a good thing for me." (Mt. 26:7–10)

As he passed by the Sea of Galilee, he saw Simon and his brother Andrew casting their nets into the sea; they were fishermen. Jesus said to them, "Come after me, and I will make you fishers of men [and women]." Then they left their nets and followed him. (Mk. 1:16–18)

When it was evening, after sunset, they brought to him all who were ill or possessed by demons. The whole town was gathered at the door. . . . Rising very early before dawn, he left and went off to a deserted place, where he prayed. Simon and those who were with him pursued him and on finding him said, "Everyone is looking for you." He told them, "Let us go on to the nearby villages that I may preach there also." (Mk. 1:32–33, 35–38)

On the first day of the Feast of Unleavened Bread, the disciples approached Jesus and said, "Where do you want us to prepare for you to eat the Passover?" He said, "Go into the city to a certain man and tell him, 'The teacher says, "My appointed time draws near; in your house I shall celebrate the Passover with my disciples."'" (Mt. 26:17–18)

HERO

Each of us has a pattern within us of being a hero. It is operative whenever one sets out with determination to achieve one's personal goal or to free, liberate, or save another or others. The qualities associated with the pattern of the hero are single-mindedness, courage, fortitude, fearlessness, and assertion of will. The hero is involved with personal power and his acts are outstanding, extraordinary, and impressive. To be a hero one needs others to free and liberate. It is easy to see Jesus the savior as the hero. The hero can bring new values and shatter the fabric of old ones.

John summoned two of his disciples and sent them to the Lord to ask, "Are you the one who is to come, or should we look for another?" . . . At that time he cured many of their diseases, sufferings, and evil spirits; he also granted sight to many who were blind. And he said to them in reply, "Go and tell John what you have seen and heard: the blind regain their sight, the lame walk, lepers are cleansed, the deaf hear, the dead are raised, the poor have the good news proclaimed to them." (Lk. 7:18–19, 21–22)

I came so that they might have life and have it more abundantly. I am the good shepherd. A good shepherd lays down his life for the sheep. . . . and I will lay down my life for the sheep. . . . No one takes it from me, but I lay it down on my own." (Jn. 10:10b–11, 15b, 18)

"Why does your teacher eat with tax collectors and sinners?" He heard this and said, "Those who are well do not need a physician, but the sick do." (Mt. 9:11–12)

Woe to you Pharisees! You love the seat of honor in synagogues and greetings in marketplaces. Woe to you! You are like unseen graves over which people unknowingly walk. . . . Woe also to you scholars of the law! You impose on people burdens hard to carry, but you yourselves do not lift one finger to touch them. (Lk. 11:43–44, 46)

FATHER

When one speaks as though one's word is law, when one's words challenge others, empower someone, correct or admonish, give just praise or due esteem, the archetype of the father is at work. The father is Lord, spiritual director, judge, counselor, guru, protector. He knows you and conveys that knowledge in word. The father challenges you to live up to your potential and to be all that you can be. The words of the father put you in touch with your own power; the father empowers you. Jesus fathered many people.

During the fourth watch of the night, he came toward them, walking on the sea. . . . Peter said to him in reply, "Lord, if it is you, command me to come to you on the water." He said, "Come." Peter got out of the boat and began to walk on the water toward Jesus. (Mt. 14:25, 28–29)

Jesus said to them, "Come after me, and I will make you fishers of men [and women]." Then they left their nets and followed him. (Mk. 1:17–18)

So he went in and said to them, "Why this commotion and weeping? The child is not dead but asleep." . . . He took the child by the hand and said to her, *"Talitha koum,"* which means, "Little girl, I say to you arise!" The girl, a child of twelve, arose immediately and walked around. (Mk. 5:39, 41–42)

He said to him the third time, "Simon, son of John, do you love me?" Peter was distressed that he had said to him a third time, "Do you love me?" and he said to him, "Lord, you know everything; you know that I love you." Jesus said to him, "Feed my sheep." (Jn. 21:17)

SAGE

While the father puts one in touch with one's own gifts and powers, the sage puts one in touch with one's deepest Self. The sage has the power to put one in contact with one's own unconscious depths because he is in touch with his own true Self. We can, in a true sense, follow him. The words of the sage come from genuine experience. The sage can contact our inner depths and unleash their transpersonal love and capacity for union with nature, God, and all living creatures. Transcendence is the gift of the sage. Jesus called us to love of God and neighbor. In this, he was doing the work of the sage. Jesus also called us to the "kingdom within," the domain of the Sage.

> Do not be afraid any longer, little flock, for your Father is pleased to give you the kingdom. Sell your belongings and give alms. Provide money bags for yourselves that do not wear out, an inexhaustible treasure in heaven that no thief can reach nor moth destroy. For where your treasure is, there also will your heart be. (Lk. 12:32–34)

> So do not worry and say, "What are we to eat?" or "What are we to drink" or "What are we to wear?" All these things the pagans seek. Your heavenly Father knows that you need them all. But seek first the kingdom of God and his righteousness, and all these things will be given you besides. (Mt. 6:31–33)

> Everyone who drinks this water will be thirsty again; but whoever drinks the water I shall give will never thirst; the water I shall give will become in him a spring of water welling up to eternal life. (Jn 4:14)

> Remain in me, as I remain in you. (Jn. 15:4a)

> And behold I am with you always, until the end of the age. (Mt. 28:20b)

5

Mid-Life Spirituality

J ung's psychology is a psychology of the second half of life.
For Jung, growth does not cease with the development of
the ego in the first half of life. He saw the development of the
ego in childhood and in youth as essential for the development
of the larger personality, the Self, in the mid-life and the mature years (Jung, *Modern Man in Search of a Soul:*70–71). "Before
individuation can be taken for a goal, the educational aim of
adaptation to the necessary minimum of collective standards
must first be attained" (Jung, *Psychological Types:*590).

It is essential for one to be holistic in one's approach to
personal and spiritual growth. The development of the ego and
the development of the Self are both holy tasks, as they are
responding to "the duty of one's state of life."

The child and the youth must be about the things of childhood and youth. The mid-life person must be about the things
of mid-life. As for the person in the mature years, she must be
about the things of the final maturing. The mid-life years are,
in essence, much closer to the mature years than they are to
youth.

The development of the ego in childhood and youth is a holy
task and a holy adventure. But as the archetype of mid-life is
evoked in the multifaceted outer and inner experiences of mid-
life crisis the person is being called to embark upon a whole
new journey. This holy pilgrimage is truly new. One cannot put
new wine into old wineskins.

Because the psychology of the second half of life is different
from the psychology of the first half of life a counselor or
therapist immediately takes a person's age into consideration. A
person's problem in the teens or twenties is going to be cen-

tered in the task of the first half of life: ego development, adapting to the outside environment, achieving some autonomy in choices of relating to persons, places, and things. The person's problems in mid-life are centered in the problem of becoming a Self. One's difficulties will primarily be in dealing with one's inner world, the layers of the personal unconscious that have not yet been assimilated, the blocking of energy that needs to be released from the different layers of the collective unconscious, namely, the archetypes. One half deals with a necessary adaptation to outer reality, and the other half deals with adaptation to inner reality.

It follows that the spirituality of the second half of life will be vastly different from the spirituality of the first half of life. The spirituality of the mid-life person corresponds to the psychological tasks and the personal growth required of the mid-life person.

Spirituality: A Way of Life

One's spirituality is the way one lives one's life. Everyone, therefore, has a spirituality. The mid-life person's spirituality is the way the mid-life person lives life.

> What is spirituality? It is the spilling out of an inner reality. It is the incarnation of a spirit. In the first half of life our spirituality flowed from how we perceived ourself and other things. It flowed out of our ego, our consciousness. If we look at where we put our psychic energy we discover our values, what is of prime importance to us, what sets our spirits on fire, and how we enact or incarnate that spirit. We discover our spirituality (Brennan and Brewi, 1985)

One mid-life extravert in her early fifties came to a workshop. She was someone we knew personally. Both of us were surprised that she came to the workshop alone. Ann was someone who was always with people. Not only that, Ann was an extraverted sensing type. She had a love for laughter, fun, and play. Neither Ann nor anyone else had ever experienced a serious side of Ann. But lately she had been experiencing changes. She found she wanted to be alone, without people, for the first time in her life.

Ann had been a member of a religious order for twenty-five years. In all this time she had had many opportunities to be solitary, to develop a reflective side, but she was never inclined to do so. She had rarely felt the need. She had felt the opposite need, for activity, people, projects, enthusiastic causes, friend-ships galore, searching out community needs to meet, and always with a light, humorous, jovial way that delighted others.

Yet last year, for the first time, Ann to her own surprise told her friends she would not join them for a two-week camping trip they enjoyed each summer. They were shocked and did everything to get her to change her mind. But Ann quietly insisted, not even sure of why she was doing this. Instead she made plans to stay on in a remote area of Appalachia after she finished a four-week volunteer project there. When the college students whom Ann was supervising left, she took two weeks alone by herself in a little hermitage connected to the com-munity her students had served for the past five years.

For the first time in her life, Ann found herself alone, pon-dering why she had done this. The quiet at night and during the day was sometimes terrifying, sometimes depressing, and still at other times she absorbed it eagerly. She sensed her body and its movements in a way unknown to her. She felt as though it were a stranger, despite the fact that she was an athletic, outdoors person and always physical and energetic. Emotions and feelings came to her that she never knew she had. As she poured over the Psalms in prayer she related to them in a way that was foreign to her. Ann was thirsty for intimacy with God.

Ann left Appalachia that summer knowing that she had come in touch with an Ann she had never known existed. Coming alone to our workshop, Ann was pursuing the person who wanted to know how to be, without always being with people. She had a gift that had to be set aside to rest for a while so that she could contact other dimensions of herself. Ann's Self was calling her to a new journey, a new adventure.

A forty-year-old lawyer came up to us at another workshop. He pointed to the diagram of Jungian typology on the board. "Do you see this?" he asked, pointing to the functions of feeling and intuition. "Twenty-five years ago," he went on,

> I consciously made a decision that they would have nothing to do with me or my life. Fortunately, I married both of them.

But now it is not enough for me that my wife has them. I feel
a need, a deprivation. Still, I wonder what will they do to me
personally. What will they do to my career?

We had no doubt that this forty-year-old lawyer was being
awakened to another side of himself. The Self was making itself
known. Just his being at the workshop was witness to the response he wanted to make.

Mid-Life—A Call to Conversion

The following lines from Walt Whitman's poem "The Song of
the Open Road" tell the story of the second journey and of mid-
life spirituality.

> Listen! I will be honest with you,
> I do not offer the old smooth prizes, but offer rough
>   new prizes,
> These are the days that must happen to you.
> You shall not heap up what is call'd riches,
> You shall scatter with lavish hand all that you earn or
>   achieve,
> You but arrive at the city to which you were destin'd,
>   you hardly settle yourself to satisfaction before
>   you are call'd by an irresistible call to depart,
> You shall be treated to the ironical smiles and
>   mockings of those who remain behind you,
> What beckonings of love you receive you shall only
>   answer with passionate kisses of parting,
> You shall not allow the hold of those who spread their
>   reach'd hands toward you. (185)

The mid-life years call for a fundamental spiritual reorientation. The purpose of the mid-life crisis and transition is to
effect that re-orientation or conversion. The conversion of mid-
life is to shift the focus, the center of attention and gravity from
the ego to the Self.

Whitman's poem mirrors the conversion and transformation
that is called for in mid-life. There is an imperative in one for
this second journey. It and it alone will be life giving now. One is
called into a whole new way of being. There is a new kind of
generativity and integrity here. These are the years for personality development, for "culture" not "nature" (Jung, *Modern*

*Man in Search of a Soul:*70–71). These are the years for unity with the Self, unity with the cosmos, unity with the Kingdom of God. This is the work of the second half of life, mid-life and the years of maturity.

One is being called in mid-life to a new way of being in the world. In childhood and in youth the outer world called us forth. In mid-life and the mature years the inner world calls to us. The outer environment gives place to the inner environment. If one does not heed this call one becomes spiritually sick, one can "lose one's soul."

It follows that mid-life spirituality will be more inner directed than outer directed, more into the unconscious than the conscious. A mid-life spirituality is more about becoming one's true Self than about the ego and following the dictates of the collective. It is more about asking the question, Who am I really? and looking for an answer within one's inner environment than about being named by one's outer environment of people, careers, professions, commitments, education, and relationships. None of these outer factors is negated, but they shift in emphasis and can no longer be priorities. Mid-life spirituality is more about being than doing, waiting than achieving, spirit food than body food. "Not on bread alone does man live" (Lk. 4:4).

All this is a radical departure from the tasks and goals of youth and their accompanying spirituality.

> For a younger person it is almost a sin, and certainly a danger, to be too much occupied with himself [or herself]; but for the aging person it is a duty and a necessity to give serious attention to himself [or herself]. (Jung, *Modern Man in Search of a Soul:*109)

Mid-life spirituality flows from a new attitude and a new orientation. The change of life at mid-life is a revolutionary change. As one enters mid-life the Self becomes the center, in place of the all-important ego. A new standpoint and attitude arises in the person, with accompanying new values:

First half of life	Second half of life
• ego	• self
• conscious personality	• unconscious personality

- outer events
- outer environment
- achievements
- doing

- inner events
- inner environment
- integration
- being

As the person goes through the mid-life years, and that could be for many people three or four decades of a lifetime, there is a new spirituality for a new stage of development. One is called to contact and integrate the neglected aspects of the personal unconscious. One must claim and own one's own story. One must objectify one's past. The collective unconscious and the archetypes become the sources of new growth and integration. The call is to become the unique individual that one is and, from a faith perspective, that God is calling one to be.

Many women and men find the empty nest the cause of deep depression, alienation, and disorientation. They are usually people who have found great satisfaction in their home and family life, and in the excitement and challenges of bringing children through the years of childhood, adolescence, and young adulthood. Full participation in all that this involves fills some women and men with more than enough energy and enthusiasm for life. One woman sobbed softly, "I just love my four girls. The thought of being without them is killing me. I don't want the time to end. But I know it is here and there is nothing I can do about it."

Another man confided in me, "My wife is in a bad way. Our youngest boy, the last of seven, went off to college. I don't know what to do with her."

Ruth shared with me the fact that she had made a major decision. Her husband had been given his company's condominium in Hawaii to use during the Christmas week. He was thrilled and wanted to go. Ruth was torn between her own desire to go and give him the opportunity he wanted, and her feeling that Christmas was family time and that they should be with their children and grandchildren. They also had to think about his parents and her mother: "How could they not be with them at this time. Perhaps it would be their last Christmas," she thought.

Ruth was smiling when she told me her decision to book their flight to Hawaii. She said,

I know that I'm going to find it hard. Many people are going
to be disappointed and feel let down. But this is right for Pete
and me now. We need time together. We need to discover
ourselves as individuals outside of the family. I have neglected
our relationship in favor of other responsibilities. This is a
great opportunity and Pete and I deserve to give it to ourselves. I know it would be wrong for me not to take this gift.

Another man had for a decade wanted to change his position
as superintendent of schools. The job required a long drive,
sometimes six or seven days a week. He was great at his work
but in the last few years found it hard to hold on to the
"persona" of superintendent. He wanted to take a simple job
lecturing at a small Catholic campus near home. Last year,
when he approached the family about his dream, his son said,
"Pop, you can't do that. How can you change the style of life we
are accustomed to?" He gave in after that. But now he knew this
was his last year. He handed in his resignation at the end of that
week.

Individuation

Individuation, as Jung saw it, is primarily a development of
the second half of life. As one enters into this growth process
consciously, one is aware that one is trembling to be born. The
Self is in the process of becoming. The Self is both conscious
and unconscious, encountered in both inner and outer events,
and embraces the ego and so much more than the ego. One's
ongoing creation takes place in and through this project of
individuation just as one's initial creation took place in and
through the lovemaking of a man and woman. Individuation
must also be a work of love. Like lovemaking, it too must be the
coming together of opposites. Speaking of human development Pierre Teilhard de Chardin said, "It is the collaboration,
trembling with love, which we give to the hand of God, concerned to attire and prepare us" (97).

The process of individuation is the process of becoming
oneself. The initial stage of this process is ego development.
The built-in pattern for ego development in the first half of life
is no less holy than the growth that is called for in the second
half of life, but it is a gift only begun.

The individuation process of the mid-life years calls for the same devotion and commitment once given to the first half of life. The mid-life person surrenders herself to allow herself to be fashioned anew. One needs to be molded anew through one's life story (past); one's inner world, unique experiences, and (present) reality; as well as the discernment of the Spirit leading one toward new hills and valleys (future).

Mid-life spirituality embraces the continual need to know one's story at deeper levels. Mid-life spirituality calls for giving more and more attention to one's own living experience within and without. Mid-life spirituality calls for a continual growing need to become more and more centered and in touch with the living streams within. Each of us has within us hills and valleys filled with demons and angels. These archetypes are the source of all energy and growth in mid-life. Like Dante, one must be willing to enter in.

Dante's journey brought him down into hell. Each person's journey in the second half of life will lead him down into a hell. So the mid-life person will have a need to bear the darkness and terror of the unknown. But through that dark valley one discovers a newness, a connection to the Spirit, to resources yet unknown, the living stream.

> Where can I go from your spirit?
>   from your presence where can I flee?
> If I go up to the heavens, you are there;
>   if I sink to the nether world, you are present there.
> If I take the wings of the dawn,
>   if I settle at the farthest limits of the sea,
> Even there your hand shall guide me,
>   and your right hand hold me fast.
> If I say, "Surely the darkness shall hide me,
>   and night shall be my light"—
> For you darkness itself is not dark,
>   and night shines as the day.
> Darkness and light are the same.
>
>   (Ps. 139:7–12)

These words resound in one at mid-life, as do these: "You shall not heap up what is call'd riches." Turn your mind to other matters. Turn your eyes and your heart within. Enter the heart-shaped door. "The Kingdom of God is within you." Explore the less forgotten world, follow the road within. But we might ask, as Jung did, "Are there schools for forty-year-olds to prepare them for the second half of life?" The first step for each of us is to learn the secrets of the heart, to find the secret of the mid-life years. Out of this will emerge one's personal spirituality for the mid-life years. For there is no one mid-life spirituality; there are many mid-life spiritualities. One's spirituality is carved out of one's uniqueness during these mid-life years. The individuation process is unique for each individual; so, too, is the spirituality of each one.

The Religious Function and Mid-Life

The spirituality of the mid-life years calls for a religious attitude. Freud, through his psychological studies, released us from repressed sexuality. The works of Jung call for a release of the religious function. As dangerous as repressed sexuality can be, a repressed spirituality is no less dangerous to the fullness of human life. For Jung, the spiritual life of the human person was exactly what made us human. Freud saw "God" as an infantile projection of the father, and prayer as a desire to return to the life of the womb. Jung saw "God" as a projection of the God archetype within, and prayer as communion with God, and communion with the Self, the archetype of God. For Jung, the God image was innate in each of us: denial and repression of that does violence to one's nature and limits the person and one's ability to relate to the "supernatural," archetypal realm of the psyche.

As a believer, one is aware that the psychic God image within is no "proof" of the existence of God, but it does support one's belief and opens one to the personal encounter with God that our nature calls for. One understands better the connection between the "God out there" and the "God in here," God as transcendent and as immanent. The idea of "divine indwelling" takes on new psychic meaning. Freud put us in contact with our basic human sexuality and its force; Jung put us in contact with our repressed spirits. Once one contacts the world within, the Self at one's center and the divine indwelling, one is compelled to live a more spiritual, wholistic life. This attention to the Self and to the God within is an illuminating experience that both separates and connects, depletes and empowers, calls us within and without, creates and re-creates us.

Jung realized that the modern person's encounter with the psyche, the encounter with the Self, is a mystery that cannot be distinguished from the experience of God. The mystics of all ages have given witness to the "cathedral within." Spirituality is a constant expansion of the divine potential that is the very constituent of being human. The mid-life person is called to an intense participation in religious life. Inner experience and the encounter with the figures of the unconscious are religious experiences. According to Jung, the unfolding of the personality in the second half of life takes place within this great encounter and in the archetypal realm.

> The seat of faith . . . is not consciousness but spontaneous religious experience, which brings the individual's faith into immediate relation with God. (*The Unconscious Self:*100)

> No matter what the world thinks about religious experience, the one who has it possesses the great treasure of a thing that has provided him [or her] with a source of life, meaning, and beauty, and that has given a new splendor to the world and to mankind. He has pistis and peace . . . (*Psychology and Religion:*113)

Finally, let us turn to the Gospels and ask whether they offer a word for those who find themselves in the midst of the mid-life experience of crisis and transition. The Gospels depict Jesus as the new Moses, calling us out of bondage and into new being. The Gospels, like all the Scriptures, are accounts of the living experiences of people. They reveal primordial experiences, religious experiences, numinous experiences, transformations, conversions, human pathos, divine pervasiveness, all the heights and depths of the human spirit. The Scriptures reveal the many facets of human nature, the evil lurking in each of us, the heights which we long and to what we are called. The Scriptures can mirror us at any moment and this can be consoling, challenging, instructive, and refreshing.

Through the Scriptures the Spirit can evoke in us growth, healing, transcendence, confession, integration, and wholeness.

The Scriptures put us in touch with the spiritual dimension of life: the unconscious, angels, dreams, evil powers, visions, divine messengers, passovers, exodus, deaths, and resurrections. In times of orientation, disorientation, and reorientation we find the Scriptures mirroring us and addressing us. In times of dislocation and relocation, in times of well-being and wholeness we may find the Scriptures addressing us in a profound, life-giving way. The Scriptures can put us in touch with ourselves. They can re-create us in mind and heart. We can encounter the divine Other here.

The Scriptures can put us in touch with our own religious experiences. For a person at mid-life this is essential. What were my religious experiences in the past? Which experiences of mine are memorable, which have been the sources of my decisions and make me know more about who I really am, as God knows me to be?

Speaking of his work with mid-life people Jung said:

> Among all my patients in the second half of life—that is to say, over thirty-five—there has not been one problem in the last resort that was not that of finding a religious outlook on life. It is safe to say that everyone of them fell ill because he [or she] had lost that which the living religions of every age have given to their followers, and none of them has really been healed who did not regain his [or her] religious outlook. (*Modern Man in Search of a Soul*:229)

Only the Spirit can awaken in one's heart a religious attitude about life. The Spirit breathes where and when the Spirit wills. But the Gospels tell us that the Christ stands at one's door and knocks. He invites us to come in and sup with him. He reminds us that he is the vine and we are the branches. He reveals our secrets to us and numbers the hairs on our head. He goes after us like a shepherd after a lost lamb. He speaks to the pharisee in each of us, challenges the Martha, protects the fallen woman, admonishes the Thomas, and takes the child in us into his arms.

The Scriptures and the primordial human experiences of mid-life open us to our unconscious inner depths and can call us to life. Speaking of the unconscious and the spiritual life Ann and Barry Ulanov say:

Without access to this vibrant underlying current of human experience—raw, undifferentiated, and mixed with the physical as it may be—the procedures of spiritual growth become dry, mechanical techniques, that effect no transformation of soul. Instead, a legalism and a moralism, a list of "shoulds" and "should nots," come to usurp the place of the genuinely religious attitude, an attitude that is always marked off from other human attitudes by its easiness, its flexibility, its sweetness of feeling, its openness to the new. (1975:50)

As one looks at the Gospels one can find so many sections addressing a person in the mid-life experience. In this regard, the story of the raising of Lazarus is particularly poignant. It is a story about process. It is a story of death and resurrection, and mid-life is a time for death and resurrection. It is a story about human emotions, fears, and heartbreaks, and the unexpected. So, too, is mid-life. It is a story about the need for involvement and a call for full participation. So, too, is mid-life a call for intense personal involvement in growth and a call for full participation. No doubt the raising of Lazarus is a source of inspiration and consolation to people in situations other than mid-life. That is the power of Scripture: it can be for us a Word of God again and again at different times in life.

The Raising of Lazarus

Let us consider the story of Lazarus as it addresses one in mid-life. Perhaps nowhere in the Gospels is Jesus more fully depicted as someone capable of deep personal love for another than in John's account of this story (Jn. 11:1–44). The shortest verse in the English Bible is found in this chapter: verse 35, "And Jesus wept" (Moulton:40–41). John is making a declaration here that Jesus is one of us and that he has deep human emotions.

The raising of Lazarus as told in John's Gospel has deep significance to the person in the midst of the mid-life experience. At one of our mid-life retreats the participants gathered together for a closing prayer. Each one brought along a Scripture passage that spoke of where they were at that moment in life. One woman read the Lazarus story, "I feel that I am dead," she said through her tears, "and I am waiting for Jesus to call me forth." She was in the heart of her mid-life crisis experience. Other people, in the mid-life transition stage, have referred to being like Lazarus "set free" or to experiencing being unbound. Many others, having experienced the third birth and being in the period of mid-life itself, identify with Lazarus because they have known themselves to be raised up and set free. Whether in crisis, transition, or the mid-life period itself, people in mid-life find that the story of Lazarus speaks to them and gives them hope in sorrow or mirrors the new life they have received.

As one prays over the Lazarus account, the spirituality of mid-life can be discerned. Jesus is at the Jordan and word comes from Martha and Mary, the sisters of Lazarus, that Lazarus is sick. Immediately we know of Lazarus's privileged place in Jesus' affection. The wording of the report reveals this to us from the start: "Master, the one you love is ill" (Jn. 11:3).

As one reaches mid-life one begins to feel one's lack of wholeness, incompleteness, sinfulness or shadiness, inferiority—one's shadow side. Only a short time ago it may have appeared that all was well. One felt a sense of maturity, rightness, being in command, superiority, completion, but now one feels like Humpty-Dumpty. Depression, despondency, or a dark night of the soul may descend upon a person, out of the blue or triggered by some outer or inner event. One feels sick. A malaise has set in that cannot be diagnosed or relieved. And one is called to wait in darkness.

What is the significance of the waiting in the Lazarus story? Jesus does not respond immediately. He knows about the sickness of Lazarus, yet he delays for several days. Again the account tells us of Jesus' great love for Lazarus. "Our friend Lazarus is asleep, but I am going to awaken him" (Jn. 11:11). Lazarus's home is in Judea, where Jesus has many enemies; nevertheless, they set out. John's Gospel leaves no doubt in our mind that Jesus loved Lazarus.

How important it was to Lazarus to be loved in this way! When one is struck by the mid-life crisis experience—when the rug, as it were, is pulled out from under—it is important to have been loved. A strong ego is just as essential in the second half of life as it is in the first half. Despite the fact that the ego appears to be shattered in this mid-life crisis it must have the strength to hold on, to wait, even without hope or a sense of hope. In total darkness, the soul awaits the word. Waiting is creative. The word is creative. Genesis tells us the Word of the Lord creates:

> In the beginning, when God created the heavens and the earth, the earth was a formless wasteland, and darkness covered the abyss, while a mighty wind swept over the waters.
> Then God said, "Let there be light," and there was light. (Gn. 1:1–3)

The archetypal image is that creation comes from nothing. Many a man or woman feels like a wasteland at mid-life. A great insurmountable abyss appears, a darkness of mind, soul, and heart descends, and violent winds threaten. Having once known oneself loved, one can wait.

"When Jesus arrived at Bethany, he found that Lazarus had already been in the tomb for four days" (Jn. 11:17). Lazarus is both dead and buried. There is no hope of life. The four-day period tells us that decay has already set in. Martha and Mary have reason to be without hope. Lazarus is long dead. Both Martha and Mary reproach Jesus with the same words: "Lord, if you had been here, my brother would not have died" (Jn. 11:21, 32). Once again John tells us that in the presence of the grief of the sisters Jesus "became perturbed [literally, "snorted in spirit"] and deeply troubled" (Jn. 11:33).

The person in a mid-life crisis is no stranger to grief. There is a dying. The "beloved Lazarus," the beloved ego, the person one has worked hard to become, the one who has won the love and affection of family and friends, this diligent, hard working, decisive personality and character, this one is dying and dead. First Lazarus was sick, and then dying. Now he is dead. Sometimes the ego has a sense that some aspect is sick, and several aspects are dying, gone, dead.

Even now, at this moment, the reader can ask the question, What part of me is sick, dying, dead? Jesus can be for me a symbol of the Self. Jesus represents the greater personality, in each of us, that one is called to be. The Self needs the ego. The Self wants to come alive in and through the ego and use its strength to carry on the work of becoming and integrating in the years ahead.

Jesus, once again troubled in spirit, approaches the tomb. There will be a partnership, a marriage between this ascending Self and descending ego. "Take away the stone" (Jn. 11:39). The power of the word of Jesus will bring Lazarus back to life. "Lazarus, come out!" (Jn. 11:43). Lazarus comes out with his hands and feet bound, as the custom was, with linen strips. His face is wrapped in a cloth. "Untie him," Jesus told them, "and let him go" (Jn. 11:44b).

Oh, the marvel of it all. It is a perfect story. The mid-life person often does not know what it was that "rolled away the stone" from one's lifeless body. Sometimes the change comes as quietly as a gentle wind: one is faintly aware of a change, one dares not mention it lest it go away. At other times it is a striking, sudden, dramatic moment, out of the blue: "Lazarus, come forth." The self commands the ego to arise, live, join me in the journey and the adventure before us. A new attitude has been born. The self is the primary mover and actress in the life story to be enacted. The ego has a necessary but a subordinate place.

Jesus asked the others to enter into the great act of raising Lazarus from the dead. He asked others to join him by rolling away the stone and again by unbinding him. The Self employs both inner and outer life in the great act of being set free. Individuation not only calls for the ego and the Self to interact, to respect and love each other; it also calls for a participation in both the inner and outer life. It calls for participation in the inner and outer lives of other people. The Self is not a proud, isolated, arrogant individualistic monarchy. She engages others, even shadowy characters, in her great task of wholeness and freedom. She engages others in her tasks of becoming a leaven for others and of joining in the re-creation of the earth.

Jesus called Lazarus forth with his mighty voice and he called on others to set him free. All throughout the story there is the most intense participation, even in the waiting.

What can the mid-life person learn about mid-life spirituality from the story of the raising of Lazarus? Here are some suggestions:

- Dying always precedes new life, new birth, a transformation.
- New life comes from decay, from what is undesirable, from a "stench."

- Waiting is part of the process of moving from one stage to another, part of the transformation process.
- Part of the darkness of the mid-life crisis is that the ego is giving way to the Self, the conscious to the unconscious.
- The Lord truly loves me and feels my pain. I am not alone.
- The Lord has the power to call me forth.
- The Self, the image of God that I am, is with me at this time of dying.
- The Self will call me forth, give me living waters.
- Full participation is demanded by the Lord, the Self, and others in this process of rebirth.
- The Self will use other people, places, and things to enter into the process of individuation.
- The second half of life is a continual process of becoming one's true Self.
- Sickness, suffering, dying, and even death itself is redemptive. Everything can be put to use in the process of growth, sanctification, and glorification.
- My growth, sanctification, salvation, and glorification are worked out in time and history by the Lord and by the Spirit.
- I must be willing to enter into both the giving and receiving of great love.
- I need liminal times.
- My own liberation is a call to set others free, to unbind them. Each one of us is called to participate fully in the liberation of the oppressed.

6

Reflective Exercises

This chapter contains a series of reflective exercises for the issues discussed in chapters 1 through 5. A few suggestions first may help you get the most benefit from the exercises in this book.

Before you begin, get yourself a special book to write in while doing the exercises.

When you are about to begin a reflective exercise, enter the date, time, and place on the top of a new page of your special writing book. Perhaps for future reference you may also wish to jot down a phrase about some significant event going on that day or in the days immediately surrounding the day of doing this reflective exercise. (For example: "April 1, 1987. At home, Joy Street. Doctor yesterday—six-month check-up, all fine. Joe buried last week.")

Dialogue or journaling facilitates reflection, self-knowledge, and growth. If an event, memory, attitude, image, or person is part of your life it is also a part of you. You have a personal relationship with it. Thus, to write about it, to write a letter to it, or to write a dialogue with it recognizes both the subjective and objective aspects of that relationship. Such a dialogue allows you to release the potential energy and healing power to be found in this past, present, or future part of yourself. To personify an event or work for example and speak to it allows you to finish any unfinished business with it. (For example: "Wedding day, I wish now that you had never dawned," or "Engineering, thank God I never chose you.")

As one dialogues with a past event one brings one's present

circumstances to bear upon the dialogue. One comes to new insights to bring to one's interpretation of the past event. Circumstances and perspectives that did not yet exist at the time of the past events are brought to the surface and a new relationship with a living part of oneself is effected.

Remember that whenever you are asked to dialogue with something you must prepare yourself. Here are some suggestions:

- Get yourself in a relaxed state of mind and body.
- After finding a comfortable position do some simple breathing exercises. Pay attention to your breathing.
- Choose a word or phrase as a calming word and repeat it slowly and rhythmically as you breathe. (For example: *life, love, Abba-Father, peace.*)
- Finally, when you are ready, bring to your mind whatever it is you are to dialogue with.
- Spend some time with that memory, thought, attitude, person, event, or whatever you have chosen.
- When you feel ready, begin your dialogue. Your dialogue can be a simple writing to the "other" (to the memory, attitude, person, or whatever), as in the form of a letter. Or it can be writing about it. Or it can be a direct dialogue where you speak to it in written form and it does the same to you, back and forth. Always choose what comes most naturally at the time.

The Exercises

1. List the decades of your life and recall:
   a) the things that gave you the greatest joys during that time
   b) the things that gave you the greatest sorrows during that time

2. One by one focus on each of the people, joyful and sorrowful events, and achievements, and dialogue with them.

3. Dialogue with each decade.

4. Dialogue with your relationship or nonrelationship with God during each decade.

5. List the greatest disappointments of the first half of your life. Dialogue with each of them.

6. Reflect on the two halves of your life: the first half (child-hood and youth), the second half (mid-life and the mature years). Think of two flowers: one to symbolize for you the first half of life and another the second half. Think of a tree to symbolize the first half of your life and another to symbolize the second half. With each symbol ask yourself: What does this symbol mean to me? List the meanings. (For example: Buttercup: "yellow, small, close to ground, our front lawn, bright, warm.") Finally, dialogue with the flowers and then the trees about their possible rela-tionship to the first and second halves of your life.

7. Take a brown paper bag (from a supermarket). Cut it open and you will have a large sheet of paper. Draw a large circle, or with a cake plate trace a circle and cut it out. Divide it in four sections, one for each of the four stages of life: childhood, youth, mid-life, and the mature years. Using crayons, colored pencils, or paints, color in the four sections. You can draw, doodle, write, or just color in each section with your impressions and feelings about each of your four stages, those past, present, and yet to come (future).

8. Ponder the archetypes we discussed: mother, companion, solitary, visionary, eternal youth, hero, father and sage. Each one is a pattern of being human, a style of being, relating, acting and ministering. You have experienced each in your lifetime. Reflect one by one on those experi-ences.
   a) Mother
      (i) What people in your life have given you the most support, have helped to nurture you?
      (ii) Recall a time when you nurtured and cared for someone else or for something else.
      (iii) Have you encountered pseudomothers, ones who overprotected, suffocated with sweetness, wanted to keep you helpless and dependent, wanted to devour and possess you rather than free you? Who were they?
      (iv) Have you experienced in yourself or another the distortion of the mother-style that allows one to be

consumed? She can never say no. She is always the first to volunteer and she cares for others at the cost of terrific psychic loss and pain.

(v) When and how have you experienced God as mother?

b) Companion

(i) Many of your close, personal friendships offer you opportunity to develop your companion style. Mutuality is a characteristic of genuine companioning. Who have you companioned (and they you) in the past? At this time in your life who are you companioning (and they you)?

(ii) As you look at this companioning history what are your satisfactions? Your dissatisfactions?

(iii) Have you been involved in pseudo or anticompanionship—either allowing someone else to provide for you, or you for them, a climate without mutuality, and calling it friendship or companioning?

(iv) When and how have you experienced God companioning you?

c) Solitary

(i) What people do you know whose style is predominantly that of a solitary?

(ii) Is this your predominant style? Can you recall times in your life when you were a healthy solitary?

(iii) An unhealthy solitary is emotionally immature and unable to enter relationships. Are you aware of this in yourself or others?

(iv) What about solitary time? At this time in your life do you have too much time alone or not enough time alone? If you answered yes, what can you do about it?

(v) If you had a day, a week, or a month to be solitary (alone), how would you spend it?

d) Visionary

(i) A visionary gives witness to what is emerging in the culture. When have you been a visionary? Whose visions have you shared in?

(ii) Who has helped you to see what lies beneath the

surface in you, to discover the inner depths of yourself?

(iii) When and with whom have you yourself been a visionary, helping someone else to discover inner depths?

(iv) What Scripture passages have served you in the archetypal capacity as visionary, pointing you to personal inner depths or connecting you to what is new and emerging in society?

(v) Events in life can be archetypal and have the same effect on us that a visionary can have. What has happened in your life to awaken you to new horizons or awaken in you new ideas and visions?

(vi) The pseudovisionary uses her psychic powers recklessly. Are you aware of this in yourself or others?

e) Eternal Youth

(i) How many projects are you involved in: five, ten, twenty?

(ii) How often do you ask people to join you in your projects: never? seldom? frequently? usually? always? (Pick the answer that best describes your behavior.)

(iii) How often do you ask someone to assist you so that you can be free to work on a project that is dear to you: never? seldom? frequently? usually? always?

(iv) Have you ever willingly or unwillingly mothered (helped out) an eternal youth? What people do you know who are predominantly eternal youths?

(v) How do you feel about the fact that Jesus often acted out of the eternal youth archetype?

(vi) If you are not an eternal youth, imagine ways your life could change if that archetype became more operative in you.

(vii) A negative eternal youth can be promiscuous and find fidelity and commitment impossible. Are you aware of this in yourself or others?

f) Hero

(i) Have you ever been in a situation where your own inner courage emerged, giving you unusual

power and strength to help set someone free, per-
form an extraordinary act, or stand up for someone else?

    (ii) When have you been heroic in regard to your own
self?

   (iii) Who are the most heroic people you know?

   (iv) Who has freed you? Whom have you freed?

    (v) Are you a compulsive hero or heroine?

g) Father

    (i) Each human person has the capacity to father.
The father knows you, what you can do, and what
is right for you, and communicates that to you.
Who has fathered you?

    (ii) Do you long for a father to clearly point the way
for you or put you in contact with your potential?

   (iii) When and with whom have you yourself acted out
of the father archetype?

   (iv) The pseudofather is a dictator. "Where love rules
there is no force." Have there been pseudofathers
in your life?

    (v) When and how has God fathered you?

h) Sage

    (i) For the sage, personal growth comes from deep
and meaningful experiences. What have been
your deepest and most meaningful experiences?

    (ii) The sage evokes the deepest aspirations and spir-
itual aims in others. What are your deepest
aspirations at this time in your life?

   (iii) Who has evoked spiritual aims in you in the past as
you look back over your life?

   (iv) The sage awakens others to transpersonal love
and values (truth, love, beauty, freedom, oneness,
and so on). Who has done this for you?

    (v) The sage experiences the transpersonal and lives
and practices what she experiences and teaches. In
what way are you a sage?

   (vi) At this time of your life what awakens in you the
greatest transcendence?

9. Plan a day or a series of days to celebrate your own mid-
life. Include doing something you have never done, some-

thing you always wanted to do. Change something about yourself (for example, your hair style or clothes). Buy something to symbolize your hope for your mid-life. Plan, create, or just participate in a religious ritual for the occasion.

10. Make this year a special celebration of your life cycle:
    a) Make a pilgrimage to significant places in your childhood.
    b) Put together an album of photos or mementos, with sections for the four stages of your life.
    c) Visit and talk with people from your past who can give you their perspective on different aspects of your personal history.
    d) Celebrate your roots in some way (for example: a trip to the country of your ancestors, learning their language or studying their customs).
    e) Attend an ethnic festival or read poetry or prose from or about places connected to your origins and history.
    f) Buy and play recordings of music that has been significant in each stage of your life.
    g) Plan a special day to celebrate your own childhood and another day to celebrate your youth.
    h) Help someone else to celebrate a day for their childhood, youth, mid-life, and mature years.

PART II

My Shadow as a Source of New Growth: The Shadow as Archetypal

by Anne Brennan

7

Mid-Life Shadow: Emergence, Upheaval, and Encounter

M ark's eyes were angry, his temples grew red under his graying hair and his voice cracked under the weight of his angry words.

> "My mother was almost thirteen when she had me. She could have raised me if only they had let her try, but they wouldn't let her do it. My twin and I were just bounced from one foster home to the other. My twin died from it at three but I've had the agony of living on to forty-seven!"

For the first time in his life this serene parole officer was allowing all that pain to surface. He was feeling the fury of that repressed rage. He was becoming aware in a whole new way of the terrible feelings of rejection and frustration inside that good little boy and self-sacrificing young man who had for so long taken it all for granted and "made do."

At forty-seven Mark was grieving over his childhood. For the first time in his life, he was allowing himself to feel and own the pain of the baby, the little boy who did not have one or two pairs of loving arms to receive him, cherish him, and rejoice in his birth and his person.

At this stage of his grieving, he could not yet honestly objectify and see what anyone looking at the situation from the outside could see. He was too angry about the pain of the baby to see realistically that his mother was only a twelve-year-old little girl herself and could never have taken on the responsibility of her twins or even of one of her babies. However, after all these years of taking it for granted, he was finally admitting the situation to himself with all its existential and emotional impact. He was standing with the infant whose human right to parenting was so poorly met and he was screaming at the injustice and deprivation.

This was the same strong, caring man who had stood, so often before, in solidarity with the innocent, imprisoned, or rejected reforming parolee.

For three years Mark's life had been in turmoil. His own four teenagers and young adults had seen their formerly rather easygoing father outraged, deeply hurt, and then sullenly quiet over every disagreement and misdemeanor of theirs. He had become fanatical about enforcing rules and had severely punished any infringement. This was placing each of them in an intense combat stance against him. Their own breaking-away process, already normally stormy as each was testing leaving the nest, was becoming more and more hostile. His youngest, at sixteen, had just been picked up for stealing a car, taking it for a wild ride, and abandoning it a block from where he took it.

There had been trouble in a rather good marriage as his wife, already drained herself, grew more and more impatient with his uncharacteristic behavior. Mark was having a great deal of trouble sleeping and had begun to take medication for high blood pressure. Meanwhile, at work, he had realized his dream and had been promoted to district supervisor and faced still greater responsibilities.

Mark was overdue. It had long since been time for a moratorium, a breathing space to take a look at his life. For at least three years he had been goaded by his own agitation and outbursts at home into reclaiming this inert part of himself. The unconscious psychic energy that had been used to keep his lifelong hurt hidden from himself was now needed for other growth. It has been crucial to his future development as a person that he now own this cut-off part of himself.

In Mark's life deprivation and numbness had served a purpose in allowing him to move into a rather healthy and magnanimous lifestyle and build a strong ego. His own early lack of love and care had been like an underground force, pushing him to give love and care to others who had so little. He had held two jobs so that he could earn a master's degree in social work. He had become a really creative social worker. His numbness about his own early life had prevented self-pity from swallowing him and crippling his ability to move beyond it into the roles and commitments in which he grew in identity and adaptation. Both this numbness and this motivation had been almost completely hidden from him until now.

In these three years in the Shadows of his own unconscious a bitter forgotten part of him was stirring. It had been making itself felt in his very uncharacteristic behavior and even, perhaps, in his physical problems.

This injustice, this evil, in his own early story was beginning to erupt at a time in his life when, in an equally shadowy way, the "great injustice and evil" at the other end of life was beginning to press in upon his consciousness. Mark was in mid-life and mortality had begun to impinge on him from many directions.

His daughters and sons were daily more and more becoming women and men with ideas, directions, and dreams of their own. His own early dreams had been more or less fulfilled and were wearing thin. He had some measure of career success but still not much power to change things. He and Marie had bought their home but it soon would be too big and too empty. His marriage was still there, if rocky. His sex life was more boring and routine. His religious life was still flickering, if recently more empty. His health was in jeopardy. His only friend from his teen years had just had a fatal heart attack.

Another friend, a forty-four-year-old airline captain, had stunned Mark at the wake: "Death," hissed this always affable, strong pilot, "is the greatest ripoff. All this stuff about a Good Shepherd is a crock! Everything we've ever worked for is just wiped out." Mark knew that this man had not so long ago been a more than weekly churchgoer.

It was in the days after the funeral that Mark went looking for someone to talk to about this mid-life crisis of his.

Mark's problems seemed at first to be connected to his present and his future, and indeed they were. However, Mark had *lived* forty-seven years and so he had a long past clinging to him. As he had been knit in his mother's womb, so he had been knit in this past and it was the fabric of who he was.

To be entering mid-life is to have lived thirty-five, forty, fifty years. It is to have accumulated millions of experiences of which one was more or less conscious and millions more which were too subliminal, too incomprehensible, or too painful to have become conscious. Yet, all these experiences, too, have somehow registered so that even an odor out of our past can stop us midsentence and carry us back to another time.

To have entered the human race well on in the course of its evolution is to have inherited a body with vestiges of prehistoric forebears. It is to speak a language that has evolved and has roots in other languages. It is to learn words, symbols, thoughts, behaviors, rituals, beliefs, and aspirations of long-dead forebears. It is to use artifacts and furnishings that can be traced to ancient underpinnings. It is to be aware of newly discovered mysteries of the universe that were always there but were unknown for most of the fifty-two billion years of its history. It is to thus be the embodiment of patterns of being and ways of relating that are typically human and so, archetypal.

To be in mid-life is to somehow be the heir and guardian of humanity and of all this human experience as well as of our own years of experience. My life is, I am, a continuum within a continuum. My life is, I am, emerging out of an unfathomable darkness and incomprehensibility. My life is, I am, the result of a pulsing urge toward life and consciousness. I am impelled not only to live life but to love it, that is, to chew it, digest it, and make some meaning of it, to make consciousness of it. I am gifted to make a gift of that dark but brilliant consciousness and love, that Self, to all that has gone before and will come after and ultimately to the mysterious Source and End of life and love.

Mark had come to that crossroad, that transition, to the edge of that "dark wood" fearful and fascinating. He had come to his own dark night of the soul where he was to wrestle with all this, to wrestle with himself and lose himself to find himself. He had come to the point of development where to go on was to go within as well.

Were Mark to read this he might call it a far too dramatic description of what had begun for him. Yet, the Mark of ten years later was a very different man in countless ways. That Mark had spent all his anger, though not his pain, about his childhood. He could talk about it then with words that tenderly embraced both the child and the others and even the very flawed foster homes. He could see that some of his own greatest accomplishments and most lovable and fine traits flowed directly in some mysterious way from the injustice and evil of those early beginnings.

Ten years later, Mark had found an abyss of evil done to him and had engaged it. He had stopped sweeping it under a rug of oblivion. He had chewed the reality of all of it, truly grieved it, been aghast at it. He had encountered the callousness and selfishness. He knew the meanness and brutality that time after time was heaped on a wide-eyed obedient, frightened little boy who kept having knocked out of him, time after time, any sense of being wanted or worthy.

The Mark of ten years later had not only wrestled with his unconscious response to the evil done against him, he had encountered the abyss of his own evil. He had seen not only his own deliberate acts of callousness, brutality, and selfishness but even some of the evil he had done in the process of what he had seen as good.

He came face to face with his own husbanding and how he had robbed his wife of a great deal of her own personhood and freedom. He saw how his need for nurture, his opinions, and his wishes had directed their lives even from the earliest days of their marriage. Sure, there had been concessions, but never any real sacrifice for her. She had sacrificed time and again for him and his need to be approved.

That terrible need, almost an obsession to be loved and approved, even by his clients, was one of the most telling new insights he came to as he surfaced more and more of his unconscious motivations. He saw how manipulative he had been, how often his overzealous courting of some parolee's esteem and gratitude had been the cause of his losing sight of the other's best interests. How often had a report for a judge been skewed? How often had he not used tough love for fear of being disdained? How often had he gone too far for one client to the neglect of others?

He recognized the same pattern in his relationships with coworkers. He had always issued insincere invitations, to keep on the right side of everyone. He often had dreaded a lunch or a day off spent with one of them because of this unconscious playacting.

Injustice and lack of honesty were everywhere he looked. His parenting had been full of it. He had neglected the children and used them in the same way as he had used his too patient wife. It was not that he had not tried to give them everything he missed. It was that somehow he had seen them as part of himself and so had sacrificed their needs and their time so often to the needs of outsiders.

Had Mark not opened himself to make this very unconscious side of himself conscious, he could have gone on directing his anger at his adult children, promoting a vicious cycle of self-righteous, accelerating ugliness. He could have wrecked his marriage by backing his wife out of his life, blaming her for her defense of herself and their children. He could have been eaten up and abandoned his job as he began to feel rancor for the evil system and the ingrates he had worked to help.

Moreover, once he had begun to look within and back at his past, Mark could have gotten stuck there. He could have gone on for forty years blaming his mother and all who had victimized him. He could have become in the process a more and more closed, one-sided, cynical, and bitter old man. The encounter of the unconscious, or Shadow side, is as risky and dangerous a business as the refusal to encounter it.

The bleak picture of evil in others and in himself that Mark contacted could have destroyed him. It could have swallowed him whole. It could have eaten up and blotted out any self-respect and appreciation of the good he had done. Yet it didn't. Mark did not identify himself with all of this evil, all of this sin against himself and others and God. He recognized that evil and owned it, accepted its reality, mourned it, and grieved it, as he did that done against him. He even saw how one evil had caused the other, was related to it, and had extended the power of the other.

For a time, the horror he felt at the realization even prolonged his sickening feeling of being forsaken. A cry of the crucified Jesus came into his head as though welling up from deep within: "My God, my God why have you forsaken me?"(Mk. 15:34b).

His anger at this forsakenness grew worse as he reflected on each of his children. He could see the results of his needs and his failures in them. He had forsaken them. The youngest's latest problems were such an obvious result of his unconscious angry behavior during those three years when all this hidden rot had begun to surface and changed him from an affable easygoing dad to the gestapo.

All this uncharacteristic behavior, all this overreaction to his children's misdemeanors, all these emotional outbursts had been what Jung called Shadow experiences. They were like Dr. Jekyll and Mr. Hyde. They were signs that there was a whole other unconscious, unlived side to strong, serene Mark, belatedly demanding anger and justice for his childhood. There was a whole other side to this mild-mannered, charitable seeker of mercy and justice for those who had paid their debt to society. All these emotional outbursts came from a more primitive, inferior, unadapted side of Mark. At times it was as though another personality had taken hold of him.

Emotion, Jung says, is:

> not an activity of the individual but something that happens to him. Affects occur usually where adaptation is weakest, and at the same time they reveal the reason for its weakness, namely a certain degree of inferiority and the existence of a lower level of personality. *(Aion:8–9)*

Overreaction, overkill, and excessive emotion are sure signs that something unconscious has been touched and is finding expression. When people overreact to something in another person they are casting their own Shadow on that person. The point is not that there is nothing wrong with the other, but that they are adding their "own stuff" to what is wrong out there. That which people most vociferously and emotionally despise in the others is most surely that which is there in themselves of which they are completely unconscious. Overkill is usually fueled by unconscious defensiveness. The offense one most rages against out there in another may look very different in oneself because each of us has our own style. Yet, at root something will be the same. One projects on others that which one most dislikes in oneself even while one is totally unaware that the despised thing is active in oneself.

Mark had begun to discover a much more profound dishonesty and injustice in himself than any he had seen in his children. His children and his wife had suffered his contempt. It had been his anger and the chaos it caused at home that first sent Mark back to his story and his undiscovered self. Mark had then done some real wrestling with his Shadow.

3)   The encounter with the Shadow is for each person the archetypal narrow way of entrance to growth in the second half of life.

> The meeting with oneself is at first the meeting with one's own shadow. The shadow is a tight passage, a narrow door, whose painful constriction no one is spared who goes down to the deep well. But one must learn to know oneself in order to know who one is. (Jung, *The Archetypes and the Collective Unconscious*: 21).

GM Hopkins

4)   Mark's outbursts had been a form of defensiveness, the tip of a kind of iceberg within. Each step of self-discovery that he took after that still seemed to him to be the tip of the iceberg. He was often tempted to draw back and foreclose as he saw the abyss opening beneath him. When he really touched the raw unhealed pain of the baby, the child within, when he found himself blaming everyone, screaming out at God and to humanity for an answer, a vindication, he wanted to bury the pain again. He wanted to annihilate the reality of his childhood. He so wished he had never been born that he read Job and identified with Job's lament:

> May the day perish when I was born, and the night that told of a boy conceived. May that day be darkness, may God on high have no thought of it, may no light shine on it. May murk and deep shadow claim it for their own, clouds hang over it, eclipse swoop down on it. (Job 3:3–5, J.B.)

It was as though he totally shared Job's experience and everyone and everything important in his present life had been wiped out, so little did he value present realities while caught into emotion about his past. It was not as though Mark's everyday life ceased to exist or that he stopped everything while he went back to take care of this unfinished business. He focused

"Wait for the fruits..."

exclusively on it for only one hour a week but it was there with him, he was there with it, whenever he had a breather. Eventually, he had begun to be painfully conscious of it. He had finally felt the emotions so long buried. The pain began to subside and some new realizations began to take its place.

Mark heard about a wilderness rehabilitation program for criminals with extremely antisocial behavior. He recognized how improvement could be seen in a short time because nature was not as easily manipulated as people could be. He was aware how often he had been manipulated by the convicts. He was musing about being "conned" when he suddenly saw himself "conning." The little boy had learned to manipulate by pleasing those in his hostile environments. He saw how this had paradoxically contributed to making him the obedient, hard-working, and eventually successful person he was.

It was fortunate for Mark that he came to his own evil and the good in it simultaneously. For many mid-life people coming face to face with their lifelong Shadow takes a long painful wrestling with the Shadow before the secret good that it has simultaneously contributed to their growth and goodness is revealed.

Yet, Mark was to grapple with the true evil his own manipulating had caused. Eventually, this began to be a greater source of grief than the evil done to him had been. All the time seeing himself as righteous and good, he had sinned against many, in so many situations. He began to see how his own blind spot had grown bigger in him with every decade. He recalled a parable of Jesus that he had never really grasped before because he had never seen himself as a sinner. Surely, he had sinned often but he had seen himself as a basically upright person and not a sinner. As he saw layer after layer of the destruction so much of his building had left in its wake, he heard welling up within him: "Lord, be merciful to me a sinner." He went searching for the words and found them in Luke's Gospel:

> He then addressed this parable to those who were convinced of their own righteousness and despised everyone else. "Two people went up to the temple area to pray; one was a Pharisee and the other was a tax collector. The Pharisee took up his position and spoke this prayer to himself, 'O God, I thank you

that I am not like the rest of humanity—greedy, dishonest, adulterous—or even like this tax collector. I fast twice a week, and I pay tithes on my whole income.' But the tax collector stood off at a distance and would not even raise his eyes to heaven but beat his breast and prayed, 'O God, be merciful to me a sinner.' I tell you, the latter went home justified, not the former; for everyone who exalts himself will be humbled, and the one who humbles himself will be exalted." (18:9–14)

The Mark who now identified with the sinner in the story had never before seen himself as the Pharisee either, and now he knew he had been both. Paradoxically, now that he owned his sinfulness, he was becoming a more honest, generous, and forgiving person. All this self-criticism and interpretation had transformed his thorny relationships and was resulting in the resolution of many of his problems. The new Mark was a different person. He was far more at ease with himself than he had ever been before. His work as district supervisor was being noticed because of the success he was having in relating to the people in his district and the success he helped them to have with their case loads.

8

Shadow as Archetypal: Friend or Foe?

Even though Mark's birth and beginnings are particularly unfortunate, and his need to get in touch with, grieve over, and reinterpret his personal story is particularly crucial, Mark's mid-life initiation process is still paradigmatic. His is the archetypal mid-life initiation process. Deep within each person who has done a fairly healthy job of adaptation, who has a rather healthy ego development, the Shadow, a kind of alter-ego, begins to stir and push toward consciousness at the time of the mid-life transition.

A person's Shadow is the whole of the unconscious parts of that person's story. It is the part of oneself that has been denied life; it is all the possibilities good, bad, and indifferent that could have been lived but have not been lived. It is all that one dislikes about oneself so much that one hides it from oneself as well as from others. It is the totality of the weak, dark, unpleasant, ugly side of oneself.

> The personal unconscious contains lost memories, painful ideas that are repressed (i.e. forgotten on purpose) subliminal perceptions by which are meant sense perceptions that were not strong enough to reach consciousness, and finally contents that are not yet ripe for consciousness. . . . By the shadow I mean the "negative" side of the personality, the sum of all those unpleasant qualities we like to hide, together with the insufficiently developed functions and the contents of the personal unconscious. (Jung, *Two Essays on Analytical Psychology*:66)

The Shadow is not only personal but archetypal because, while much of the contents of my Shadow are personal to me, the fact of the Shadow is a universal phenomenon. An archetype is a psychic organ, an inherited mode of psychic functioning present in all of us. The Shadow is a psychic organ. One cannot be human and be totally conscious of every perception or of every element of one's past. Our human experience would overwhelm us if our psyche were not constantly screening and selecting, among the bombarding sensations and emotions, what will be conscious and what unconscious. One cannot be human and develop every human potential simultaneously. Human potentials tend very much to divide themselves into opposites, and while one develops a strength on one side of a pair of opposites, one necessarily pays for it by leaving the other side relatively underdeveloped and so unconscious. A person in youth cannot be simultaneously very zealous and very laid back, for example. A differentiated Shadow is the product of a differentiated ego. As each of us chooses ways of being, we reject the opposite ways. As a child grows, the shadow, as it were, grows with it, duplicating in its flat, dark self every curve and contour of every inch of growth.

As an archetypal component of the psyche, the Shadow is neither simple nor static. To have a differentiated shadow which is a negative of our ego personality is, as a matter of fact, an achievement of individual psychological maturation. The Shadow of an immature personality is not clearly organized or defined and only becomes so as the ego is more firmly established and the total personality attains form. Thus the emergence of the Shadow as an essential component of the psyche, a kind of psychic organ, is a positive entity in personality development and in its own peculiar way can be creative.

The turning point that begins with the transition from the first to the second half of life summons up the more-or-less unconscious, hitherto neglected sides of the psyche. In this process the Shadow plays its great creative role.

> By the time that mid-life comes, a person has usually settled into familiar psychological patterns and is ensconced in work and family. And then suddenly, a crisis! You wake up one day and you are unexpectedly out of gas. The atmosphere of

personal ownership sinks; the sweet milk of achievement is sour; the old patterns of coping and acting pinch your feet. The ability to prize your favorite objects—your works; children, possessions, power positions, accomplishments—has been stolen and you are left wondering what happened last night? Where did it go? (Stein, 1983:4)

It is the Shadow who is responsible for such a shocking theft. It is the Shadow who has come when the mid-life person begins to experience himself or herself in such a whole new way. Jung calls the realizations of the Shadow an "eminently practical problem." This growing awareness of the inferior part of the personality cannot be twisted into an intellectual activity; it has far more to do with:

the meaning of a suffering and a passion that implicate the whole man [or woman]. The essence of that which has to be realized and assimilated has been expressed so trenchantly and so plactically in poetic language by the word, "Shadow" . . . Even the term, "inferior part of the personality" is inadequate and misleading, whereas "Shadow" presumes nothing that would rigidly fix its content. "The man [or woman] without a Shadow" is statistically the commonest human type, one who imagines he actually *"is"* only that he cares to know about himself. (Jung, *On the Nature of the Psyche:*178)

The ego consciousness of the human child develops from a state of unconsciousness, but it always remains in relation to the unconscious. There is always more to us than we know we are. As we mature what is quite unconscious in ourselves may be quite obvious to others. We are always becoming more than we have been. All of this is still the Self. The ego or consciousness that we have at any one time is always there in relation to the more, or the Self. This ego-Self axis is the relation of the part to the whole, or the conscious part of the psyche to the totality of the psyche.

Even more mysteriously, the Self is always in relationship to a greater whole. I will always be in relationship to my half-animal roots and to the large collective or objective psyche and spirit of the human race.

At mid-life, this great unknown, this Shadow, has a sufficiently developed ego personality to engage, without immediately swallowing, that ego consciousness whole. However, at
this same time in life the ego personality is in danger of closing
in on itself and getting stuck, precisely because of this same
strength. It is the Shadow, then, as the unconscious parts of the
personality that the conscious ego has tended to reject or ignore, which begins to emerge as a kind of number-two personality. Is it friend or foe? This is the mid-life question.
Answering that question in fidelity to my Self, as the unique
image of God that I am called to be, as I wrestle with it in each
real situation that presents the question, is the spirituality of
mid-life. Mid-life spirituality is lived on the stage of life, not in
the auditorium. One acts integration and holiness. Here one
cannot be a spectator.

These encounters with the Shadow are never an easy or
simplistic affair. Yet, the word *Shadow* may give a name to all
kinds of inexpressible new experiences of oneself that are totally individual. Trying to capture these very complex and subtle experiences in a word necessarily reduces them. However,
having a word does place these sometimes frightening and
always disturbing experiences within the horizon of human
experience and, it is often infinitely comforting to know that
one has had many Shadow experiences and is not "simply losing
one's mind." As one is contacted now by both the psychological
zoo and the embryonic beginnings of new greatness within, the
result is a kind of chaos. Only when the lion and the lamb have
come together in some area does one begin to glimpse the
kingdom within.

The experiences of Shadow, however, necessarily overflow
the word and so the word can be a kind of catch-all term in a
psychology of the second half of life.

> It would be misleading to conceive of the Shadow as a clearly
> defined archetype. In Jungian writings the concept is
> shrouded in confusion and the more one reads about it, the
> more one is left with the impression that "the Shadow" is a
> portmonteau term which has been used to accommodate all
> those aspects of the Self which are not evident in the con-
> scious personality. Jung himself sometimes evinced exaspera-

tion with attempts to clarify the concept: "This is all nonsense!" he once exclaimed after a long discussion on the subject. The shadow is simply the whole unconscious. (Von Franz, 1974:5)

One cannot fail to be ambivalent about this part of the human psyche because it inevitability inheres all that is worst and best in mankind. (Stevens:215)

The Shadow in Developmental Psychology

Usually, the first side of the Shadow encountered is what Stevens called the "worst" in humanity. Roger Gould in his fine work on adult developmental psychology, *Transformations*, points to this phenomenon and to the archetypal nature of the Shadow as a mid-life encounter. Gould claims that the developmental task of the mid-life years is to come to terms with the childhood illusion: "There is no evil or death in the world. The sinister has been destroyed." Time, he says, has made us vulnerable. We have come to the end of naiveté, we stand exposed before our own mortality as we challenge this last major false assumption. Yet he points out that it is our very vulnerability that gives us access to the deepest strata of our minds that we have ever examined.

It is our final natural opportunity to deal with that deeply buried sense of our "demonic badness" or worthlessness that has curtailed us from living as legitimate, authentic creatures with a full set of rights and a fully independent adult consciousness. To achieve an adult sense of freedom, we must pass through periods of passivity, rage, depression and despair as we experience the repugnance of death, the hoax of life and the evil within and around us. To enjoy full access to our innermost self, we can no longer deny the ugly demonic side of life, which our immature mind tried to protect against by enslaving itself to false illusions that absolute safety was possible. (Gould:218)

If we do not let go of this childish desire for absolute safety by walking through the fire of the reality of death and evil, we will continue to reassert our invincibility and innocence. We will continue to use the same protective devices to cast our Shadow on "all those evil others." We will continue to shield ourselves from the demonic side of ourselves and of life, but we will have "to relate to others as cardboard figures rather than as passionate, hurting, and loving human beings" (Gould:218).

We will continue to be good girl scouts and good boy scouts but we will define life, work, and relationships too narrowly; we will take no chances; we will continue in our conspiracies of cutthroat competition or deadening repetition. Eventually, our closed, one-sided, innocent judgmentalism will sour and cynicism may engulf us.

In *Seasons of a Man's Life,* Daniel Levinson draws even more explicitly than Gould does on Jung's theories about growth in the second half of life. In his chapter on the mid-life season Levinson uses Jung's archetypal theory to organize his reflections on the experiences of mid-life. He refers directly to Jung at the beginning of this section (196).

In his discussion of the process of reappraising the past (which he sees as crucial for the man in mid-life), Levinson underlines the need to deal with illusions. He speaks of mid-life individuation and dealing with major polarities: young/old, destruction/creation, masculine/feminine, and attachment/separateness. All four of these polarities are in some way experiences of the opposites of conscious and unconscious. All four are very much about the encounter with the Shadow.

In discussing the destruction/creation polarity, Levinson recognizes that no one gets to age forty without some experience of human destructiveness.

> In reappraising his life during the mid-life transition, a man must come to a new understanding of his grievances against others for the real or imagined damage they have done him. For a time, he may be helplessly immobilized by the helpless rage he feels toward parents, wife, mentors, friends, and loved ones who, as he now sees it have hurt him badly. And, grievances against himself—for the destructive effects he has had on others and himself. (223)

Each of us must rework painful feelings and experiences and come to terms with ourselves as victims and villains in the large continuing tale of our human inhumanity to one another. This coming to terms is no small struggle. It is hard to acknowledge that we can be unwittingly destructive. It is even harder to admit our hostile, destructive wishes toward others, even most intimate others. It is harder still to own our bitterness and hatred expressed in the cruel, disparaging, petty, controlling, hurtful things we have done even to loved ones and with sometimes frightful consequences. This kind of learning has to go on within the fabric of one's life. It comes by going through "intense periods of suffering confusion, rage against others and ourselves, grief over lost opportunities and lost parts of the self" (225).

As we each live our own tragic story, we come to the sense that great misfortune and failure comes not only from outside but from the tragic flaw within each of us. It is in this new relationship to one's own destructiveness—and to the mysterious, life-affirming, living aspect that rises out of the ashes of this fire-walk—that the creativity of mid-life has its genesis.

In *Passages*, Gail Sheehy looks at the "deadline decade," age thirty-five to forty-five, and invites us to have a "full-out authenticity crisis." She too warns about what sounds like the Shadow and the archetypal evil lurking in the gateway.

> But first, letting the dark side open up will release a cast of demons. Every loose end not resolved in previous passages will resurface to haunt us. Even chips off the archaic totem pole of childhood will come to the surface. Buried parts of ourselves will demand incorporation or at least that we make the effort of seeing and discarding them. These demons may lead us into private hells of depression, sexual promiscuity, power chasing, hypochondria, self destructive acts (alcoholism, drug taking, car accidents, suicide) and violent swings of mood . . . If we do admit that dark side, what are we likely to see. We are selfish. We are greedy. We are competitive. We are fearful. We are dependent. We are jealous. We are possessive. We have a destructive side. (1974:247–248)

All these researchers into the experiences of mid-life adults happen on the same phenomenon that Mark, Jung, and even (the Gospels hint) Jesus happened on in his temptation experience. It is a paradox and a mystery that stepping humbly and honestly into this dangerous abyss of one's own experience of evil can break open the personality and transform it for the better.

Jung, in his own mid-life period of disorientation, encountered his Shadow and gave us his personal revelation of the role of the Shadow in the growth process of the second half of life.

In his autobiography, Jung dates a watershed dream that occurred in Advent 1913, when he was thirty-eight.

> I was with an unknown brown skinned man, a savage, in a lonely rocky mountain landscape. It was before dawn; the sky was already bright and the stars fading. Then, I heard Siegfried's horn sounding over the mountains and I knew that we had to kill him. We were armed with rifles and lay in wait for him in a narrow path over the rocks. (*Memories, Dreams, Reflections*: 179–80)

Jung goes on to tell how they indeed killed the hero Siegfried, and that he was filled with disgust and remorse at killing something so great and beautiful; he was filled with a feeling of unbearable guilt that would not go away. He felt a great urgency to understand this dream, and suddenly the meaning came. Siegfried is the hero and represents the heroic mode of operation ("where there is a will there is a way"). Imposing his will was what Jung had wanted. However, the attitude embodied by Siefgried, the hero, no longer suited him. Therefore it had to be killed.

> After the deed I felt an overpowering compassion as though I myself had been shot: a sign of my secret identity with Siegfried, as well as the grief a man feels when he is forced to sacrifice his ideal and his conscious attitudes. This identity and my heroic idealism had to be abandoned, for there are higher things than the ego's will and to these one must bow ... The small brown skinned savage who accompanied me and who had actually taken the initiative in the killing was an embodiment of the primitive Shadow. (180–81)

Thus Jung came to see that the Shadow leads one and invites one into a rite of passage that requires that one kill one's heroic idealism and one's dependence on one's own will characteristic of the first half of life. There is now the Self and the Self's alpha and omega to which one must bow. It is the Shadow who blows holes in the heroic mode, as Jung's shadow blew holes in Siegfried, with whose beauty and greatness he had so identified. It is the Shadow that blows holes in the ego, that deflates and dethrones it at the time when ego development has reached its zenith. This death of the ego, however, is an invitation to lose life in order to preserve it. The ego has been "sailing the ship"; now it must move out of center to make room for the Self, which will be the coming together of both the conscious and the unconscious.

Mid-Life Transition

How important it was that the ego rose up out of the unconsciousness of infancy and proclaimed its first tiny voiced Me! and No! How important for that little girl who affirmed her identity and will by calling out her no each time her young parents warned her not to get her feet wet in the lake, even though she still did exactly what they told her to do.

Jesus must have been referring to her and all of us in the Gospel of Matthew when he tells of two sons and their yes and no responses. The one had said yes, and then proceeded not to go to work in the vineyard, as the father asked. The second said no, and then went and did what he was told (Mt. 21:26–31). How strange it is that at such an early moment in our lives we learn that sometimes a no spoken or acted out will be precisely doing the will of the Father in growing toward that degree of autonomy and ego development where we will have the strength of will to act decisively.

At mid-life we know that by exercising our willpower, we have achieved a great deal. We have sacrificed for our values. We have been able to be relatively loyal to our commitments. We have overcome laziness and been able to stick to something and work hard. We have bit by bit put something together, no matter how successful or unsuccessful we or others judge ourselves to be. The first me and no have developed into a differentiated and differentiating ego identity. Now, just when we have finally reached this pinnacle, we must be shot down. How so? Mid-life is, they say, "getting to the top of the ladder and finding that it is against the wrong roof." Thirty-five-, forty-,

forty-seven-year-olds scream this out. It is the first interpretation of the mid-life crisis of negative feelings. It is also an
inkling that one is feeling the need to start over again.

Of course, the most dangerous misinterpretation of this painful loss of meanings, values, and goals is a literal interpretation.
It is obvious from so many modern tragedies of regression in a
frantic effort to hold on to one's lost youth that many make this
mistake. Many people jump to the most obvious literal solution
to the pain at the "top of the ladder": they abandon everything
and start over.

But this is no call to raze everything that has been built up, to
run amok and tear down the personality, roles, relationships,
and commitments that have piece by piece been put in place by
so much effort. One *is* being called to make earth-shattering,
tremendous changes, to rework the entire personality around a
new center, which will profoundly affect every role, relationship, and commitment. One is being asked to exchange
one's identity for a larger, truer identity. One is being called to
surrender that ego to the Self, which will somehow incorporate
the Shadow. One does not lose one's life just to lose it. One does
not literally slay the ego but teaches it how to bow to the higher
things.

When one learns, as Mark did, to integrate the Shadow into
the conscious personality, the personality is leavened and it
grows. One's life will be different but it will still be built on the
foundation that has been there from the beginning. When one
holds on until the opposites come together in some way that
transcends the opposition, without losing either side, one becomes more real. One's lifestyle may look profoundly different
(there may be geographic or career moves, inauthentic commitments may be exchanged for new ones); or, things may appear
much the same on the surface. Yet, deep down all will be new.

At mid-life, as the second half of life begins, a need rises up
in each of us to let go of a modus operandi, a way of operating,
a smallness of conscious attitudes and style, even a narrowness
of relationship that will suffocate us if we live with it after we've
outgrown it, as surely as the womb would have suffocated us
had we remained there after we came to term. When the hour
comes for us to be delivered the labor pains begin.

At this time one needs to bear the tension of opposites. One

"Relationship to Past" - How?

needs to somehow hold on to that ego, that identity, that one's life has built, *while* holding on to the new awareness of one's Shadow. Thus, there are two great catastrophes possible at mid-life. These catastrophes threaten everyone who comes to this juncture in the life cycle. There are two ways of being swallowed alive. One can close off awareness of the tremors, the hints of one's Shadow and the sense that the earth is shaking under one. One can deny that a volcano is erupting and just freeze in one's place and become a petrified, hardened fossil. One can die at forty and not get buried until ninety. This would surely be a catastrophe.

Yet, just as terrible would be to begin to discover what had been unconscious and proclaim that everything one has been to this point has been a lie. One could just throw everything over and begin to live out one's Shadow personality. It seems that many people move in both of these unfortunate directions.

> Whoever protects himself [or herself] against what is new and strange and thereby regresses into the past, falls into the same condition as the man [or woman] who identifies himself with the new and runs away from the past. The only difference is that one has estranged himself [or herself] from the past, and the other from the future. In principle both are doing the same thing, they are salvaging a narrow state of consciousness. The alternative is to shatter it with the tension inherent in the play of opposites—in the dualistic stage—and then build up a state of wider and higher consciousness. (Jung, *Modern Man in Search of a Soul:* 102)

Those who close off the future are people who panic at new ideas or feelings that come to them or rise up in them. "I've heard about this sort of thing. Not me! I'll have none of it," they think. They will deny and effectively repress again any inkling of their own Shadow that has the boldness to knock on the door of consciousness. Closing off this way can play havoc with themselves and those around them.

In her book, Barbara Hanna tells the story of a well-known lawyer, an intelligent man of good reputation who was one who got stuck because he would not allow the encounter with his own shadow to come to consciousness (183ff.). His story was one that his only surviving child had to make conscious for herself at mid-life as part of her own healing and individuation process.

This father was the dominant of the two parents, self-righteous, always knowing exactly what was right and what was wrong. Yet, apart from this early sign of rigidity, he had been, as a younger man, generally amiable, loved, and esteemed. He certainly felt that he loved his gentle wife and three children. Yet, this man who seemed well-equipped to live a rather normal, healthy, happy life had a highly dangerous Shadow of which he remained until his death totally unconscious.

When the children were young, the father, who worked late in the evening, often slept late in the morning. One or another of the children was sent to wake him and would play with their lazy father to make him get up. It was on one such occasion that the middle child, a girl of about three or four, had her first experience of her father's unconscious incest desire. He never touched the child but he wounded her spirit of harmless playfulness. He exposed himself in front of her and frightened the child severely by the expression that she saw come over his face. In this strange way the three-year-old was overwhelmed by this participation in her father's sexual desire. He never saw the seriousness of what had happened and buried the whole thing.

When he was in mid-life, the lawyer's wife died. The daughter was then fourteen. On two occasions, the now more righteous father, still unconscious of his own temptation in regard to his daughter, grossly invaded the young girl's privacy and violated her modesty, again scarcely concealing his own strong emotions. Because he never crossed the lines of his own taboo against sexual intercourse, in his own eyes nothing ever happened and he never grew in awareness.

His daughter had a terrible time through her life growing beyond the enthrallment of these early sexually charged experiences. She became a successful professional musician in spite of her father's great contempt for her because of her terrible shyness in social situations. He grew more and more judgmental.

He died at seventy-eight after a slow lingering illness. In his last six months he was hospitalized and his daughter, who continued to love him, went to see him every day. In the last days of his life, his mind began to fail. As his still self-righteous consciousness began to be slowly extinguished, he once asked his daughter to undress. As she bent over to hear his feeble voice he grabbed at her blouse and tried to unbutton it. He was angry with her for several days because she had escaped his grasp. He was a pitiful sight in those last days, filled with dreams and hallucinations. He kept saying that he was imprisoned and in chains because he had murdered both his daughters (the second daughter had committed suicide). He was positive that the murders had been reported in all the papers.

Such stories of aged people undisguisedly revealing a never integrated Shadow are not uncommon. Many a nurse or doctor has stories of old people who reveal an unbridled lust after a lifelong sexual repression or of the aggressive and violently abusive behavior of formerly cultured, genteel people. In "stuck" aging people a maudlin sentimentality may reveal the other side of a lifelong impersonal, distant, formal way of being. Constant preaching and condemnation may reveal a lifelong unowned and unintegrated thirst for joy and pleasure. There are endless variations on this theme of lack of integration of the Shadow and admission to consciousness.

The key here is *unadmitted*. Unconscious, unknown, unowned, unacknowledged parts of oneself are one's unbefriended Shadow. There is all the difference in the world, however, between befriending, admitting, owning, acknowledging a Shadow and collapsing totally into it and living it out.

In mid-life, Shadows begin to contact each of us in many different ways. Unresolved parts of our stories meet us in the last sickness and physically dependent days of an aging parent. Tears well up for a marriage broken fifteen years before. Old sibling rivalries rear their ugly heads after twenty-year separations. Faithful spouses find themselves drawn to some not-so-faithful behavior. A crooked deal has a new appeal after twenty-five years of honest hard work. Jealousy of one's own children's freedom and opportunities pulls at one. A long-buried atheist emerges in a committed churchgoer. Instincts emerge under the influence of alcohol that betray a whole other side of the sober personality.

As important as it is to make these as conscious as possible, own them, and even surface the guilt one feels and own that, it is just as crucial that one not totally identify with any one of these new parts of oneself. A great temptation at mid-life is just this kind of identification and overthrow.

> "I've just discovered who I *really* am, and by God, you'll discover her too."
> "I never loved you, all these years I've been living a lie, I finally know who I really am and what I really want!"
> "I'm no good, I've always suspected this. Now I may as well go on proving it."
> "I really hate you and this life I've been living."
> "This whole thing has been a facade. I became a lawyer to please my father. I'm sick to death of it."
> "How could I have been such a fool as to think I was called to sacrifice marriage for a religious life. No more!"
> "I've always hated it, only I didn't know it until now and I won't tolerate it another minute."
> "I never wanted these children, they're yours and by God you can have them."
> "All you've ever wanted from me was money. Now you can all go to hell!"
> " 'I have sinned in betraying innocent blood'. . . . and [Judas] went off and hanged himself." (Mt. 27:4–5)

All these announcements indicate the identification of the whole of oneself with a part and the collapse into this newly discovered part of oneself. Often such statements are only screams of pain at the dawning consciousness that, indeed, there has been some lie in my choices, some hate in my loves. They usher in collapse when the announcement is quickly transformed into action and the whole of one's new reality. This is a whole other thing than the recognition and owning of a new part of myself and bearing the pain and tension of the conflict. One needs to bear the tension until somehow this new element can be integrated into who I am, without totally destroying who I have been. Bearing this conflict within oneself is no easy thing because the opposites experienced are apparently irreconcilable. It becomes a kind of crucifixion in which one feels torn limb from limb. Holding on in agony until they come together to create a new whole is indeed a core of mid-life spirituality. It is an asceticism that far outstrips the asceticism of youth which called for so much delay of gratification and hard work; so much faith, hope, and love. The fact that one is no longer young adds to the pain and to the reality of the faith, hope, and love.

This is precisely the time then when new values begin to surface and draw one. Becoming one's true Self, becoming integrated and becoming holy means trying to internalize conflicting values and becoming, like Christ, a sign of contradiction.

> The transition from morning to afternoon means a reevaluation of the earlier values. There comes the urgent need to appreciate the value of the opposite of our former ideal, to perceive the error in our former convictions, to recognize the untruth in our former truth, to feel how much antagonism and even hatred lay in what until now had passed for love. Not a few of those who are drawn into the conflict of opposites jettison everything that has seemed to them good and worth striving for; they try to live in complete opposition to their former ego. Changes of profession, divorces, religious convulsions, apostasies of every description are the symptoms of this swing over to the opposites. The snag about a radical conversion into one's opposite is that one's former life suffers repression and thus produces just as unbalanced a state as existed before when the counterparts of the conscious virtues and values were still repressed and unconscious. . . . It is, of course, a fundamental mistake to imagine that when we see the non-value in the value or the untruth in the truth, the value or the truth ceases to exist. It has only become relative. (Jung, *Two Essays in Analytical Psychology:* 75)

Continuing to see the non-value or the untruth where before there was only value and truth, continuing to see the ugliness where before there was only beauty, and all the time holding fast the value, truth, and beauty poses the greatest challenge of discernment that can occupy persons in the second half of life. Yet, Jung goes so far as to say that whether we destroy the planet in a nuclear war will depend on how many people can bear this tension of opposites. Here is a motivation and spirituality worthy of any of us committed to the love of God and neighbor, who have lived only part of the image of God that we are. This is again the spirituality of the kingdom where the lion and lamb lie down together.

9

Owning One's Shadow
in Mid-Life

When the Shadow personality erupts and overwhelms consciousness and begins to live itself out in the life of a
person, that person has identified with its unconscious contents.
One can be at risk of this whenever one is the man, or the
woman, without a Shadow. When one's head is too much in the
clouds, one's roots reach down to hell.

Jung tells of a man from a peasant family who had risen very
high in academic circles very quickly and who had his sights set
for still higher summits. He suddenly began to have symptoms
that corresponded in every detail to a malady that overtakes
some mountain climbers at high altitudes. At the time of his
visit to Jung for treatment he had had a dream in which he saw
a train climbing a steep mountainside. The engine cleared the
last of several sharp curves and ascended to an open stretch of
straight track. The dreamer saw that the cars in the rear were
still proceeding around several sharp curves and hoped the
engineer would not "forget his tail" and plunge full steam
ahead. When this was precisely what happened, the dreamer
awoke in a cold sweat (Jung, *Analytical Psychology: Its Theory and
Practice*:90).

Obviously, the message from his unconscious was that this
man who now saw himself as an intellectual superman should
not allow "his head to forget his tail." He needed to slow down
and get back in touch with his instinctive peasant self before
ascending any higher. Other dreams seemed to confirm this
same danger; however, the man would not see it and went on
with his plans. Jung concludes this story by saying, "It took him

integration.

about three months to lose his position and go to the dogs" (105).

We all necessarily have a "tail," or unconscious side, a primitive, unadapted, underdeveloped, instinctual side that has been neglected while we pursued our ego ideals and built our many roles. A Shadow is not something we choose to have or not have; we cannot afford to deny or ignore it anymore than we can deny or ignore a hand or foot.

Consciousness grows out of unconsciousness and the ego complex is the knowing subject of that consciousness. Building that ego and holding on to consciousness are no small achievement. As each child comes to the days of dawning consciousness and begins to recognize and name the objects of the world with all the awe and excitement of which a baby is capable, adults can be thrilled again in the child's discovery. We know the wonder it is to know and be self-conscious and the precious event consciousness is.

> As with each person's arrival at consciousness so the immensity of the arrival of consciousness in the history of the evolution of our solar system. All the worlds that ever have existed before man were physically *there*. But they were a nameless happening, not a definite actuality, for there did not yet exist that minimal concentration of the psychic factor which was also present, to speak the word that outweighed the whole of Creation: this is world and this is I! That was the first morning of the world, the first sunrise after primal darkness when that inchoately conscious complex, the ego, the son of darkness knowingly sundered subject and object, and thus precipitated the world and itself into different existence, giving it and itself a voice and a name. (Jung, *Mysterium Coniuntionis:*107–8)

It is not surprising then that we can so hold on to consciousness as to deny our lowly unconscious roots and perhaps even deny the existence of an unconscious. Not only that but each of us instinctively knows how precarious our hold on consciousness is since we were once unconscious and still slip into unconsciousness every night. We fear loss of consciousness and the specter of mental illness when unconscious contents can totally take over the personality. Thus, the journey into the unconscious—encountering, befriending, and integrating the

Shadow—is not to be undertaken lightly. Nor can it be under-taken at all until one's ego development is strong enough and consciousness truly valued and secure. Here is the great para-dox and irony. It is only when we so believe in our con-sciousness that we almost see it as all there is that we can come to see, respect, and value the Shadow for its danger and its trea-sure. With each encounter with the Shadow, consciousness needs both to hold its own and surrender only when sufficiently convinced. The dance of bearing the tensions of opposites is always intricate, the goal is always the widening of con-sciousness, integrating what was formerly unconscious and pos-sibly seen as evil. This is never done directly. It happens through an intermediary. The opposites unite in a third, a child of both, a symbol of transcendence. The lion and the lamb come together in the Kingdom; black and white come together in gray. The integration of the Shadow and consequent growth in consciousness will take time. It will happen in stages.

In the eyes of friends and enemies alike, John was always extremely aggressive, belligerent, even brutal in his verbal as-saults when he believed himself right. For years he had been totally unconscious of this brutality. In his own eyes, he was an absolutely honest person and had the courage of his convic-tions. He despised those "weaklings" who "chose peace at any price" and who "would not call a spade a spade." He was proud of the fact that he fought to defend his country and fought in the civil-rights movement. He had championed many causes, on both "left" and "right," once he had been convinced of their justice and rightness. It never dawned on him that as welcome as he had been as a strong fighter in these movements, he was equally unwelcome when his companions in causes wanted a little peace and quiet. He was so volatile and argumentative that others shunned his company because they knew that they could not be with him for longer than ten minutes without being drawn into controversy.

Then John began to encounter the Shadow. One day in his late forties it dawned on him that he had been saying angrily that his department of the plant was a "war zone." He gave some serious thought to quitting his job because he was, "sick and tired of so much opposition and stupidity." Yet, the benefits and pay made him hold on. It was then that he had the insight to stop being part of the war. Tomorrow, he resolved, he would not be caught into any of that "flack and hassle no matter what." "Do you know," he told the bartender that first night, "I went in there today determined to stay out of the war and by quitting time they had all begun to change."

It was some time after his first faltering encounter with his own "warmonger" within that John was honestly able to see that it was not "they" who needed changing. There is a great gap between first seeing a bit of one's Shadow and beginning to live out its "gold." The John who eventually could review his life in the light of this formerly unconscious side of himself suffered some painfully embarrassing hours as he recalled years of terrible conflicts and pain that his own overbearing brutal "honesty" had caused. It took time before he could move beyond both the impulse to do battle and the strong resistance to "never open his mouth again." By bearing the tension and integrating John became a true peacemaker, both the man who could fight for a just cause and the honest but gentle man who was a far more welcome guest and companion.

The Hebrew Scriptures paint a somewhat similar picture of what can be read as the gradual integration of the patriarch Moses. The young Moses who is to be the representative of the Liberator God first seems to have the liberator rise up in him in a very unintegrated way.

> On one occasion, after Moses had grown up, when he visited his kinsmen and witnessed their forced labor, he saw an Egyptian striking a Hebrew, one of his own kinsmen. Looking about and seeing no one, he slew the Egyptian and hid him in the sand. (Ex. 2:11–12)

Later the liberator was there again when Moses, who had fled into Midian lest he be punished for his crime, came to the defense of some shepherdesses who were being roughly driven away from a well: "Then Moses got up and defended them and watered their flock" (Ex. 2:17).

This is the same Moses who will with courage, strength, and great control face Pharaoh and lead the people out of Egypt and through the desert. Eventually, he becomes a leader. He is free himself, and a true liberator who time and again puts up with the fickleness and complaining of the people he is leading to freedom.

Projecting the Shadow

The things one cannot admit about oneself are often projected onto others. As the shadow one's body casts is always projecting in different sizes and in different directions depending on the light, so one projects one's unconscious Shadow on other people. One finds in others what one hates in oneself, what's denied and unknown about oneself. Since one's Shadow is all that is unconscious about one's personal story, parts of one's story that have never been owned can show up in these projections on others.

Mary Ellen had worked in the same place with Joan for some time and the two had a rather pleasant relationship. Then, their lunch breaks were changed and they began to arrive in the cafeteria at the same time. Day after day, Joan carried her tray to whatever table Mary Ellen was at. From the very first day, Mary Ellen found Joan's table manners offensive and was bothered so much that she became cold and curt with Joan. "She is repulsive and I can't stand her," Mary Ellen thought and she eventually began to say just that to others.

One day, Mary Ellen was saying this to a coworker and the other woman looked her in the eye and said, "I've eaten with Joan and you're crazy, she's not as finicky as you, but you certainly are overreacting." When another person walked away from her complaint a few days later, Mary Ellen was furious. One after another, her relationships at work were being affected. The last straw came for her when her husband yelled, "I don't want to hear another word about Joan; you're just like your mother." She was stunned by his tone. "You know how wonderful my mother was, what are you saying?" "You and your sainted mother," he said. "Will you never see her clay feet; haven't you seen yet that she tore every ounce of dignity from your father's mother?"

Mary Ellen's grandmother had a stroke in her sixties and her grandfather took care of his partially paralyzed wife for ten years. Not once in those ten years would Mary Ellen's mother even have her husband's parents to dinner, nor would she even attend a family dinner at their little house or any other place where her mother-in-law would be eating. "She looks so horrible when she's eating that I almost get nauseous. I will not eat with her," she told her husband, and that was that.

Mary Ellen had loved her mother, who had died three years before. Indeed, she had been a good and generally well-loved person. People who knew her would hardly believe she could be so stubborn and so blind to the pain this one issue caused not only her mother-in-law but her husband, who continually tried to make excuses for his wife.

Mary Ellen never allowed this question to cross her mind. Now her husband was trying to jar her into consciousness. Her husband's voice softened, "Can't you put yourself in your grandmother's place, even now? You, who have done so much for the rights of the handicapped?"

It was sometime before she could do as he suggested and really get into her grandmother's feelings. It was weeks before she could let her mother fall from the pedestal and see her as a woman who, like herself, had done evil as well as good. It was as though she feared that if she let it come to her consciousness that in this instance her mother had been hateful and cruel she would forever only see the evil and would lose her mother.

There is just as great a temptation to equate others with their Shadow as there is to equate oneself with one's Shadow when it is contacted. So Mary Ellen had to deal with this before she could see both sides of her mother. She had to bear the feelings of guilt for condemning her mother's actions before she was able to reclaim her own healthy guilt in regard to Joan.

She had been projecting on Joan; an unknown, hidden part of her own story and Joan's careless behavior carried for her all her hidden ambivalence and anger about her mother. Because she repressed the knowledge that her perfect mother had been in this instance really cruel, she was being cruel to Joan.

Mary Ellen had been a child during the last ten years of her grandmother's life. Helpless and dependent small children cannot risk irrevocably offending the powerful people who take care of them. If Mary Ellen's father could not confront his wife, how much less so the child.

In our Shadows are hidden all those ideas, feelings, and wishes whose expression would have placed in jeopardy our most significant early childhood relationships. Since we cannot survive without developing a somewhat consistent and disciplined ego, we have no choice but to unconsciously disown those parts of ourselves which threaten our life supporting relationships. It is unsafe for us to be aware of their existence.

Sometimes "teenage rebellion" takes the precise form of exhibiting the very actions and values rejected by one's parents. In these cases the adolescent will sometime live out the Shadow of the parents. Everything the parents consciously believe, value, stand for, the youngster will disbelieve, devalue, and stand against. In the extreme, this reaction is not a healthy way of separating, since to the degree that the young adult continues to make choices in exact opposition to the parents, it is still the parents who control his or her life.

None of us is able to achieve a total separation from the meanings, values, goals, language, body language, ethnicity, culture, and events that were the second womb in which we grew. It is only in mid-life that we begin to really approach such a separation from and consciousness of what was so all-pervasive in those early years.

As we adapted to the outside world in the first half of life, the more unacceptable anything about us was to a parent or to some other important social group to which we belonged or to a role which we chose, the more it had to be repressed. "We don't do [or think, say, feel, bother with] that sort of thing." Thus the Shadow gradually becomes the repository of the negative side of our personalities. This is not to imply that the Shadow includes only characteristics that are bad or worthless. It simply means that in the Shadow are hidden the parts of us that some significant others in those early surroundings seemed to find unacceptable. As a constituent of ego development, the Shadow is that which we have unconsciously measured and found wanting.

> The existence of the Shadow is a general human archetypal fact since the process of ego formation—the clash between collectivity and individuality—is a general human pattern. (Whitmont:153)

The development of ego is the encounter between inner potential individuality and external reality or the outer collective. The child and young adult has to "fit in." "The ego cannot become strong unless we learn collective taboos, accept super-ego and personal values and identify with collective moral standards" (Whitmont:163).

Those tendencies relegated to the Shadow may be the op-posites of the collective moral values we internalized, but they may also be merely neutral tendencies that in our personal history were frowned on or forbidden. In innumerable ways each of us "gets the message" that something is "bad" or a "no, no." We learn which neutral tendencies or behaviors will not be tolerated.

In young adulthood we move into groups and settings of our own choice but here, too, as in our early families, there are "no, nos" that have nothing to do with morality or real evil. Each profession, each corporation, each office has its own unwritten mores, even its own language and dress code. There are telling furniture arrangements, rites of initiation, and periods of pro-bation and internship everywhere in society. Again we uncon-sciously repress what doesn't fit in. Any one of us in shaping our personality may have had to select between such polarities as being verbal or action oriented, controlled or impulsive, passive or aggressive, warm or cold, intellectual or emotional, loud or quiet, rough or gentle, prodigal or frugal, effusive or restrained, and a host of other neutral "virtues" and "taboos." The more one-sided our conscious ego became the more un-developed and therefore unconscious the opposite tendencies would have become.

Edmond was an impulsive, happy, outgoing child. His par-ents were both very quiet, serious, controlled, cold, and distant. Gradually, Edmond's spontaneity, enthusiasm, and natural dis-play of affection grew dulled. On growing up, Edmond gradu-ated from West Point and became a career army officer. His rise in rank was steady. His marriage was good, at first, but slowly the couple became more distant. Their sex life became per-functory and dull. There was no real intimacy between them, yet they kept up appearances. Edmond's career kept him away from home for long periods. His wife made a life of her own. Upon retiring, Edmond became a licensed masseur in the same health spa where he had his own first massage only a few years before. This choice of second career shocked all who knew him, but Edmond seemed to be genuinely happy in it. He was listening to some classical music one day about a year later when he suddenly saw himself as a child of three in his grandfather's lap, with those huge gentle arms around him. He realized that his grandfather, who had died when Edmond was four, had been the only one who ever really touched or held him. Edmond remembered a scolding he got for running around during his grandfather's wake; the scolding had given him the idea that if he had been a better, quieter boy his grandfather would not have died.

Locked up in Edmond's Shadow was a noisy, impulsive, warm, affectionate, sensitive child. When he contacted his repressed human contact and human touch, positive energies, lost vitality, and creative possibilities opened for Edmond. There were some uncomfortable doubts about his masculinity that he had to bear as he went about his new career and grew in warmth and spontaneity. He still had a long way to go in reworking his marriage to break down patterns of years.

When such good or neutral contents are contacted they can bring a great new dynamism. Of course, Edmond could have gone a destructive route, as have others who contacted this denied relational side and the repression of human touch. Edmond, however, found a healthy outlet and way of integrating this other side of himself.

In his book *In Mid-Life*, Murray Stein tells of a woman who came into his analytic practice and eventually reported that she had been afflicted for a year with an unmanageable compulsion to steal small articles from cosmetic counters in dime stores (73). She was married to a prominent member of the community and had several fine children. She came from a rigorous religious upbringing. Her religious life had slipped in recent years as her husband became interested in another woman and her grown independent and autonomous children no longer needed her. She was in mid-life now. For years her self-esteem had rested on being the "good wife and mother," putting herself and her wishes after the needs of her husband and his career, her children, her parents, and her in-laws. Now she felt the foundations and roots of her life giving way.

Her thieving originated in a repressed piece of her personality crying out for integration. Yet, it was making itself known in such a peculiar and indirect way that she could not understand what it was and what it demanded. Consciously, she did not know what she was doing or why.

> Perhaps because the structures of defense against the unconscious are less able to hold the unconscious out, or because the unconscious is more strongly charged with energy than usual and is able to break through them, or a combination of these two reasons, the impulses, drives, fantasies, longings and wishes that were previously repressed make a powerful reappearance during mid-life. (Stein, 1983:74)

An impulse disorder such as kleptomania is one of the innumerable forms the outbreak of the Shadow can take. June Singer, in *Boundaries of the Soul,* recounts a similar instance: a well-respected high school principal in mid-life combined intermittent nights of heavy drinking with kleptomania. He never stole anything he really wanted and always returned it when he sobered up. He took a used briefcase, a picnic table, benches from a park, and odds and ends from glove compartments.

In the case of the woman, cosmetics were the only thing she repeatedly and compulsively stole. Her severe denial of her own wishes in order to respond to other's wishes had reached such a degree that she no longer had any idea what her own wishes or preferences might be, or if indeed she might be wishing for something at all. When she was able to understand the message of her behavior, she was again in touch with her own wishes. The cosmetics for her represented charm, female attractiveness, and personal value. Here was the place to start: she needed a makeover.

In the principal's case he had a need to "show them he didn't have to keep their damn rules." He would go on until he was ruined if he did not find a more appropriate way of letting go his too tight conformism.

There are many forty-year-olds who feel an unconscious desire to "show them." There are many mid-life women and men who have lost touch with their own needs, desires, and wishes. This loss is the fast lane to despair. Many just become ill and die.

Bob had a heart attack. In intensive care he found himself writing imaginary letters of resignation to all the committees he chaired and, most surprisingly of all, a letter to his boss. He was about to be promoted to vice-president of his company but he requested to stay where he was. During those months of re-cuperation he made an amazing change. He did write all those letters. He saw that he had not been able to take control of life, and realized that the goal of vice-presidency that he had made the center of his striving for his whole career did not fit him anymore. He saw that he had heeded none of the previous signs and wondered if he hadn't brought that heart attack on himself because he hadn't done what unconsciously he knew he must do. There was a whole neglected person in Bob longing for a chance to live. In Bob's Shadow were a gardener, a reader, a jogger, a traveler, a human-rights advocate, a husband, a father, and a grandfather, a pray-er and player who had all been denied the right to really live.

Louise, a stunning woman in her fifties, stood up at a mid-life workshop and volunteered her "Shadow story." She wanted it to be shared so that others might learn from it the way she had.

Louise was an obviously feminine, sophisticated, and cultured woman. She was a published author and extremely well-read in Eastern philosophy and religion, Christianity, so-ciology and history. She was also a social worker in a woman's prison.

As Louise's mother aged and grew less capable of living alone Louise and her husband decided to invite her to live with them. Louise and her mother had never had a close relationship but she felt this was the best thing to do.

The mother had been with them for eight years when one night Louise was sitting alone in the living room. Her husband and her mother were somewhere else in the house. Louise had just turned off the television set when suddenly she vividly imagined herself with a knife in her hand wildly slashing out at her mother.

> I saw this so clearly and felt the violent emotions and hatred so strongly that I was in a cold sweat and shaking when I finally came to myself. I know that if my mother had walked into the room during that time, I would have killed her. When I could pull myself together, I ran to my husband and asked him to hold me and pray with me. Over and over, for days, we

asked what this could mean? How and why could such a thing have happened to me?

Eventually I realized that while I had taken such good care of my mother for eight years, while I have been such a dutiful daughter, I had not taken good care of myself. Worse, I had not allowed my husband to express his care for me. Time and again, I had refused his suggestion that we get away or even go out for dinner because of mother. I had neglected not only myself but him.

Something else happened to me as well. When I went to the prison the next day, I found myself, for the first time, sitting with women who were my "sisters" and not just inmates. These women, many of whom were there for having committed serious crimes—one had murdered her child—were now not so very different from me. I hadn't killed my mother, but I knew then that I could have. This experience has opened a whole new part of me, a compassion that is far more real than any I had ever felt before. Time has gone by and I am a different person. My "universalism" is far more real than I thought it was when I was reading Eastern philosophy. Now I experience a real kinship with all people.

The Shadow that rose up in Louise was far from being neutral or good. She contacted the violent, brutal murderer within. This other was such a complete contradiction to everything she consciously was, and yet it was there in her as it is in any of us. We tend, however, to deny that we could ever even imagine doing such a thing, let alone do it.

10

Integrating Shadow
Manifestations

This is precisely the reality and meaning of the Shadow: Each of us could imagine and could commit any atrocity or achieve any greatness of which humanity is capable; the Shadow is the rest of who we are. For every virtue we have espoused, the opposite has had to remain undeveloped, unconscious. While we have the right to consider the murderer, thief, adulterer, terrorist, prostitute, blasphemer, drug dealer, extortionist, or racist in us sinister and evil, we do not have the right to consider any one of them absolutely nonexistent in us. We cannot deny the possibility; we cannot "forget our tail." We dare not forget that we have, as Christ said, a "least one" inside as well as outside: it is this least one and all the other primitive, inferior, undeveloped parts of each of us that have paid the price of neglect for the virtuous, capable, superior, skillful parts. Their neglect, suppression, and repression made possible the cultivation of their opposites.

> Its not easy to admit that you are capable of thoughts, feelings, behaviors so foreign to the way you usually think of yourself. But like it or not, the personal ego that establishes your everyday conscious image of who you are, represents only a small portion of everything that makes up yourself. The rest of you is hidden in the shadow of your unconscious. Not that you shadow is made up of nothing but forbidden evil impulses. It simply includes all the personal characteristics that your conscious personality cannot acknowledge. (Kopp:28)

116

We find the Shadow parts of ourselves doing things in dreams that "we would never do, never think" in waking life; things we can hardly admit to ourselves because of their inane or immoral character. We see ourselves or symbols of ourselves doing things we would never want anyone to see us doing. Usually, hostile or disliked dream figures, especially those of the same sex, are symbols of our shadow selves.

Each of us recalls times in our waking life when we had fleeting thoughts or feelings so foreign to our conscious self-image that we needed to reassure ourselves immediately with phrases like: "What a crazy idea! Where did that come from?" "That's not like me at all." "What a shocking way for anyone to feel!"

Perhaps there were other times when we had more than just a passing thought or feeling but were "beside ourselves," possessed, as it were, by this "other personality," so that even now we feel uncomfortable just thinking about how we behaved. "What could have gotten into me?" "What came over me?" It was as though we were, for a time, someone else. To be able to live with it, we've said, over and over to ourselves and perhaps to others who witnessed the spectacle we made of ourselves, "You must know, I was not myself that day."

If the Shadow personality has taken over or threatened to take over for an extended period of time, we feel "like we're going to pieces." "We're coming apart." We're even, perhaps, more willing to be declared temporarily insane than to admit and acknowledge that these unacceptable aspects could be part of who we are.

The fact that these kinds of "slips" and the defensive clichés associated with them are so familiar and universal points to the Shadow as archetypal. It is an integral part of our human structure. It cannot be eliminated. The central psychological task and the core of a genuine spirituality of mid-life is to build the bridge between two great archetypal structures: the one, established and dominant, the ego complex; and the other, the Shadow side, newly emergent from the unconscious.

It is a fundamental fact that the Shadow is the door to our individuality. Now is the time to separate myself from the collectivity, not for the sake of alienation but for the sake of the unique image of God that I am and a newer, richer freer commitment to the collectivity. God help those who are being served or "reformed" by a mid-life person who is not in some way trying to repossess and own his or her own Shadow. And God help our earth if more and more of us who are living longer than even before in history do not get in touch with and make conscious our areas of blindness, darkness, and neglect.

It is not as though we do not have Shadow experiences in the first half of life, or even that they do not serve a salutary purpose then. But at mid-life the archetype of the Shadow beckons us with greater intensity, for a wholly different reason, and needs to be dealt with in an entirely different way.

> No wonder that many bad neuroses appear at the onset of life's afternoon. It is a sort of second puberty, another storm and stress period; not infrequently accompanied by tempests of passion—the "dangerous age." But the problems that crop up at this age are no longer to be solved by the old recipes: the hand of the clock cannot be put back. What youth found and must find outside, the man [or woman] of life's afternoon must find within himself [or herself]. (Jung, *Two Essays in Analytical Psychology*:74–75)

The first half of life is, as it were, for the growth and differentiation of the Shadow. The whole second half of life is for the greater and greater integration of the Shadow. Thus, the beginning of mid-life becomes the time for the initial, intense "banging on the door" of the crisis-transition period. Stein calls it a liminal period (1983). It can seem like a floating period, on the boundary, neither here nor there.

A young college student who is normally studious can have a Shadow experience where, for example, the other side of his personality knocks and he lets go of his normal, sensible behavior pattern and "goofs off," abandoning all much needed study for a whole weekend before a very important final exam on Monday morning. Of course, the consequences are predictable. He fails the test. He comes face to face with this real fact of life: he is not a god. He must study. He has put his degree and his future in jeopardy. He has done a foolhardy thing. He learns a fact about his own psychic equipment and character: he has "feet of clay." He can learn from the experience that he needs to shore up his willpower. He needs to be aware of and eliminate, as far as possible, sources of temptation. He needs to be more single-minded and "shape up." In other words he needs to get on with building a strong ego. The experience may even open him further to the possibility that since he is so vulnerable to temptation and failure, he might need some divine assistance and prayer. He may grow in humility. He may also grow simultaneously in empathy and in contempt for those who "goof off" all the time. At this point since he needs to "get on with it," he can hardly become too aware of his own weakness or identify too closely with these "others."

Another young adult, a medical student resident in dermatology, may have the exact same kind of experience and go through the same process, and still time and again break her resolutions to study and work harder. Eventually, she may come to the conclusion that she just can't keep making and breaking resolutions. Perhaps she does need to stop driving herself. This may lead her to see that she had made a mistake in choosing dermatology and that what she really wanted was cardiology. She makes the decision to change her specialty.

These kinds of experiences—in vocational choices; marriage; staying physically fit; building trust, honesty, chastity, patience, or a hundred other virtues, skills, and roles—need to be dealt with in youth. This is part of the asceticism and spirituality of the first half of life.

If these experiences have done their work in us in some area or areas of our life we have been heroic in our efforts to succeed. We have poured ourselves out, hardly counting the cost because the goals or values involved have been so crucial to us. In the process we have built our strong willpower and identity, our conscious personality.

Now comes mid-life with perhaps an onslaught of experiences of the other side of the personality. We may be hit on many fronts at once. When we use the "old recipes," as Jung says, they fail time and again.

The archetypes are spoken of as primordial patterns and images. The archetypes are not inherited memories, representations, or images but inherited *possibilities* of representations. They are like "channels or predispositions, riverbeds into which the water of life has dug deep" (Jacobi, 1959:52). Yet, this ground plan or primordial pattern or potential axial system or inherited form is at first characterized by no specific contents. To be manifest they must first be clothed by the conscious mind and partake in the concrete outside world, and then they are no longer what they were. An archetype as such is invisible, it cannot be seen. The perceptible, actualized, "represented" or "archetypal image" is born when it is expressed by individual psychic material. Only then can it enter into consciousness.

From infancy we steadily differentiate and grow by developing innumerable habits, qualities, virtues, taboos, typical ways of responding, and patterns of perception and judging; by mid-life we have a well-defined conscious personality. The opposite of each of these habits is also well-defined: both the ego and the Shadow have been clothed through our interaction with the concrete outside world.

In mid-life one is called to individuation: to become one's own true Self, to discover more of oneself, to expand and not stay closed, stuck, or one-sided. A whole new world of exploration awaits within. One needs slowly and carefully to uncover the value in every nonvalue. One needs to stand outside one's habits, qualities, virtues, taboos, and patterns of perception, judgment, and belief. One needs to loosen one's hold on, one's captivity in, these ways of being and experience their relativity. One needs to expand one's consciousness, raise one's consciousness, stand outside oneself, critique oneself, laugh at oneself, and mellow. One needs to find the lost, despised parts of oneself and acknowledge their existence within. One needs to reinterpret one's life in light of this new stance.

It is only to the unconscious, both personal and collective, that one can go to discover all the opposites and neglected and unknown parts of one's character. It is here that one will begin to come to a new kind of individuality no longer measured overagainst the others out there or named by them. The more one now takes possession of the whole of oneself the more one will begin to give up competition with others as a way of affirming oneself, the more one will see the unique value of others, not identifying them with their conscious or unconscious personalities, their good or their evil. Owning one's Shadow opens the possibility of a new and more Godlike, unconditional kind of love of oneself and others.

Until now the ego has always had to defend itself furiously against too much of such dangerous realizations lest it be compromised and inundated. This defensiveness has served a good purpose. One still needs to be wary of the darkness and danger of the Shadow even as one now begins with fear and reverence to know and own and befriend one's Shadow. Resolutions, willpower, running away, making alternate choices that worked relatively well before—none of these are as effective as they once were. One meets oneself wherever one turns, brings oneself wherever one goes.

Now it is time to stand still and face oneself, for these Shadow experiences and this new awareness of evil everywhere and death at the end are real and powerful and a witness that there is much more to each of us than we are aware of. Each of us begins to sense our own complexity in a whole new way. Each of us begins to sense what a bundle of paradoxes we really are. Who am I really? There is a whole new kind of humility in the questioner asking this now than in young adulthood when one first asked this in the face of innumerable choices. Now that one has a long list of things one knows about oneself—a list so long that it could be rolled out across a transcontinental highway—one awakens one day to the realization that one doesn't know oneself at all!

A tremendous shift of power is in preparation within us. Jung called it the shift from the ego being in control to the Self being in control. From a theological perspective one has come closer to the hidden dark holy place at one's center where one grows out of God. Now one contacts one's own powerlessness. One is being invited to lose one's life to find one's life, to lose oneself to find oneself (Lk. 17:33; Mk. 8:35).

> Amen, amen, I say to you, unless a grain of wheat falls to the ground and dies, it remains just a grain of wheat; but if it dies, it produces much fruit. Whoever loves his life loses it, and whoever hates his life in this world will preserve it for eternal life. (Jn. 12:24–25)

The ego is letting go, not to be annihilated but to germinate. It will indeed feel like death but it will be an expansion of consciousness, of love, of Self.

Every experience of one's personal Shadow, every new awareness of the collective Shadow manifested in the evil in the world, can be fuel for the shifting of power. When one is able to take the perspective of the Self rather than just the ego, the good and evil in one's life and in life itself will be reinterpreted. Evil will be seen where before one saw only good and good will be seen where before one saw only evil.

The Self incorporates both the ego and the Shadow and despises neither. In loving both it redeems both. Only the inflated Self turned away from God could have contempt for the ego. This true Self despises neither the ego's concerns with eating, drinking, working, dressing, and so forth, nor the primitive ways of the Shadow. The Self wants to reclaim what has been cast out by the ego and projected ŏnto others. It is the ego speaking when a chronic fighter says to the bartender after one day of peacemaking, "*they* all began to change." It is the Self who is able to say, "Lord, be merciful to me a sinner."

Projection

Projection is seeing out there in the world and in others what I am totally unconscious of in myself. We all have scapegoats: those characteristics that we can't abide in others are the things we despise in ourselves, but we can't see them in ourselves. We can't admit them to ourselves. We can't own them, so we project them onto others. It is not that there is nothing objectively wrong in others, yet these qualities, to the degree that they are present in others, seem all the more glaring when we add our own darkness to theirs. Our excessive emotional reactions are indications of our own lower level of personality, our Shadow.

A Catholic priest in his late thirties took part in a program of preparation for hospital chaplaincy. He was well-loved and received splendid reports from all his instructors and supervisors. Then, one day, after a week on a new floor, a supervisor sent for him. She told him that she had been having complaints about him from nurses, doctors, and other personnel, She had observed him herself and thought that she was going to recommend him unfit for hospital chaplaincy. However, when she spoke to the director of his program and other supervisors, she found they had nothing but the highest praise for him, his kindness, tact, and ministry to the patients. She told him she wanted to talk to him about all this before she filed her report.

As they discussed what she had observed, he realized that the place where his cold, curt, cynical manner had been the subject of such criticism was the abortion wing. At first, he blamed his behavior on his moral objection to abortion but even as he said this he was ashamed that he could have been as brutal as the comments of the staff made him appear. It took this realization of his self-righteousness and failure to minister to shock him into the realization of what was going on. He admitted that he had always found his celibacy hard. He said that his virginity, chastity, cost him a great deal. He became aware of his feelings of anger that these women, especially the young unmarried ones, could take sexual behavior so lightly. He was angry that they dared indulge so freely, then abort the consequences. This anger and its cause underlined for him how far he still had to go to freely love and accept his celibacy as part of who he was. When he came to this as a free choice of his true self he would no longer see it simply as painful sacrifice: he would no longer need scapegoats.

When projections happen, there is usually some hook to hang them on, something objectionable in the other to which we add our Shadows. There is a wonderful story of Jesus unmasking projections in John's Gospel: Jesus was confronted by the scribes and Pharisees who brought to him a woman caught in adultery whom they were about to stone. He was reminded, as a test, that stoning was the law. He did not engage in disputing the law, he simply said, "Let the one among you who is guiltless be the first to throw a stone at her." One by one they went away, beginning with the eldest. Alone with her Jesus asked "Woman, where are they? Has no one condemned you?" "No one sir," she replied. "Neither do I condemn you," said Jesus. "Go, and from now on do not sin any more" (Jn. 8:1–11).

It is significant that the issue here was literally throwing stones—"projectiles." Jesus was surely asking each of them to withdraw his or her projections. When he turned the spotlight off the woman's sins and back on the accusers' own sinfulness, the stones fell to the ground, the anger dissipated. They left not as a "lynch mob" but as individuals. They left beginning with the eldest, the one most likely to have the longest history of sin and the greatest ambivalence about good and evil.

Projections are part of our lives. The question we need to keep asking is not Am I projecting? but, Where am I projecting now?

The pacifist who is ready to kill those who do not see things his or her way is projecting. The weapons manufacturer who sees all peace demonstrators as "communists" is projecting the antifascist who treats his wife and children like a dictator is projecting. What is projected may be moral evil or it may be a neutral quality that becomes an evil in the projecting.

Sara was a pretty woman with beautiful children and a wonderful husband. The two were happy after twenty-five years of marriage. They had always had to struggle financially but managed to do a great deal on very little.

Sara worked with Kay, who was married to an addict and had nothing but trouble with her children. Kay was plain looking but was always well-dressed and had her hair done every week. Day after day, as Kay came to work, Sara would comment sarcastically to her about whatever new pieces of jewelry or clothing she wore. Because of Sara's projection, Kay's one source of pleasure became a source of deep pain in her life.

George was a very accomplished administrator. He had great natural talent and a gifted personality. He was outgoing, energetic, and artistic. His life was filled with remarkable achievements. George, however, kept one great secret known only to his wife. Even his children did not know that he had never gone to college. Circumstances wouldn't allow it in his youth and he had been too busy getting ahead to go back to school later. As years passed he grew more embarrassed by this fact until it was blown out of all proportion.

One day a customer had a rather small complaint about a member of George's office staff. It was the first time George had ever had a complaint about Jim. In the industry Jim was highly regarded and many envied George for having him as a staff member. When Jim left George's office that day, he felt as though he had been stunned by an explosion. He had thought he and his work were highly valued by George, now he felt he was not even respected. Jim looked at his watch and realized that he had spent two hours in George's office experiencing an intensive cross-examination and controlled but unmistakable anger all about this one small complaint. What Jim didn't know was that his Ph.D. was at the root of the whole thing. George had projected his imagined inferiority on Jim.

Sheldon Kopp tells about a therapy group in a prison hospital. Everyone in the group was a sex offender. "In my mind," Kopp says,

> I lumped all the sex offenders in one category and all us good doctors in another. Unconsciously intent on maintaining the bastion that separated the good guys from the bad guys, I paid little attention to the ways that people *within* each category were different from one another. (1982:42)

He began to discover both his own Shadow projections and the Shadow projections within the group when a fight broke out and each began with contempt to call the other a name associated with the other's sex crime.

> Under the oppression of the collective shadow cast by the allegedly non-perverted community (of which I considered myself a charter member), each of these men was reduced to basing his self-esteem on comparing his offense with that of some other group member. If he had to identify himself as a sex offender, at least he did not have to consider himself the lowest form of pervert. (1982:44)

A woman in her fifties who had never committed a crime or been really abusive of her children recalled that when her children were small, especially when her twins were around two, she had been horrified by terrible scenes in supermarkets when parents would scream at and beat their children. She realized, she said, that now she hardly notices such scenes. She knows now how strong her temptation to lose patience and take it out on the babies truly was and how she was projecting her desire on those others.

Jesus said:

> Why do you notice the splinter in your brother's [or sister's] eye, but do not perceive the wooden beam in your own eye?

> How can you say to your brother [or sister], 'Let me remove the splinter from your eye? You hypocrite, remove the wooden beam from your eye first; then you will see clearly to remove the splinter from your brother's [or sister's] eye. (Mt. 7:3-4)

We put others down so that we can raise ourselves up by standing on them. We see the splinter out there in others and miss the great logs within ourselves. Probably we change the splinters out there into the greatest of logs because we are adding our projected inferiorities to what is there in reality. Withdrawing projections is a way of moving within. In a sense, we have received ourselves back from another when we catch ourselves in the act of projecting. If we can begin in mid-life to explore compassionately the great logs within, we may come closer to knowing and loving our whole Self and our neighbor as ourselves in a way we never could have in earlier stages of our lives.

> At first we cannot see beyond the path that leads downward to dark and hateful things but no light or beauty will ever come from the man [or woman] who cannot bear the sight. Light is always born of darkness, and the sun never yet stood still in the heaven to satisfy man's longing or to still his fears. (Jung, *Modern Man in Search of a Soul*:215)

Finding Gold in One's Shadow

There is no doubt about it, it is less fearful to see the dark and hateful things out there in others and keep ourselves as far away from their contamination as possible than to discover and own our Shadow. Yet, there is no light and beauty of mid-life spirituality without this bending low to embrace the ugliest, meanest, most hateful parts of ourselves. There is no question of a mid-life spirituality if we do not withdraw, repossess, and own the good and beautiful in ourselves that we have projected on heroines and heroes.

A speaker once made this point of our projecting our own goodness after our standing ovation for her finally subsided. "Thank you," she said,

I deeply appreciate your applause and affirmation. However, I want you to realize that you were really applauding yourselves. For you would never be so enthusiastic in your response to me if what I said wasn't already there in you. You would not be clapping so hard if I hadn't touched something there deep inside each of you.

Besides these "light" Shadows of our untapped potential for goodness and beauty there is also the possibility of discovering a pearl of great price (Mt. 13:45–46), a treasure hidden in a field (Mt. 13:44) in the midst of our own most despicable parts. Jesus saw both in every sinner he met. He saw the untapped potential and the gold in the wickedness.

Jesus saw in Zacchaeus, the wealthy thieving senior tax collector who collected extravagant amounts of tax so that he could pocket the surplus, a potentially extravagant philanthropist (Lk. 19:1–10). Jesus tells the short man who has climbed a tree to get a glimpse of Jesus to come down and invites himself to stay at Zacchaeus's house. Jesus shocks everyone, but probably Zacchaeus most of all by seeing something more in him than the outcast and traitor who stole from his own people in the process of collecting Roman taxes.

Jesus saw hidden there in the midst of that ugly extortionism, a genius and zeal that, if turned around, could be transformed into great good. Jesus saw in Zacchaeus's curiosity and effort to see him not merely the idle curiosity others might sneer at but the opening for his own extravagant kind of response. Jesus' fanning of this little spark pays off. Zacchaeus said to Jesus, "Behold, half of my possessions, Lord, I shall give to the poor, and if I have extorted anything from anyone I shall repay it four times over." (Lk. 19:9)

Our projections keep us from fanning this kind of spark, from even seeing the spark. Projections blind one so that not only is more evil seen than there is and evil is seen where there is none but also they blind one from seeing the possibility of good even in the midst of one's own or an other's evil.

In Jung's view assimilation of projection takes place in five stages *(Alchemical Studies:* 247–48). At first, a person experiences projection simply as the perception of reality, as though what one sees is what's really there. Next, doubts arise from within

and if the behavior of the other is in any way in conflict with the
ideas we have about him or her, we begin to differentiate
between the projected image we have and the actual person. In
the third stage, we make a moral judgment about the contents
of the projection. Fourth, we usually explain the projection as
having been an error or an illusion. Finally, we ask where the
faulty image came from; then we can recognize that we are the
source of the illusion and then recognize it as the image of a
content that originally somehow belonged to our own personality. However, if it was not and still is not evident how or what
in us is being projected, the cycle starts all over again.

11

Jung's Typology
and the
Archetypal Shadow

Projections are not the only way that one contacts one's own Shadow, but they are a very important one. They are invaluable as a practical aid in reappropriating the energy of our inferior attitude and functions of our psychological type.

In Jung's important work *Psychological Types,* he explores this issue at length. His type theory is his psychology of consciousness. He saw that human beings could be divided into conscious types according to how each of us develops certain potentials common to all of us because they have a built-in attraction for us, and consequently leave other common human potentials in a less developed, more unconscious state.

Introverted, Extraverted

In his type theory Jung first divides people by their typical attitudes: those who are *more* extraverted and those who are *more* introverted. Extraversion and introversion are both human potentials. In other words, all human beings have both an outer and an inner life. Our extraverted life is our life of involvement in the outer world of persons, places, and things. Relatively speaking all human beings orient themselves to the objective data of the outside world. Extraversion directs interests and attention to objective happenings, particularly those in the immediate environment. People and things seize and rivet our attention. Our extraversion is outer directed; yet, it is possible in the midst of much outer activity to "get lost in one's own thoughts." This is because of the other side, the introverted side, of the *human* involvement in reality. The world exists not merely in itself but also as it appears to me. There is a subjective limitation to all knowledge. The psychological reaction merges with the effect produced by any object "out there" to produce a third locus of new psychic data. Here again, because of the similarity of human equipment, the subjective factor has from earliest times and among all peoples remained to a large measure constant and is as much a firmly established reality as the reality of the world of external objects.

Thus we all have an introverted side, an inner world of our own images, insights, thoughts, emotions, values, and symbols all flowing from a human psychic structure, a psychological reaction to the "out there." Relatively speaking, all human beings are influenced by this subjective factor. Yet, it seems that from the beginning of life we are drawn more to one than to the other. There is more energy, more life, for us in one than the other. We are gifted to be *more* extraverted or *more* introverted; more influenced by the outer objects or by the inner subjective factor. One is more natural to us than the other. One becomes the determining factor over the other, seems more real than the other.

Extraverts are those who are more extraverted than they are introverted. They are magnetized more by the outer objective world. They are more energized by the outside. Extraverts' actions are more recognizably related to external conditions. Objective happenings have an almost inexhaustible fascination. Extraverts are more energized by the outside and by interaction; their psychic energy flows out to the object. They are more distractable by the stream of external stimuli. A multiplicity of relationships is more characteristic of them. Extraverts will be drawn more to breadth of involvements than to depth, to variety and action rather than to concentration. The extraverted person will tend to talk through his or her thinking rather than think through first and talk later.

Introverts are more introverted than they are extraverted. The inner subjective factors are the determining ones for them. The psychological processing of external data is more important than the data itself. Introverts find the inner world, their own agendas, more crucial and decisive than the outer world and are more influenced by this subjective aspect. Introverts are energized by quiet solitude and concentrated, thoughtful, introspective or restrospective activity. Analysis of what happened or what is going on is more crucial than what is happening out there. Interaction costs them more and exhausts them more than it does the extravert, who is more exhausted by *too much* quiet and the kinds of things that energize the introvert. Introverts are more interested in the inner dynamics, interconnections, and underpinnings than they are in outer networking or facile dealings with the outside world. Introverts are more taken by depth than breadth and more likely to have fewer, more intense in-depth interests and relationships than those that engage and energize the extravert. They need more privacy, more space. Territoriality will be more crucial than sociability. They will even need to protect themselves from the intrusion and bombardment of too many things as well as too much exposure to people and events. The many layers, multiple dimensions, infinite complexity, and great depths in limited areas of reality will invite their exploration.

If one side is our preference or natural gift or built-in tendency, then we will use that side more innately, more frequently, and more typically; we will grow in that direction. Our conscious personality will therefore be more extraverted or more introverted. Thus, if I am consciously more extraverted, my extraversion will be more adapted; if I am consciously more introverted my introversion will be more adapted. This does not mean however that the opposite side will be obliterated from my personality, but it will be more unconscious. The unconscious compensatory attitude will find expression and be crucial in maintaining psychic equilibrium.

> A normal extraverted attitude does not, of course, mean that the individual invariably behaves in accordance with the extraverted schema. Even in the same individual many processes may be observed that involve the mechanisms of introversion. We call the mode of behavior extraverted only when the mechanisms of extraversion predominate. (Jung, *Psychological Types:*340)

At the same time the *unconscious* extraversion of the introvert and the *unconscious* introversion of the extravert are inferior extraversion and inferior introversion. They are not well-adapted; they are not under conscious control and so are relatively undifferentiated. Under the influence of inferior extraversion the introvert is no longer "himself" or "herself," but is sheer relatedness, identical with the object and therefore without a standpoint. Similarly, when

> the extravert proceeds to introvert, he [or she] arrives at a state of interior relatedness to collective *ideas* an identity with collective thinking of an archaic concretistic kind. (Jung, *Psychological Types:* 1020)

The extravert also loses "himself" or "herself" in this inferior introversion, hence the extravert has the same repugnance or silent contempt for introversion as the introvert for extraversion, although both actually have this contempt for their own inferior version of the opposite of their conscious attitude.

In everyone, introversion and extraversion are both going on all the time, one in a more conscious adapted way, the other in a more unconscious way. An introvert goes to be alone by the lake, finds a seat, gets comfortable, and realizes when a dog comes by that she had been there for thirty minutes lost in her own thoughts. The lake has been a background to this deep introverting. The extravert goes to the lake to be alone and will most likely walk around it first, then on sitting down will be in touch with the whole setting, notice the beach house and the birds that fly by. He will see the dog coming from a mile off and will be much more in touch with the outer and much less in touch with the inner processes in the same half hour.

All during life all of us will need both introverted and extraverted time. Yet at mid-life, the introvert or the extravert will start to be more conscious of the lack of control he has over the more unadapted side and, instead of feeling contempt, will start to see the pearls of great price that the other side offers.

At the lake, the mid-life introvert will consciously make the effort to pay attention to his surroundings before he sits down; he may catch himself getting lost in thought and pull himself out more quickly to pay more attention to and be refreshed by the surroundings. He sees the wealth in what before was felt to be a distraction and less real. Similarly, the mid-life extravert may more quickly say to herself, "you came here now to be alone and to think things through. Forget those birds and that dog and pay attention to what is going on inside you."

Away from the lake and solitariness, in the midst of the involvement and activity of a busy office or hospital, the extravert will be at home and flourish and move easily from one involvement to the next. The introvert will move and interact and accomplish but will do it in a more introverted way, perhaps more slowly, with more intensity and more pauses for reflection. Too much relatedness with no pause to regain his standpoint will make the introvert too frazzled. People try instinctively to move into work and living environments that allow for an individually healthy balance between introversion and extraversion, or they try to find ways to compensate for too great an exclusion of one or the other.

The introvert will tend to see the similarities between objects and will find security in reducing the multiplicity of the world to something more uniform and coherent. The extravert tends to find similarities tiresome and disturbing as these actually hinder one from recognizing the object's singularity.

The outward reaction characterizes the extravert as the inward reaction characterizes the introvert. Extraverts express themselves, making their presences felt almost involuntarily because their whole nature goes outward. Extraverts react quickly and more likely have quick discharge of emotion. One can see where they come from and where they are going. The quick succession of immediate reactions produce a series of images that show the public the path she has followed and the means by which she has attained her result (Jung, *Psychological Types*:325).

Because of the extravert's readily renewed capacity for action and reaction many new themes tend to crowd into a given unit of time. Since this rapidity facilitates extensive rather than intensive reaction, affectivity is more superficial and rapid adaptation and changes of attitude are more easily possible.

A person of this type gives the impression of having an uncritical or unprejudiced attitude; we are struck by his [or her] readiness to oblige and by his [or her] understanding or again we may find in him [or her] an unaccountable lack of consideration, tactlessness and even brutality. . . . His [or her] rapidity looks like decisiveness. (Jung, *Psychological Types:*276)

Involvement in other people's affairs is taken as a matter of course because of the quickness and more superficial appreciation of values, ideas, or actions in oneself or others. For the same reason memory is poor unless interlinked with other memories. Excitability and enthusiasm can also quickly fade in the extravert; this puzzles the introvert, who in general has more staying power.

The introvert, on the other hand, reacts almost completely within. She suppresses reactions even though they may be as quick as those of the extravert. The introvert hides her personality by repressing immediate reactions. An inner elaboration goes on before the final product comes out in a more abstract and depersonalized form. The introvert's real self is not visible. This of course is not done intentionally but because of an incapacity for immediate expression. She prefers to let her work or her reputation speak for her. "What fills the extravert's heart flows out of his [or her] mouth but the enthusiasm of the introvert is the very thing that seals his [or her] lips" (Jung, *Psychological Types:*326).

Instead of impulse or ready movement toward practical life, there is in the introvert a drive or movement for inwardness. External stimuli are regarded from the standpoint of inner ideas. While for the extravert, universals tend to be names lacking reality, for the introvert the inner facts, abstractions, ideas, or universals always occupy the foreground. They are the only true realities to which she *must* relate all individual phenomena. The introvert trusts the inner world and tends to distrust the outer world. Individual phenomena are not conceived as things in themselves but as partial ideas or part of a complex of related ideas.

It is as though introverts, at the time for reaction to a given situation, at first hesitate and draw back, as it were, with an unvoiced no, and only then are they able to react. Introverts are at home in their own company but can feel lonely and lost in a crowd. The introvert's own world is a safe harbor, a walled garden closed to the public; this is not a renunciation of the world but a search for quiet, where she can make her greatest contributions to the world. The introvert will have a better relation to ideas than to things.

As one develops one of these basic attitudes in the first half of life and as it more and more characterizes one's conscious personality, one tends to see the opposite, more neglected side as strange, threatening, frightening, or simply peculiar and objectionable. In other words, projection is going on. Extraverts may call introverts names, and vice versa. Extraverts may be called flighty, superficial, shallow, loud mouth, gad about, butterfly, pushy, showy, talkative, show off, egotistic, know-it-all. Introverts are called proud, quiet, slow, egg head, aloof, too deep, inscrutable, introspective, loner, stuck up, intense, whimp. In other words, extraverts project their weaknesses on introverts and introverts project their inferior side on extraverts. The one who moves easily and without hesitation into and through the world of objects is called "shallow" and "pushy." The one who is in contact with the inner psychic realm is called "inscrutable" and "slow."

Introverts tend to be self-critical and aware of their own motives; therefore they are interested in the motives of others. The more introverted among us can teach us to view the many-sidedness of the inner self with more justice. They can lead us from a too vigorous observation of external things back into ourselves. The ego and its relative constancy is accented by the introvert. For the introvert, the "person" tends to be exclusively the ego. For the extravert the accent is on continuity of relationship to the object so that the "person" is revealed solely in its relatedness to the object. Thus the introvert discovers herself in the constant, while the extravert discovers herself in the fluctuating and changeable.

The extravert leads us to the many-sidedness of external reality. The extravert emphasizes the "becoming" aspect of the ego in its relatedness with different affects through relationships to other persons, places, and things. The extravert more freely allows people and things to be what they are in themselves.

Yet the extravert who seeks life and experience as busily and abundantly as possible is far more influenced by the inner psychic world than she suspects. While the extravert cannot see it herself, observant others will always detect the unconscious *personal* purpose, the ego purpose, in her striving. Precisely because she is so given to relating to persons and things, the critic of the extravert is liable to see through the veil that conceals a cold and calculating personal aim. Hence the extravert needs always to ask herself the question: What am I really after? What is my secret intention?

The introvert with all her careful, thought out intentions always overlooks (will be unconscious of) what others can see all too clearly, that her

> intentions are really subservient to powerful impulses, lacking both aim and object, and are in a high degree, influenced by them. . . . The man [or woman] who tries to understand the introvert will readily conclude that vehement passions are only with difficulty held in check by apparent sophistries. (Jung, *Psychological Types:*150)

At mid-life when adaptation to the outer world has reached a certain fulfillment in either an extraverted or introverted way new flowering will come from the other side, the unconscious side, the Shadow. This, of course, will not happen without resistance, risk, and danger. The seduction of the other side at this time is archetypal. With an intensity never before experienced in the development of the ego to incorporate some of the other side, the other side of the typical attitude wants to have its day.

Two women in their forties expressed it this way. Janine, the more extraverted one, said to the other with great intensity, "No more happy-go-lucky Janine. People are going to begin to take me more seriously from now on." From the other side of the room, her more introverted sister, with even more intensity said, "Not me, I'm sick and tired of being so serious about everything." Soul-felt exchanges like this, which are indeed expressions of whole new perceptions and behaviors, come from someplace in the personality beyond the ego. These women already had an objective view themselves, a standpoint from which to critique the forty-odd years of their lives as happy-go-lucky or serious. The standpoint was somewhere outside their egos. The Shadow, and at its heart, the true Self was speaking. Janine undoubtedly had once seen seriousness, as strange, morose, slow, too deep, and so on. In any case, it was not "her," it was not her way to go. Mary, her sister, had seen being happy-go-lucky as shallow, flighty, loud, or just not "her," not her way to go.

Now, the top of the ladder has been reached by both of them and they feel the ladder is against the wrong roof. The temptation is strong to collapse into the other way of being. For this seduction to have reached consciousness to the degree that it can be verbalized means that a great deal of energy is involved. For the repugnance to the other side to have so disintegrated that each woman expresses a real commitment to the other side means that blind spots have been filled with light and motivation has swelled. Dreams of wading waist-deep, or neck-deep in the water (of the unconscious) give many mid-life people a graphic picture of the surrender to the other side that is going on.

Another man in mid-life expressed the same attraction in a more negative way, "I don't know what's the matter with me, I used to enjoy going out three or four nights a week but for the last six months, I can't make myself budge out that door."

Here again, we see both the danger of collapsing what has been built up and losing everything, and the danger of resisting everything and getting stuck. However, if "happy-go-lucky" can hold on to that and to "serious" until they somehow come together and give birth to someone who is neither but both, integration will have occurred. If "serious" can do the same, a more whole Self will emerge. The man has emphasized holding on while his behavior has moved on. Many who do get stuck are simply overcome by fear of "going insane" because they are experiencing repugnance for old ways and the attraction of new needs, new parts of themselves.

In trying to focus solely on introversion and extraversion in looking at the Shadow and Jung's theory of typology at mid-life we have been making artificial distinctions. We have had to neglect the important role of the functions of sensing, intuition, thinking, and feeling. In Jung's theory one's introversion or extraversion is greatly affected by which of the four functions are more highly developed in their introverted or extraverted mode. The four functions, like the two attitudes, are all human potentials and either consciously or unconsciously all four are part of us. Like the attitudes, Jung sees the functions as divided into pairs, and thus as shadows of each other.

Sensing and Intuition

The functions of perception are sensing and intuition. The functions of judging are thinking and feeling. Jung saw that people tended to develop one function of each pair and that these two functions in dynamic relationships with one another are in dynamic relationship with introversion and extraversion to form the conscious personality. One's introversion or extraversion is colored by the primary, or dominant, function and by the auxiliary that is also more conscious. The other two inferior functions tend to be "pushed down" and, in combination with the undeveloped attitude, are part of the unconscious, or Shadow personality. If then, for example, an introvert is gifted for and develops sensing as primary, and feeling as auxiliary, that person's conscious personality would be described as introverted sensing with feeling. Primitive, unadapted, and undeveloped within, but still operative, would be the person's extraverted intuitive thinking aspects.

In order to hold this kind of typological mirror up to oneself, it is important to know what element of human equipment each function is referring to, what each attempts to name.

The functions of perception—sensing and intuition—refer to our ways of contacting reality, of perceiving what is there to be taken in. Our first and most obvious way of perceiving is through our senses. Our senses give us the facts, what we can know through our bodies. We see and hear, taste and smell, we touch textures and feel temperatures. We have extended the power of our senses by telescopes and microscopes, telephones, recorders, television, thermostats, and hosts of other ways of perceiving sights, sounds, tastes, odors, textures, heat, and cold. Every human person uses the function of sensing but those whose sensing is their greatest gift and who go with that gift will have their personality more defined by this gift. In the process of growth and development in this way of perceiving they will necessarily neglect what is diametrically opposed to it, perception through intuition. Jung defines intuition as perception through the unconscious, perception of realities not yet known to consciousness.

The sensing type takes everything as it comes, experiencing things as they are in the here and now, noticing many facts and details. In the intuitive type much that is sensed barely reaches consciousness. The intuitive ordinarily admits only sense impressions as they are related to current inspirations or enthusiasms. The sensing person can't imagine how the intuitive has missed the sights and sounds, tastes and odors, that are so obvious to him or her. "How could she always bang the door that way?" "What do you mean you don't know what color your hospital room was, you were there for five weeks!" "That's not new. It's been there since we moved in."

The intuitive is loyal to possibilities, to what is not yet but surely will or can come to be. Intuition touches into the archetypal layer and perceives relationships in the archetypal riverbeds of the psyche. The intuitive can't imagine how the sensing person "can't read the handwriting on the wall." "How can you be so literal," the intuitive will say. In a book store a seventy-year-old woman said to a clerk, "I want a book on mid-life for my son who died at forty." When the bewildered clerk asked, "How can he read a book if he's dead?" the intuitive woman just walked away. Illusions, figurative language, imagination, and symbols are the world of the intuitive, who will often be bored by the facts. Noticing the facts, pursuing the facts, remembering many facts, precision, fine print, and thoroughness will be more often the realm of the sensing person.

The extravert sensing person will tend to see things as they really are, and will be practical and tolerant. He or she will have a zest for experience and be attracted to new foods, scenery, activities, and people. The extraverted sensing person enjoys applying experience, usually enjoys physical exercise, and values material possessions. In general the sensing person is more in touch with the body than the intuitive person is.

The introverted sensing person is more patient with routine, tends to be more conservative, and enjoys using old familiar skills. The introverted sensing person is extremely dependable, thorough, hard to discourage and distract, tends to be a good rooter or fan, and has a good memory.

People with extraverted intuition are drawn by successive enthusiasms into serial projects. They will enjoy pioneering, be attracted to new ventures, and sacrifice the present for long-range projects.

Introverted intuition sees the interrelationship of ideas, the deeper meanings: flashes of insight, potentialities, outcomes, originality, and the power to inspire will combine with a stubbornness about the rightness and value of these inner perceptions.

The patience of sensing is the shadow of the impatience of intuition. Where sensing is straightforward, intuition is full of ideas about everything. Where sensing is systematic, intuition is versatile. Where sensing looks to precedents, intuition looks for originality. Where sensing sees the present, here and now, intuition sees future possibilities and outcomes. Sensing is into the particular, intuition is into the general. Where the sensing person is more likely to be technical, the intuitive is more likely to be the initiator. Sensing is stability, intuition is its shadow, restlessness. The intuitive's independence of physical surroundings, even the needs of the body and the irrefutability of the fact of time, is the exact opposite of the realistic, down-to-earth, observant, accurate inner clock of sensing.

How a person's sensing is developed may appear very different in different people. Whether it is primary or auxiliary, whether it is introverted or extraverted will make a great deal of difference. Typology should never put people into boxes; we are all unique. Yet type can help capture something of how each individual uses common human equipment and this gives us some objectivity on ourselves and others. The archetypal Self uses this archetypal equipment. These attitudes and functions are archetypal; in Jung's theory, the choice of one of these pairs of opposites is also built-in, and thus an archetypal pattern.

The more highly conscious and differentiated each choice becomes, the more its opposite defines an aspect of one's Shadow. The outlines of one's Shadow personality can begin to be sketched by contrasting the functions as they operate in oneself. In seeing the attitudes and functions as Shadows of one another one has a tool for naming one's projections. In this way one can recognize how one has made one's own "speck" into the "log" in another's eye. When the intuitive person dislikes what is seen operating so smoothly in the highly developed sensing person, she is really reacting negatively to her own inferior use of the sensing function. When the intuitive person overreacts to the "boring practicality" of the sensing person, that reaction reveals her own undeveloped, unconscious practical side. When the sensing person gets furious at how the intuitive person overlooks facts or makes a factual mistake or loses track of time, the sensing person is also furious that the other has the versatility and originality he needs. The opposition of the functions, especially of the dominant and inferior functions, is a fertile field for projections. The withdrawal of such projections discovered in the midst of conflict and explosions is a source of the greatest growth in the second half of life.

Thinking and Feeling

Jung looked at the functions of perception as the irrational functions in the sense that they are prerational. We perceive before we judge and decide. Thinking and feeling are rational functions. They name how we judge and decide. With the word *feeling* Jung referred to values and evaluation, not to emotion, though some of the emotion of the highly feeling person may be more obvious than that of the highly thinking person.

If thinking-type judgment is analytical, feeling-type judgment is relational. If thinking is impersonal, its shadow feeling is personal. Where thinking values logic and objectivity, feeling values subjective and harmonious human contact. Where thinking values truth, reason, and organization, feeling values conciliation, good feelings, and cooperation. Thinking can more readily be firm and tough and consistent. Feeling can more readily be easy, tactful, and consider extenuating circumstances.

Extraverted thinking stakes out objectives, is decisive, is convinced by reasoning, and excels at executing standard operating procedures and standing firm against opposition. It enjoys authority and administration.

Introverted thinking is detached, perservering, and given to theory and abstractions. It seeks to understand the world; it revels in research and is given to precision in thought and language.

Extraverted feeling radiates warmth and sees the value in

others' opinions. It seeks to please people, and values friendliness. It is loyal to collective values with a strong devotion and
sense of duty. *← McIntyre type / Bellah*

Introverted feeling is loyal and idealistic, and has extremely
fine-tuned values and sentiment, almost too deep for expression. It can forecast another's feelings and takes responsibility for another's feelings.

Where the thinker not only tolerates conflict but can value it
to "get all the thoughts and ideas out," the feeler hates conflict.
Thinking holds to principle and policy in the midst of objection. Feeling is crippled by antagonism and very sensitive to
praise, approval, indifference, or criticism. Where thinking is
intellectually curious, feeling needs a purpose and meaning.
Where thinking regulates, feeling appreciates. Where thinking
reforms, feeling sells. The feeler can hate the dispassionate
expression of the thinker while the thinker is appalled by the
passionate expression of the feeler. "Be coherent and unemo-
tional," says the thinker. "Be involved and empathetic," says the
feeler. Cause and effect are important to thinking; individual
circumstances are important to feeling.

Social life is incidental to the highly thinking person; comfortable charm and social adeptness are central to the highly
feeling personality. For the sake of harmony, feelers will repress
their own feeling when it conflicts with those around them. For
the sake of high achievement, the thinker will largely repress
emotional life. To meet their own standards thinkers may be
hard on themselves. Cultivating personal understanding and
intimacy, feelers may tend to lose themselves. The thinkers can
be openly critical and strict disciplinarians. Feelers outwardly
ignore the unacceptable unless a value is touched, but because
of their very differentiated hierarchy of values, feelers will be
perfectionistic and inwardly very critical of others. Because
their own criticism also falls back on themselves, feelers tend to
be less self-confident than thinkers.

(Our analysis of the functions in concrete contrast or opposition to one another, as Shadows of one another, owes much to
developments and applications of Jung's type theory in the
work of Isabel Briggs Myers and the Association of Psychological Types, and to the work of David Kiersey and Marilyn Bates.)

A spirituality of mid-life will be open to the treasure from the opposites of the attitudes and functions that characterize one's conscious personality. This openness is archetypal, but it demands much asceticism. Whereas Shadow experiences based on typological differences in the first half of life tended to strengthen one in the differentiation of one's gifted side, at mid-life they serve a different purpose and need to be handled differently.

Of course everyone has developed both attitudes and all four functions to some degree. Adaptation to the world requires that one use all these potentials at some time or other. Different environments even different nations make different demands on the development of these potentials. People often see themselves differently when they compare how they are at home to how they are at work. The tasks of the first half of life tend to be more extraverted tasks; nonetheless, schooling and study require some kinds of introversion. In societies where education emphasizes thinking and sensing, intuitives and feelers may be forced to develop their sensing and thinking more than thinking and sensing persons are asked to develop their feeling and intuition. Sexual stereotyping may also play a role here.

At mid-life however, what is called for is not just some more development of the less developed functions so that we can adapt in a better way to the outside environment. What is called for is the recognition of the undeveloped attitude and functions as the more accessible gateway to one's own Shadow and one's Shadow as the way to one's whole unconscious. This real knowing of the inferiority of one's inferior side and the embracing of it are crucial to one's adaptation to the whole inner world of the personal and objective psyche, which is the source of all personal and spiritual growth in the second half of life.

At mid-life one's own highly developed side starts to feel bankrupt, too tight, or too constraining. One begins to feel the sting both of one's highly developed functions and of one's introversion or extraversion. The introverted sensing person may begin to feel like a martyr and be very angry with those who take his or her dependability and practicality for granted. The extraverted sensing person, who has always been given to joy and pleasure and has been the source of others' joy and fun, may begin to resent always having to be the "life of the party." The introverted intuitive will start to feel the exhaustion of the neglected body that has been dragged along by all the possibilities and potentials from the world of ideas and inspirations. The extraverted intuitive will also begin to feel physically worn down and to have longer periods of loss of energy and enthusiasm; such people may begin to look around for neglected relationships that have "gone down the drain" while they followed their successive enthusiasms.

The introverted thinker may now begin to feel lonely when others turn away from his or her hairsplitting abstractions. The extraverted thinker may scream out, "Everybody wants me to chair the committee but all I want is someone to want to pal around with me." The introverted feeler may need to get away from the people who "people" him or her, want more privacy. He or she may begin to see the value in conflict and be sick of the need for harmony. The extraverted feeler will want more time alone and will feel the confinement of the shoulds and oughts that have held him or her captive.

Openness to this pain—living it rather than disowning it in more of the same kind of operating, or in alcohol, drugs, or despair—can begin to effect the kinds of conversion that one is being called to. Bearing the tension of opposites without totally letting go of either side will give birth to a new thing that is neither wholly one nor the other but somehow both. A child will be born from the union of opposites. New life will grow from the pain and asceticism of embracing this poor weak side of oneself every time one falls because of its clumsiness. Primitive sensing or intuition or feeling or thinking will be embarrassing as we walk on these tottering new legs and make many mistakes. In every instance, the Shadow of one's attitude and functions is pure gold, yet murders have been committed in mid-life because of repressing the call of the Shadow and holding on too tightly and too long to one's conscious typology—or because of not holding on at all and collapsing into the primitive side.

When each attitude and function is leavened by its opposite in mid-life, when some true integration occurs as one moves beyond the initial stage of feeling and owning the pain of one's conscious personality, one begins to mellow, to give off the aura of a new depth of personality. One is not so hard, flat, closed, and one-sided, one is not cut off from the springs of new life.

One has found the "new roof for one's ladder." Thoughts and emotions of anger and destruction of oneself or the other give way to the painful but exciting process of learning to walk again on tiny untried legs. The scales gradually fall from one's eyes and one by one the projections of the inferior side start to be withdrawn. Dislike and intimidation of the opposite type give way to real admiration of the other's facility with what is so difficult for oneself. Focus on the strengths in the other takes the spotlight off the flaws and faults. Recognition of one's own superior attitude and functions and the consequent weakness of the neglected ones, which were sacrificed so that these might have life, makes one more compassionate toward oneself and toward others, who live the same kind of archetypal pattern.

Competition gives way to generativity in the second half of life. One is interested in nurturing one's own growth and the growth of others; one is less often tempted to put oneself up by putting others down. The spirituality of mid-life is a spirituality of straining against stagnation by passing through this very dark night of inner and outer conflict. Going through these typology Shadow experiences, neither denying them nor inflating them, may indeed be the narrow gate that Jesus talks about:

> Enter by the narrow gate, since the road that leads to perdition is wide and spacious, and many take it; but it is a narrow gate and a hard road that leads to life, and only a few find it. (Mt. 7:13, JB)

12

Jesus, the Shadow, and New Life

Whether the dark night be the night of the shadow of typology, or of my own taboos, or of the new awareness of archetypal evil in oneself and others, there is new life born of this mid-life archetypal process of dying to one's ego and letting go of this too tight grip and control. This exploration through the Shadow into the Self is really exploration into God, and so it is a surrender that is active and creative.

Jesus walked into the water to be baptized—he who had not sinned. He waded with the other sinners into the water and was made sin for our sake. The womb of each of our unconscious origins is water-filled. The mother's water breaks as the violent contractions of the childbirth begin. Water always speaks to us of the unconscious. The purifying waters of the Jordan washed the sinners who came to John the Baptist to acknowledge their conscious and unconscious need of conversion, of repentance and liberation.

John the Baptist came to his place at the Jordan out of the desert and the struggle with his own unconscious. He came out of the narrow way of physical and psychological asceticism. He ate only locust and wild honey, yet he knew that Jesus, who was no ascetic (Kasper:68), must increase and he must decrease. He was generative toward Jesus. He was generative toward his own disciples as he sent them away to follow Jesus. John is well into a mid-life spirituality of the Shadow. He is the great gate figure. "Prepare the way of the Lord, make straight his paths" (Mt. 3:3). John confronted the hypocrisy of those who were blind to

146

their own Shadows and came for baptism without willingness to own their own evil and transform it. "You brood of vipers! . . . Produce good fruit as evidence of your repentance. And do not presume to say to yourselves, 'We have Abraham as our father.'" (Mt. 3:7–9) No longer can one depend on just being part of the collective. John is warning that each individual will have to produce fruit or, like a barren tree, be cut down and thrown into the fire.

Yet John goes even farther into the mid-life spirituality of the shadow:

> I am baptizing you with water, for repentance, but the one who is coming after me is mightier than I. I am not worthy to carry his sandals. He will baptize you with the holy Spirit and fire. His winnowing fan is in his hand. He will clear his threshing floor and gather his wheat into his barn, but the chaff he will burn with unquenchable fire. (Mt. 3:11–12)

These mysterious words of John's seem to refer to different kinds of fire. There is the fire of destruction for the barren trees who do not produce fruits of repentance. There are the fires for those who can never see themselves as sinners, and the fire of destruction for those who can never seek and love their own weak side. And yet there is still another fire connected dynamically to the Holy Spirit (Kasper:66). "He will baptize you with the holy Spirit and fire." This kind of fire is purifying (Bornkaam: 48–52) like a baptism in water, but even more: it is transforming like the fire that separates base metal from gold. Yet, it is very painful, for later in Luke, Jesus seems to be referring to his Passion when he talks of fire and baptism.

> I have come to set the earth on fire, and how I wish it were already blazing! There is a baptism with which I must be baptized, and how great is my anguish until it is accomplished. (Lk. 12:49–50)

The way of recognizing and befriending one's own weak side is indeed a daily crucifixion; withdrawing projections without being inundated and overcome by one's own inferiorities is a daily crucifixion. But none of these comes close to the struggle

Unaccepted (margin note)

Unacking/shadow. (margin note)

with archetypal evil that unleashed can massacre eight million Jews in the name of purity or indeed blow up the earth in the name of righteousness.

Mid-life spirituality is a dark night of the soul. Yet within the darkness of what seems like increasing conflict, loss, and struggle is a bright fire ever consuming the chaff and never going out. The fire is a transforming fire. It transforms into new life. The Holy Spirit comes in tongues of such fire and will transform the derelict Shadows into a conflagration that will perhaps not consume the earth but save it by transforming in new life one by one the aging individuals who people this planet.

"Shadow speaks" has/takes voice ~ (margin note)

positive mobilizing fn of shadow functions (margin note)

Jesus is baptized by John and John protests that he is the one who should be baptized by Jesus. Then the Spirit of God comes not like fire but like a dove descending and coming down on him and with it a voice saying, "This is my beloved Son, with whom I am well pleased" (Mt. 3:17). From the depths and the heights, Jesus knows himself to be beloved. As he acknowledges himself to be one with sinful humanity—as the hands of John, a sinner, cleanse him and lead him to repentance—he knows himself to be beloved! This is the strange paradox of mid-life spirituality. One can know the worst about oneself. One can know the worst about one's intimate others. One can have one's blinders removed and lose one's naiveté about the real evil in one's own past and in the institutions one has been part of. One can have deep awareness of the evil within one's nation, church, and world, and at the very same time one can know and even feel one's self, one's past, and one's world beloved, blessed, and favored of God.

↑ Strngth ↓ Shad- (margin note)

Paul expresses it this way in a paean of mid-life trust in God's love when he cries out:

> If God is for us, who can be against us? He who did not spare his own Son but handed him over for us all, how will he not also give us everything else along with him? Who will bring a charge against God's chosen ones? It is God who acquits us? Who will condemn? It is Christ Jesus who died, rather, was raised, who is also at the right hand of God, who indeed intercedes for us. What will separate us from the love of Christ? Will anguish, or distress, or persecution, or famine, or nakedness, or peril, or the sword? As it is written: "For your

sake we are being slain all the day; we are looked upon as
sheep to be slaughtered." No, in all these things we conquer
overwhelmingly though him who loved us. For I am convinced that neither death, nor life, nor angels, not prin-
cipalities, not present things, nor future things, nor powers,
nor height, nor depth, nor any other creature will be able to
separate us from the love of God in Christ Jesus our Lord.
(Rom. 8:31–39)

Paul is saying that, all evidence to the contrary, we must be
lovable; in spite of our misinterpretations of hardships as
punishments, we are loved. God gave us Jesus to reveal that
love and show it to us.

Jesus goes into the desert led by the same Spirit to be tested
by the devil (Mt. 4:1). The Spirit of the Lover and the Beloved
leads him. Like John he fasts in the desert. He fasts for forty
days and forty nights, Matthew says, referring to Moses
(Vawter:182). After this he is hungry. According to Mark, he
was "driven into" the desert after the heavens were "torn apart"
for the Spirit to come like a dove: the gentle dove tears apart
and drives Jesus to be tested by "Satan" (Mk. 1:12–13).

In Luke, while Jesus prays after his own baptism, the Holy
Spirit descends on him in "a bodily form like a dove." This time
the voice from heaven says, "You are my beloved Son; with you
I am well pleased" (Lk. 3:22). After Jesus identifies himself with
sinners in a baptism of repentance, the voice says, "with you I
am well pleased." According to Luke, Jesus was filled with the
Holy Spirit, was led by the Spirit for forty days, and was put to
the test by the devil. A test that lasts forty days is described by
Luke as three temptations, at the end of which, "When the devil
had finished every temptation, he departed from him for a
time" (Lk. 4:13).

Jesus in the desert is attacked by the very weak and sinful
humanity with which he is identified. He encounters all the
possibilities for sin that flesh is heir to. He encounters all the
possibilities for sin that the human spirit is heir to (Lane:123).

The ego personality of Jesus, nourished in the home of Mary
and Joseph and on the Hebrew Scriptures, had gone down to
Nazareth and was subject to them. He had adapted to his
environment. But, something had happened to move him be-

yond the adaptation that was so well done. At the river and in the desert he reaches the definitive end of naiveté, a wonder filled naiveté that was so beautiful and strong. The other side of everything breaks in on him. He knows now the hypocrisy John struck out against in the apparently holy Scribes and Pharisees. He sees the "riffraff" going into the river, the outcasts, the sinners. He is with them, dirtied by the same contaminated water. But that is nothing compared to the solitary experience of his oneness with all the sin of humanity and with a voice, not of the Father but of the devil, Satan. He experiences in his own flesh the movement that the devil voices for him: "Turn these stones into bread." A temptation is not a temptation if it doesn't hit upon a possibility, strike a cord that vibrates in one. Jesus is starving. His body has started to feed on itself and here are these stones, perhaps they even looked like bread. Was the temptation to work magic, to treat sonship trivially and turn stones into bread for his own gratification? Perhaps. Was the temptation a mid-life temptation to look for life and nourishment in stones? To turn to everything that one has rejected or undervalued in the first half of life and see that, as the only value, totally rejecting all one has valued for so many years? Was it a temptation to ego gratification, pleasure, ease, and comfort by ending his fast in a great celebration of and for himself. Later in his life he is hungry and the multitudes are hungry. In John he tells his disciples he has food that they don't know anything about. His food, strangely, is a conversation he has been having with a Samaritan woman of bad reputation in the hottest part of the day. Returning, the disciples urge him to eat. He says:

> My food is to do the will of the one who sent me and to finish his work. . . . I tell you, look up and see the fields ripe for the harvest. (Jn. 4:34–35; see also Kasper: 208–9)

In John too, he calls himself the bread of life.

> I am the bread of life; whoever comes to me will never hunger. . . . I am the living bread that came down from heaven; whoever eats this bread will live forever; and the bread that I will give is my flesh for the life of the world. (Jn. 6:34, 51)

Jesus will not collapse into ego gratification. He is true to the larger Self, to the Son, who has been fathered by heaven, who is beloved, who is led by the Holy Spirit. He does not do his own will, he surrenders the heroic mode, he does the will of the Lover who has more to give him if he hungers. The will of the Lover for the Beloved is to feed the multitudes by feeding hungry individuals. To do so he must be hungry and participate in each one's neediness. To be bread and give his own flesh for the life of the world requires that he not cut off his own neediness. If he stuffs himself on any other bread than the will of the one who sends him, he cuts himself off from all nourishment.

He answers each temptation by quoting Scripture (McKenzie: 878–79). His temptations are archetypal ones so he answers archetypally, "One does not live by bread alone" (Lk. 4:4). Human beings can transcend any deprivation when the Self is true to itself, when we do what we have to do, when the Holy Spirit leads us into it.

Now the devil leads him. This is very frightening. He surrenders to being led by the devil to a vision of all the kingdoms of the world. The devil remarks he will give Jesus all their power and their splendor. He says, "I may give it to whomever I wish. All this will be yours, if you worship me" (Lk. 4:6–7).

Did the devil then seem to be the Holy Spirit who had previously been leading? Was Jesus confused by this new inner leading? How did he know not to do homage when all this splendor and power came before him and was being given over to him? Was it really so obvious to Jesus—or to any of us—that the movement in himself of awe at the power and splendor of the whole thing was the offered gift of an evil spirit and not of the Holy Spirit? The urge to power in us is very subtle. At midlife a person knows what power and splendor can do. One knows what gets projected onto the wealthy, gifted, and powerful person and how much good could be done with all this in the right hands. Do homage, project all the good in yourself on to me, the devil says. In worshiping me, you worship your own goodness. You are the Beloved, you can do no evil. You will use all this for good. It clicks now with Jesus. "You must do homage to the Lord your God, him alone must you serve." Again, he quotes Scripture. Worshiping one's own goodness is as dangerous as worshiping one's own will (stones) or worthlessness.

Now the devil leads him again. Is he disguised as the Holy Spirit? Again Jesus goes. The devil takes him now to the most subtle disguise of evil. He brings him to the *holy* place. He brings him to the holy city Jerusalem, to the highest pinnacle of the holy temple. There in the sacred place, he acknowledges the sacredness of Jesus himself. He recognizes him as the Holy One of God. He says, "If you are the Son of God, throw yourself down from here" (Lk. 4:10). The angels will take care of you. Here, confronted with this secret of his own heart, his own person, his own incredible intimacy with God—an intimacy he felt called to share with the multitude by inviting each of them to call God "Abba"—he feels the urge to test God's favor. One can risk all, even life, and like Isaac be saved by an angel. "You shall not put the Lord, your God, to the test," Jesus finally answers. Do not identify with your baseness, he warns all of us. Do not identify with your goodness, he warns. And now finally in answer to the last temptation, do not identify with the Father. Every mid-life person needs to make these distinctions in the midst of the shadow temptations. You are not your weakness, baseness, evil. You are not your goodness, power, splendor. You are not your God. Humanity can be put to the test. Even Jesus, God living humanly, can be put to the test, but there is One who transcends. No person can be so inflated by being beloved as to forget his or her own status as creature and child.

13

Reflective Exercises

1. If you are more extraverted, dialogue with your extraversion and then with your shadow introversion. If you are more introverted dialogue with your introversion and then with your shadow extraversion.

2. Dialogue with your primary function. Dialogue with the opposite of your primary function.

3. From the descriptions of the attitudes (introversion and extraversion) and each pair of functions (sensing, intuitive; thinking, feeling) in this chapter, copy the phrases that most ring true to your knowledge of yourself. Discuss them with a friend. Finally, put them together as a portrait of yourself.

   From the same description copy out the phrases that are most unlike you.

4. List all the characteristics that you most despise in other people. Put an x next to those that are most loathsome to you. Study those that awake the most negative emotions in you to see in what way these same characteristics are present in yourself. (Remember that they are very unconscious in you and so you are very unconscious of them.)

5. Who are the people with whom you are having the most difficulties relating at the present time? Pray the Lord's Prayer for each person, inserting the person's name throughout: "Father of [name] hallowed be thy name. Thy Kingdom come about in [name]. Thy will be done in [name]," and so on.

6. Pray the Lord's Prayer for yourself, using your own name. Then meditate on how God's Kingdom needs to come about in you, and on how God's will is being done in you. What daily bread do you need? What sins need forgiveness? Who have you forgiven? What are your present temptations? What evil do you want to be delivered from? What future evil do you pray to be delivered from?

7. List the conflicts of your life that have taught you something important about yourself. Dialogue with the ones that seem most significant.

8. We come to know ourselves as much in our collapse or failures or sins as in our protestations of love and loyalty. What protestations have you made that have later collapsed in you or been discarded because you now know better?

9. Have you ever identified yourself with the evil in yourself? Have you identified anyone else with their evil? Who are those who have most sinned against you? Do you still identify them with that evil?

10. Have you opened yourself to God's forgiveness and love in the midst of your own awareness of your evil. Write a dialogue with God or Jesus about this.

11. Write a litany of your weakness. For example:

> For my inability to be lighthearted,
> Lord have mercy on me.
> For my slowness to praise others,
> Lord have mercy on me.

Do this with someone you trust.
Write a litany of your strengths. For example:

> For my ability to see what needs to be done,
> I thank you Lord.
> For my sense of humor,
> I thank you Lord.

12. Draw a portrait of your shadow.

13. Find ways to make amends to people you have harmed because of past blindness or deliberate evil, and put them on your calendar as things to do.

14. How have your gifts been a source of pain and suffering to you? To others? How have your gifts been a source of joy and growth to you? To others? List and dialogue with each one.

PART III

Keeping the Inner Child Alive: The Child as Archetypal

by Anne Brennan

14
The Child Archetype: Wonder and Contemplation

The author Lewis Carroll died at age sixty-six. He wrote *Alice's Adventures in Wonderland* when he was thirty-three, the exact midpoint of his life. While mid-life cannot so literally be interpreted as the exact year that marks the middle of a life, the words he writes as comments on his book do seem to emerge from a mid-life perspective:

> The why of this book cannot and need not be put into words. Those for whom a child's mind is a sealed book and who see no divinity in a child's smile would read such words in vain; while for any one who has ever loved one true child no words are needed. For he [or she] will have known the awe that falls on one in the presence of a spirit fresh from God's hands, on whom no shadow of sin, and but the outermost fringe of the shadow of sorrows has yet fallen, he [or she] will have felt the bitter contrast between the selfishness that spoils his best deeds and the life that is but an overflowing love. *For I think a child's first attitude to the world is a simple love for all living things.* And he [or she] will have learned that the best work a man [or woman] can do is when he [or she] works for love's sake only, with no thought of fame or gain or earthly reward. No deed of ours, I suppose, on this side of the grave is really unselfish. Yet, if one can put forth all one's powers in a task where nothing of reward is hoped for but a little child's whispered thanks and the airy touch of a little child's pure lips, one seems to come somewhere near to this. (Carroll, 1962:ii)

Carroll here betrays himself as a person in mid-life who has discovered the selfishness in his "best deeds" and in his love. He seems intimately to know about the "shadow of sin" and the "shadow of sorrow" that have not yet touched the child. He seems to look to the child to teach him again "such simple love of all living things." He tells us that he threw himself completely into *Alice's Adventures in Wonderland* in an attempt at unselfishness, hoping for no reward or fame or gain but doing it for the child's sake and for "love's sake." Paradoxically, we of the next century know that this is his most famous book and that his name and fame live because of *Alice's Adventures in Wonderland*.

The Return to Wonder

Carroll seems to intuit that it is the child who can show the mid-life adult how to capture or recapture the fullness of life, "the simple love of all things." Each of us, at mid-life, has to find the way back to wonder. The alternative seems to be that we become jaded. By this time we have been around. We have seen it all, done it all, heard it all. There is little new under the sun for us. We have been touched by the evil all around us and in our own heart. We have "made it" or we're not going "to make it" now. We have experienced the shocks and disgust of our own guiltiness and the horror at the violence of which we and every other are capable. We have been sinned against and been betrayed by loved ones and love. We have been hurt many times and our defensive crusts have grown thick. We are at great risk of becoming cynical. Cynicism and bitterness are real possibilities, real temptations, when one has come face to face with the disillusionment that is at the heart of the mid-life crisis. To be in a crisis means that one can go either way. Mid-life is, after all, the end of naiveté. In *Passages,* Gail Sheehy called it the "no more bullshit" passage.

At this point, we are at the other pole from those precious early days when everything was new. Then, everything filled us with wonder. We could sit for half an hour watching ants running back and forth on a crack; we could try the patience of the one who was trying to bathe us by our delight in just splashing water. I remember seeing a two-year-old refuse to leave an empty tub as he giggled gleefully with his ear to the drain listening to the water as it gurgled down the pipe.

Once recently, a child sitting behind me in a plane shouted

ecstatically every ten or fifteen minutes, "Clouds!" "Clouds!" jolting me into awareness of my blasé attitude about the wonder outside the plane window. I recalled my own excitement about those great clouds that were below me and above me the first time I flew, in my twenties!

I've seen a little girl who had just learned to walk laugh enthusiastically every time that she fell on a hard floor; she didn't notice the pain because she felt such joy in her chubby shaky legs holding her upright for the first time. I remember teaching a group of nine-year-olds about Christoper Columbus one morning and having one of them run breathlessly into the classroom that afternoon, clutching a book from the library and pointing wildly to a page, "Look, look, here in the book is that man you told us about, Columbus!"

As I took a seven-year-old to the circus, I asked her what she had liked most about the circus when she went with her parents the year before. She giggled into her hand and wouldn't tell me until I coaxed it out of her, "It was the man in the green suit," she said, "the little man with the broom, shovel, and pail who followed the elephants." Sure enough, he was there again this year, and there was the same glee, a year later, whenever the man in the green custodial uniform with his shovel appeared to do his "exciting" job. I often wonder whether the mid-life man who had this job could ever imagine that his was, for two years running, the best act in the circus.

What may appear lowly or even repugnant to adults, can be a beloved thing of beauty and wonder to a child. Toads, frogs, insects, and old castaway junk can fill the heart of a child. In a child's eyes the ugliest person can be transformed into a beautiful prince or princess. A woman told me that her second-grade teacher, whom she adored, was tall and exquisitely lovely in her child eyes. When she met the teacher twelve years later, the woman was both short and had a flat, rather ugly face. Since the teacher was only in her early forties, she knew that she could not attribute the new vision to the ravages of aging but only to the loss of her child's eyes. Who is to say which vision was right? Perhaps the child had seen beneath the surface.

I came upon two children, a brother and a sister; the boy, a child of four, had a small doll tucked in his belt. When I asked what was going on, he told me that they were playing "having a baby" and that it was his turn! All of life and all of living is open to the child.

Indeed, children put us in touch with a spirit fresh from God's hands. In the presence of children we can be in the presence of overflowing love and new life. The old man with the child bouncing on the "horse" of his leg, or rolling on his leather hassock turned on its side into a "wheelbarrow," becomes a child behind his wrinkles and under his forgotten arthritis. In the child's eyes, he is a playmate as young and new as she is.

The Archetype of the Child

What is it in us that sparks when we become hooked by a child? What does the child touch in me that can laugh in delight, awe, and respect with her at the man with the shovel and the elephant dung? What dead part of me comes to life when I see a cloud, or a toad, or an ugly person, or an old person, with a child's eyes? It is my Child; it is the archetype of the Child in me.

I came into this world as a human child. I was like every other human child who has ever come from a womb, even while I was like no other child who had ever been born. Like every other child, I grew from a fertilized egg through my fetal stages into an infant who was thrust into the world by birth. I came not "tabula rasa," a mere blank slate, but with an incredible pre-programmed potential to babble, to mouth vowel sounds, to imitate words in a language, and to make sentences. I came with a grasping response, to grab hold of my mother when I am frightened. A healthy baby, a few hours after birth, will reach up with arms and legs when it is frightened and make a grabbing gesture. This gesture goes back in human phylogenic history to the time of our ancient ancestors. Within a few hours of birth, babies begin to single out the human voice, particularly the high-pitched human female voice, from other sounds in the environment.

> Thus, they will quieten and reduce spontaneous movement more reliably in response to the sound of female speech than to other auditory stimuli of like intensity. Similarly, the visual

apparatus appears to be programmed to respond to the "face-ness" of stimuli, so that crude representations of two eyes, a nose and a mouth will be attended more readily than visual stimuli organized in other configurations. Most effective of all in quietening a newborn infant are the combined stimuli of human face, human voice and the tactile and proprioceptive stimuli of being held. (Stevens:87)

These observations all support the Jungian view that each child is living out its own version of the Child archetype, which is genetically endowed to act appropriately in and with the world. The most powerful social assets that the child has are its innate ability to cry and to smile. It is not an accident that the most annoying sound in all the earth is of a baby crying. Few sounds so get under the skin and are so disturbing. There is something in every one of us that knows that this crying must not be allowed to go on and that care must be given to take away the child's pain.

Smiling has the same effect of eliciting responsiveness from the world, but especially from the mother. At about the fourth week, the child begins to spend time staring up into the mother's face. This has a profound emotional impact on the mother, but can be even more powerful if the infant happens to be smiling at the same time. The mutual fascination, the intuitive rapport, being expressed is the love in this primal love affair. It is an affair with the other and thus with all others, with life and all living things, and with the inanimate world. From this secure base of love, the infant can crawl out and can scramble back from forays of exploration into the world. She will look back over her shoulder often to make sure of the loved one's presence, and in that presence will grow in trust of the surroundings. These will entice the baby more and more with their numinosity as her innate curiosity widens the circle of exploration.

The intense curiosity which motivates all young creatures to explore may be understood as a primary expression of the individuation principle, a basic drive of the self to seek encounters with the environment and achieve actualization through such encounters of the Self's archetypal endowment. (Stevens:101–2)

Stands &
stands against > choice
based
on values.

Thus, as the archetypal Self is there in embryo in the child's first crawling out into the world, the child as initiator is still there in the individuation process of the mid-life adult. I dare say that it will be the Child in one who has the curiosity, adventuresomeness, and trust to pass over the final threshold of death into further life.

The Child archetype is crucial, and as one attempts to cross the border from the first to the second half of life, it is the child who will carry forward the exploration into newness. It is the child who will not allow the adult to become stuck.

A wonderful, generative old/young woman of ninety-six was asked how she managed to be so vital and enthusiastic, and questioning and growing, at her age. She answered, "Well, my dear, never get stuck. There are people who have a heart attack at forty-eight and get stuck in it." This particular woman had encountered and integrated into herself all the losses of the aging process, including the loss of her sight. She, like children and handicapped people, had learned to compensate. A child whose short legs keep her behind her dad and big brother will call out in a loud, demanding voice, "Hey, Dad, wait up." Her insistence and loud demand will more than compensate for her short legs. I recently heard a handicapped woman who was excited over the gift of a new electric wheelchair say, right out of the Child within her, "Everyone thinks of me as permanently disabled, I think of them as temporarily abled." She was close indeed to the child who, not able to walk, crawled, and not able to keep up, opened her mouth. The Child in the handicapped woman was into individuating by "crawling" out into the environment, no matter what the dangers.

Jung was convinced that the child, far from being a blank slate submitting to life's lessons, was born with innumerable predispositions for perceiving, feeling, behaving, and conceptualizing in specific ways.

> He accepted, of course, that the extent to which the predispositions were developed or expressed depended largely on environmental factors and individual life experience but he viewed *the growing child as an active preprogrammed participant in the developmental process.* For him the slate was not blank: much was already inscribed on it before the lessons began (albeit in invisible chalk). Moreover, it would suffer

only certain forms of information to be recorded on it; and most of all, it was capable of doing much of the recording itself. (Stevens:44)

Thus, the Child in us is not merely a time of life that we outgrow; it is the archetypal beginning of human life with its archetypal equipment. It is a built-in psychic system that is ours forever. The archetypal Child pattern lives long after individual circumstances have allowed expression of all its built-in predispositions.

For Jung, the human experience presupposes the Child archetype. It is the subjective aptitude.

> Ultimately, it consists of an innate psychic structure which allows man [or woman] to have experience of this kind. Thus the whole nature of man presupposes woman, both physically and spiritually. His system is tuned into woman from the start, just as it is prepared for a quite definite world where there is water, light, air, carbohydrates, etc. The form of the world into which he is born is already inborn in him [or her] as virtual images, as psychic aptitudes. (Jung, *Two Essays in Analytical Psychology*:300)

If the form of the world into which each of us is born is already inborn in each child, it is no wonder that the child loves everything.

Archetypes are like riverbeds that dry up when the waters desert them but that revive whenever water can find and flow through again. Of all the archetypes then, the Child archetype will carry the waters whenever the world encountered touches the world inborn, whether this be for a first time or a long-forgotten world reencountered. These a priori categories are by nature collective; they lack solid content and are thus unconscious:

> They only acquire solidity, influence, and eventual consciousness in the encounter with empirical facts, which touch the unconscious aptitude and quicken it to life. (Jung, *Two Essays in Analytical Psychology*:190)

It is thus that new things in the world make us remember what we seem mysteriously to have known before, or make us realize that we knew more than we thought we knew. It is thus that sensory experiences remind us of intellectual notions that were already present before we thought them. The Child is the Wise Old Man or the Wise Old Woman in potential; the Child is the Self in potential and the Self can always rely on the Child to know what is hidden from the so-called wise and learned: "A little child shall lead them" (Is. 9:6). The child in us is first and earliest and all-absorbed in the collective unconscious; thus it is the Child who can know the source of every differentiated aspect of life as it emerges in experiences and connect it to its roots in the collective unconscious.

The Art of Contemplation

In mid-life then—when differentiation has reached a zenith; when all the world has been seen, heard, known, and experienced, and seems no longer the place to "crawl into" for wonder—it is the Child who will lead us back to the unconscious roots of the as-yet-unknown Self and to the hidden wonders and mystery within us, as well as to the hidden mysteries in the unknown world without.

> The Child motif represents not only something that existed in the distant past but also something that exists now; that is to say, *it is not just a vestige but a system functioning in the present* whose purpose is to compensate or correct in a meaningful manner the inevitable onesidedness and extravagances of the conscious mind. (Jung, *The Archetypes and the Collective Unconscious*:163)

In the *Wonderful Crisis of Middle Age* Eda LaShan says that living the second half of life well is like reading the book again, but this time a lot more slowly and with a lot more depth. The poet Gerard Manley Hopkins pointed to the "dearest freshness deep down things." In *Seasons that Laugh and Weep*, Walter Burghardt says that the key to living the second half of life well is living contemplatively. He defines contemplation as taking a long loving look at what is. He stresses that each word in the definition is crucial: "long," "loving," "look," and "what is."

The child lives contemplatively and the Child archetype is the *system within* that can teach us how to do so again. In *Adulthood*,

Erik Erikson reminds us that an ancient attitude toward the child was that if it survived at all, it must be fashioned in the adult mode. Our century of child study has changed all this:

> Only the century of the child has made us study childhood and indeed youth, not only as causal precursors of adulthood as it was and is, but also as a potential promise for what adulthood may yet become. (22)

We recall the four-week-old infant contemplating her mother's face. These long, loving looks into that adoring face are drinking in far more than "facial configuration." The *love* that pours out of the mother back into the contemplating child is mystery: mother and child as pure gift to each other from life itself and from the Source of life and love. These first acts of contemplation of the child are indeed profound ones and formative for all of life and perhaps beyond this life. In *Adulthood,* Erikson quotes a poem from Ingmar Bergman's motion picture *Wild Strawberries* and comments on it in terms of the last stage of Erikson's life-cycle theory, integrity versus despair.

> Where is the friend I seek everywhere
> Dawn is the time of loneliness and care
> When twilight comes, I am still yearning
> I see His trace of glory and power
> In an ear of grain and the fragrance of a flower
> In every sign and breath of air
> His love is there.

> The poem, the setting, the tone seem to confirm the sense in which every human being's Integrity may be said to be religious (whether explicitly or not), namely, in an inner search for, and wish to communicate with that mysterious, that Ultimate Other, for there can be no "I" without an "Other." That in fact, is the first revelation of the life cycle when the maternal person's eyes shiningly recognize us even as we begin to recognize her. And it is the hope of old age, according to St. Paul's promise. (11–12)

"What eye has not seen, and ear has not heard, and what has not entered the human heart, what God has prepared for those who love him" (1 Cor. 2:9).

If in mid-life the Child can bring us again to contemplate, to take long loving looks at what is, we will see so much more deeply; we will see so much more because we can bring to each experience of contemplation the awareness of all the years since childhood. We can know so much more, have so much more insight into what we are contemplating than we could have had at an earlier life stage. However, for this to happen we do have to let go of our ego concerns and surrender to the Child within.

I had such a contemplative experience in a large department store in New York City one day when I was shopping for a dress. I was quite hassled and anxious to find something that day. So I was tearing impatiently through the racks, getting more and more discouraged. A high-pitched, rather loud voice broke through my preoccupation. I heard a girl of about thirteen say to the saleswoman,

> Could you help me? I have to get a dress for graduation and it has to be a "knock out." You see, there's this girl in my class and when she comes into the room every eye looks at her. I want a dress that will make every eye look at me when I walk down the aisle!

I surrendered to the Child within and let go of my conscious ego concern and just watched, listened, and enjoyed. This was a "slice of life" too precious to ignore. The girl went on, "This girl is *so* beautiful and *so* smart and she is *even* nice, and if I could get the right dress people would see me too." The saleswoman asked her size. "I don't know. I haven't worn a dress since I was in the sixth grade," she said. I followed the two as she gasped at prices and rejected dress after dress until she took three into the dressing room.

I knew I had had a deep contemplative experience when I realized that I was smiling and relaxed as I went on in a whole new attitude with my own search. I know that fifteen years earlier and much closer to my own adolescence I might have thought, "such vanity," as I ignored the whole scene and went about my business. Now, however, I have so much more living to bring to such experiences and when my Child gets me into them, the adult can find so much mystery and beauty there from my mid-life perspective. I know now from experience what it is to have lived through those painful teen years of trying to fit in, of trying to be as worthy as the next. I can bring stories of all the young adults I have known to the appreciation of such a moment in a girl's life.

I really consider such moments to be deep prayers of contemplation. They are prayer because in them I am put in touch with my deepest gratitude for life and for "what is." So, I am in communion with the Giver of life and what is. Gratitude is an essential way of praying. Here the Child can lead us, for the Child is always open to surprise, never ceasing to be amazed at one thing or another. The Child sees everything as a gift; that is why gratefulness makes us feel younger. At one time each of us had the kind of recollection a Child has. We were whole and full of wonderment.

> We need only to watch little children in their playpen to realize how perfectly they combine concentration with wonderment. Often they are so concentrated on sucking an ear of a toy rabbit or simply on wiggling their toes that you might have a hard time trying to divert their attention. . . . How often adults destroy that gift with the best intention. Children have a need to stand and look. . . . But then, you see everywhere adults pulling children out of their wonderment and concentration. "Let's go. We have no time"—and a long arm pulls the poor child along. No wonder that so many marvelous children turn into dull adults. No wonder their wholeness is scattered and their sense of mystery lost. (Steindl-Rast:45–46)

It is never too late to recapture that prayerfulness that is like breathing to a child. We can finally allow our own inner Child to have its way. We need to allow ourselves to recognize the moments in a typical day when we are already recollected. We need to be aware of those things that we enter into already with concentration, wonderment, and so, gratefulness. Is it the morning coffee or an evening walk? Is it a smiling person we meet everyday? Is it a part of our work? Walking the dog? Stopping by a schoolyard or a playground? Taking a swim? Throwing snowballs? Gardening? Attending a class? Painting? Listening to music or playing an instrument?

When we become aware of how we feel when the Child

within us is playing and praying at any of these moments we will be able to expand the moments until we "pray always," until we begin to feel more really alive, until we are living contemplatively again. Our formal prayer life will be deeply affected by all this contemplative living. Our prayers will surely swell with gratitude as we allow our child to be free to pray in us in these special times of focusing on the Giver of Gifts.

15

A Little Child Shall Lead Us

This freeing of the Child needs to be distinguished, however, from a Pollyanna approach to life and from childishness. Jesus told us "unless you turn and become like a little child, you will not enter the kingdom of heaven" (Mt. 18:2). He did not say to become a child but to become *like* a child. The Adult is in charge even when it allows itself to be led for a time by the Child. The Adult knows enough to be "wise as serpents and simple as doves." The Adult will discriminate the weeds from the wheat, will recognize danger and evil. After all, the mid-life adult has had many encounters with evil and is having many encounters with the evil potential of the Shadow. However, there is still a way of seeing even an evil situation as an opportunity to work for transformation and so a reason for wonderment and gratitude.

There is a danger that the mid-life adult might allow the imperfection in everything, the sin in the world, to block her vision of the beauty that is. Many mid-life people focus on the imperfection and allow that to be so big that they identify the whole with it and miss the wonder that *is* there. "How can I look at the beauty of that green pasture without being reminded of and made sad by the fact of world hunger?" such a person might say, and God would cry that besides the horrible fact of world hunger, now there is the fact that another green meadow has been blocked out and written off. We need to bless the Lord for what is, for the evolution and goodness that has been achieved, and the blessing will have its own power to further that evolution and to energize us to work for it.

171

When the metaphors of seriousness, work, morality, responsibility are used to interpret life as a whole it becomes difficult to play, dream, loaf, love, wonder and accept grace.

When the world is seen as divine play and life a game, it becomes difficult to confront the tragic limitations and wage war against the blatant evils of hunger, injustice and carnage. (Keen:110)

The Child then puts us in touch with the outer world, but in a different way, precisely because we are mid-life adults and no longer children. We can no longer see and name objects for the first time. We can't be Adam and Eve in paradise in a primordial naming of the animals, nor can we be the baby who cries excitedly in first recognition, "Dog! Dog!" or "Elephant! Elephant!" But with our Child we can finally have eyes that really see and ears that really hear; if we have lived life for thirty or fifty years with any real engagement, we can now be struck by the mystery, the meaning, the "more" in our experiences.

Getting up early so that I can spend an hour really enjoying my morning coffee in pure gratitude, or spending an evening having a truly grateful sharing of stories with good friends, can be a meaningful and so mysteriously holy experience. One needs to ask: What is it that I can do that makes me feel most alive, to discover a place where Child and Adult come together to move me into more wholeness?

Ask twenty different people to name something that they have always loved, something that has always meant a great deal to them, and their responses will surprise you and will also seem perfectly natural coming from each personality. They will name things like fabric, dinner out, railroads, ocean, snow, resting on the earth, sports, dogs, skiing, sand, cooking, tinkering with a car, knitting, drumming, fishing, camping, biking, arboretums, museums, sailing, antique shops, horseback riding, driving, mountains, waterfalls, making bread, zoos. As their eyes light up and their faces become animated when they are expanding on "their love," Spirit is alive and meaning is being manifest. When we experience the deepest meaning we often cannot put that meaning into words, or into words that are equally meaningful to anyone else. The experiences that touch and carry one spirit into Spirit may not be the ones that carry another spirit into Spirit. Yet at such moments we all are so obviously fully human and fully alive that we can almost touch and see the one Spirit that unites this plurality of spirits; we can know that life does have meaning.

> When our heart rests in the Source of all meaning, it can encompass all meaning. Meaning in this sense, is not something that can be put into words. Meaning is not something that can be looked up in a book like a definition. Meaning is not something that can be grasped, held, stored away. Meaning is not something. . . . Maybe we should stop the sentence there. Meaning is no thing. It is more like the light in which we see all things. Another psalm calls out to God in the thirst of the heart: "With you is the fountain of life, and in your light we see light" (Psalm 36:9). In thirsting for the fullness of life our heart thirsts for the light that lets us see life's meaning. When we find meaning, we know it because our heart finds rest. (Steindl-Rast:34–35)

The Child and Pain

While gratitude and meaning and concentration and wonderment are as near as the morning coffee and while we need to be open like a child to as many moments of transcendence as possible even *in the midst* of the greatest sorrow, pain, and evil, there is another sense in which gratefulness and meaning are ultimate, not proximate, experiences. Here, too, the Child can lead us. Here, too, we need to become like a little child. Earlier we noted that a child has two built-in weapons of survival and growth, the smile and the cry. In focusing so far primarily on one style of "living contemplatively" that the Child archetype can bring to life in us, we have been looking at the smile. The child beholds, smiles at, and loves everything in gratitude. Yet, the cry is a seductive, powerful, effective, and very real built-in potential in every child. The child cries when it faces hunger, discomfort, pain, or fear, and it cries even louder when it feels frustration, anger, or hostility. The cry of the child is a powerful way to bring relief. When the mother begins to recognize the language of the different tones and strengths and lengths of those cries, effective communication has been established.

The cries of the child speak to others around it, too. It takes an incredible amount of exhaustion and frustration to silence the unanswered cry of a child. It is a terrible moment in the history of the universe and the human race when a human baby has been so neglected as to cease forever its cries for help. It signals the failure of all of us and it signals the child's death or almost irreversible incapacitation. However, even very neglected, damaged, and brutalized children voice a hope of survival and some hint of basic trust when they still can find an outlet in sobbing quietly in hidden corners.

As adults we more and more do our crying within ourselves or take our crying to hidden corners. It is a fortunate adult who has some other person to receive his or her crying. It is the Child in us who at mid-life, in the heart of our dark night of the soul, will help us to rediscover the voice for our hidden cries.

The Child can free us to sob and groan and moan and growl and yell and scream about the pain and injustice and evil in our life and in the life of the world. Some of our cries will need to find human ears. We will need to find effective adult ways to protest evil and injustice and put our time and selves on the line personally and politically to change things. We may need to grieve with a dear friend or with a counselor or spiritual director over the losses and sorrow of our life because unexpressed grief is one of the major causes of depression in adult life (Fairchild:113–15). Yet, even if we make use of all of these outlets, the Child in us will still need to "cry out to heaven!"

Mid-Life and the Prayer of Anguish

Our prayer and contemplative living will need to allow our Child to own and express feelings of anger, frustration, hostility, aggression, sexuality, despair, and alienation that have not yet found rest in meaning and gratitude. The Psalms are filled with such cries and screams and curses and questioning of life and of God.

> O Lord, my God, by day I cry out;
>   at night I clamor in your presence.
>
> You have plunged me into the bottom of the pit,
>   into the dark abyss.

You have taken my friends away from me;
   you have made me an abomination to them;
   I am imprisoned, and cannot escape.

Do they declare your kindness in the grave,
   Your faithfulness among those who have perished?
Are your wonders made known in the darkness,
   or your justice in the land of oblivion?

Why, O Lord, do you reject me;
   why hide from me your face?
                (Ps. 88:2, 7, 9, 12, 13, 15)

It is not so hard to put this into a modern idiom and see that
it sounds like a mid-life scream:

     My God! I'm sick to death of trouble;
     I've hit rock bottom.
     No one gives a damn about me;
     I'm repulsive in their eyes
     For God's sake, will you wait until I'm dead to show
        me a drop of pity or good luck?
     Do you have a thing for corpses?
     Why me?
     Why do you reject me?
     Do you exist at all?

We can also see Psalm 94 as a mid-life scream against the evil
in the world.

     God of vengeance, Lord, . . .
     your people, O Lord, they trample down. . . .
     Widow and stranger, they slay;
       the fatherless they murder. (vv. 1, 5–6)

The cry of this Psalm is something like:

     God damn them! the murderers of widows, babies, and
     homeless victims of greed.

We need to cry out and we need to cry out in prayer. Much
that calls itself prayer is sheer dishonesty. Trust in a relationship
allows for honest pouring out of feelings. Trust in God means

that we can trust that real feelings will be received. Every human feeling and attitude is appropriate in the context of prayer. Nowhere else can we so strip ourselves and know that we are known and received as we are. The God who knows these human depths is the God who intimately knows all the archetypes or the built-in patterns that each of us is. That God, like all of creation, groans with us until these patterns are brought to birth.

> We know that all creation is groaning in labor pains even until now; and not only that, but we ourselves, who have the first-fruits of the Spirit, we also groan within ourselves as we wait for adoption, the redemption of our bodies. . . . In the same way, the Spirit too comes to the aid of our weakness; for we do not know how to pray as we ought, but the Spirit itself intercedes with inexpressible groanings. (Rom. 8:22–23)

There is much unconscious praying that goes on in mid-life. People are always groaning and sighing, asking, Why bother? What's it all for? What's the use? Who cares about me? They are searching for answers, screaming for meaning. Many such people would never imagine that their cries for answers or help or release unconsciously imply an unknown ear that hears, an unknown Other who hears. They would never imagine that these spontaneous cries of the heart are prayers to an Other who cares. Yet, when people realize that such expression has been a kind of unconscious prayer, it seems strangely right. The child, who after all does everything unconsciously, has no problem with this; and so the Child archetype in the mid-life person has been leading and now the adult has caught up.

Carl Jung had carved in stone over his front door, "Called or not called, God shall be there." Perhaps this could also mean, "Consciously or unconsciously, God shall be there." God is no "big daddy" or "good mommy" in a mid-life spirituality. He or She can no more take away all the pain and discomfort and loss than a human parent can always "kiss and make better" a wound, a cancer, or a death. What does "make better," however, is the kiss, the presence, the receptivity, and the crying out in trust.

Rediscovering One's Heart

Living contemplatively means praying always. It also means sometimes saying prayers, that is, taking time out or building time in. Of course, this need not mean set prayer formulas or verbalizing or vocalizing at all. Yet, there is something archetypal about those prayer formulas that have survived the test of time. The Psalms, Berakah, the Lord's Prayer, the Hail Mary, the Magnificat, the Jesus Prayer, the Prayer of St. Francis, the Prayer of Serenity: they last because they touch deep well-springs in the human psyche. The corollary, then, is also true: one can meditate on such words to recapture some once-known and ancient truth. If something was once true for so many human hearts, it can be true for mine. The problem may not be in finding the truth or the belief, but in finding my heart again, finding my Child.

In Dickens's *Christmas Carol*, Scrooge finds his heart, his faith, and his truth by finding his Child. The Ghost of Christmas Past takes him back to the child he was in the orphanage. The adult Scrooge thus sees himself objectively as a child and passes the painful judgment on him, that he "made do." The degree of pity that rose up for his own childhood becomes evident only when, after following the Ghost of Christmas Present, he fears that the child Tiny Tim will die. Scrooge gives the Child free reign when he wakes from his long nightmare of a life spent with a dead Child in him. *A Christmas Carol* is a resurrection story as well as a Christmas story. It is so fitting that the birth of the Christ child should be celebrated year after year by this myth of the rebirth of the Child in an aging man! This, of course, is the point of Christmas celebrations.

> For a child is born to us, a son is given us; upon his shoulder dominion rests. They name him Wonder-Counselor, God-Hero, Father-Forever, Prince of Peace. (Is. 9:5)

As part of our mid-life spirituality we need to look with the eyes of our Child on such archetypal stories. The Bible is a particularly rich archetypal mine for our prayerful con-templation. We need to identify with the flesh-and-blood human beings in these stories, with their depth and their primal human experiences of birth, love, conflict, sexual union, marriage, passages, sickness, ecstasy, agony, singing, dancing, success, homecoming, loss, death, and resurrection. As we identify, we will be able to find our hearts and feel the faith, hope, and love of these people stir once more in us. These stories are in the Bible because the peak experiences, the religious experiences, and the prayer experiences of the people who walk through those pages are among the most noble and at the same time most common in our human history.

There may be some parts of Scripture that we love and have always loved, and other parts that we hate and have always hated. Both of these will tell us things about ourselves that we are unconscious of, if we take the time to look and do not let our long-armed Adult drag us away prematurely. Perhaps we will have to carry a scene, a passage, a person, or a word with us, sucking and chewing it until it yields up some unconscious content and we come to new faith, hope, and love for our life, and so to the God of our life.

I have always loved the Scripture line, "the love of God is poured out into our hearts through the Holy Spirit that has been given to us" (Rom. 5:5). I am an introverted feeling type, and the implication that God's love is poured into the depths of me, seemed to perfectly express my God experience. In my early twenties, I learned that Aquinas defined charity as an outpouring of this same love of God. So I attempted to go about putting love where there was no love indiscriminately. I tried to be God, and love everyone equally.

Concurrently with this, I always hated the Scripture story of the workers in the vineyard. In this story, Jesus tells of a vine grower who pays those who came late to work in the vineyard the same wage as those who worked all day. I can remember the place in a church where I was sitting when I first heard this story. I was about eight or nine years of age when I first got angry at the injustice in this story. I was right on target for a preadolescent stage of moral development, and things would have been fine had I outgrown my hatred of the story. But in my thirties, I think I still had a secret sorrow at being in the vineyard so early and still unconsciously felt superior to those who came late. Only since then have these two passages of Scripture come together for me. I have seen that, indeed, I have been unconditionally loved early and long, and have *known* that love. Yet I had not loved others unconditionally, but with much superiority. I put love where there was none in a pseudomaternal way, and expected love back as payment.

The most incredible part is that, when I began to let go of wanting so desperately to please and be loved by others, I was showered with more real love than ever before. My childishness had surrendered to my Child, who helped me to contact the unconscious Shadow that was operative here, and has showed me the "gold" in that Shadow. The simplicity of the Child sees through our self-deceptions, and the humility of our Child brings us to laugh at ourselves.

I have read stories to children and have watched the look on their faces. I have seen that same look when I read a Scripture story to a group of adults. The extravagant, poetic more-than-rational language of Scripture captures the Child in people. Somehow the Child archetype in us knows about truths deeper than the rational ones. At some level below consciousness, the contradictions at work in a person's life are revealed in the childlike simplicity and humility present in so much of Scripture, and this childlikeness hooks the Child in adult listeners.

16

Peter Becomes
"Like a Little Child"

The story of Peter in the Gospels and in Acts is one that can easily hook the Child in us, since Peter is a man in whom the Child is supremely active. As we meet Peter early in the Scripture account of him, he is told by Jesus, who was no fisherman, to take his almost clean nets and go back out again after having fished unsuccessfully all night. In this moment we can almost taste, touch, and see the struggle of the adult Peter with his Child: the Child wins out. Peter goes, probably somewhat grudgingly, and has a catch so big that he has to call another boat to help him. That does it for him—he has tarried long enough around this Jesus: "Depart from me, Lord," he says, "for I am a sinful man" (Lk. 5:8b). Peter identifies himself as Jesus had in his baptism with sinners. Again, this is an adult act that takes a child's simplicity and humility. Jesus takes this unlikely moment, as heaven had done for him, to show how pleased he was with Peter. He asks Peter to follow him, and become a fisher of men and women. Peter receives a call to mission, to his life myth which shares in Jesus' life myth. Peter lives out his intimacy with Jesus in his own rocky way. He tries to walk on water but has doubts and sinks. He was the one with the courage to speak to what seemed like a ghost walking toward them on the water: "Lord, if it is you, command me to come to you on the water" (Mt. 14:28). He takes the first step in childlike faith, but then the adult doubts. Peter later becomes acquainted with his unconscious and so with his Shadow in many ways.

180

Three Denials, Three Affirmations

Peter hears Jesus speak of going up to Jerusalem to suffer and tries to stop him. Jesus uses some of his harshest words ever to his friend. He says, "Get behind me Satan!" You are not voicing God's words, Peter, you are asking me to turn away from myself, from who I am and what I have been about. If I back down because my life is threatened then I surrender my new consciousness, my integration, my revelation, and capitulate to the status quo. That is not the will of the One who sent me.

Jesus is strongly putting Peter in touch with his Shadow of fear and cowardice at this very moment when Peter presumes such courage as to give Jesus this strong advice. Jesus may just as well have said, You are not talking about *my* not going up to Jerusalem, you are talking of *your* not going up to Jerusalem.

When the time came, Peter was there in Jerusalem for the last meal in the upper room but he was still not in touch with his fear and cowardice. Jesus, very in touch with the Child in himself, stoops to wash the disciples' feet. Jesus' gesture is one of supreme tenderness and respect for each of these common men and women who have *walked* with him and will spend the rest of their lives walking all over the world for him. The menial nature of the thing Jesus wants to do for each of them is a small sign of all the physical and psychological stripping he will soon undergo. They will participate in this stripping each in his and her own way.

Again, Peter tries to stop Jesus: "You will never wash my feet" (Jn. 13:8). Jesus has to persuade him by showing how integral this is to their mutual love and to their love of others. Jesus again puts Peter in touch with the Child and assures him that as Jesus has served, he too will serve.

Toward the end of the meal, in response to Jesus' saying, "Where I am going, you cannot follow me now," Peter retorts: "Master, why can't I follow you now? I will lay down my life for you." (Jn. 13:36-37) He has such great faith in his will power, in his conscious ego development. It has gotten him this far. He has even been through the ritual bath that Jesus asked of him and has eaten this bread, his body, and drunk this wine, his blood. How could he, like Judas, go away if Jesus were in danger? Here is childishness, but not the Child, in Peter.

In the garden, Peter is asleep. He is unconscious. Three times Jesus tries to wake him. When he finally awakes, in John's account, he is violent. He cuts off the ear of Malchus the Centurion (Jn. 18:10–11). Jesus restores it and warns Peter about this violence, telling him again about the necessity of his suffering (Brown, 1983:133).

Around a charcoal fire, Peter finally relinquishes his ego as defender. Three times Jesus tried to wake him. Three times he denied that he even knew Jesus. He lived out his Shadow, a weak, cowardly, unloving traitor. Yet, perhaps an almost immediate merciful synchronicity saved him from hanging himself as Judas did. He hears the cock crow and remembers Jesus' warning: "The cock will not crow before you deny me three times" (Jn. 13:38).

It is the Child in Peter who takes this "mere coincidence" seriously. He bursts into tears and somehow the tears of this Child drown the temptation to stay back in the Shadow. He does not identify himself with his baseness.

All the Gospels recount how a chastened Peter remained with the others. He is there with the disciples after the death and he is there in the resurrection narrative. He is on the lake fishing with the others when Jesus suddenly appears at another *charcoal* fire on the shore. Jesus is cooking fish for them now. The Child Peter jumps into the sea and swims to Jesus. This time he knows that he cannot walk across the water to Jesus (Brown, 1976:81). Peter grabbed his coat to cover his nakedness before he jumped into the water. We may imagine he was also covering his embarrassment about his betrayal with this little piece of persona. There on the beach Jesus leads Peter three times to undo his denials (Fuller: 152). Jesus asks him:

> "Simon, Son of John, do you love me more than these?"
> "Yes, Lord, you know that I love you."
> "Feed my lambs."
> "Simon, Son of John, do you love me?"
> "Yes, Lord, you know that I love you."
> "Tend my sheep."
> "Simon, son of John, do you love me?"

> "Lord, you know everything; you know that I love you."
> "Feed my sheep." (Jn. 21:15-17; see also Fuller: 149-52)

Peter is not God. Jesus reminds him by making him face himself three times with probing ultimate questions. He has failed miserably to love. Yet he now has the credentials to feed others as Jesus feeds them. Now he not only knows his fishing mission but his pastoral concern (Brown, 1983:152). He is in touch with his Shadow, and the Child in Peter has allowed him to make friends with his Shadow. He has taken it on himself and been merciful to his own weakness, therefore he can now, as Jesus does, see the sinner, and never identify the sinner with his or her sin. He can see the sin in himself and not identify himself with it. He can know that though he was and is a sinner, he is loved and loves. In the Acts of the Apostles we learn of Peter's miracles: sick people were carried out into the streets and placed on beds and mats, so that at least Peter's shadow might fall on them as he passed by (Acts 5:16)!

Peter and Mid-Life Spirituality

Peter's spirituality is like the spirituality of Jesus, filled with hints of a mid-life spirituality of the Shadow and of the Child. In the Acts of the Apostles we see Peter transformed, open to living contemplatively, open to the revelation that came to him both in historical outer events and in his inner psychic events. We see how the Child in Peter helped him to be recollected, reflective, attentive to inner and outer events, and faithful to his individuation and his mission, which were one.

In Caesarea there was a Roman centurion named Cornelius, who was a religious man. Cornelius had a vision in which he was told to send for Simon Peter. He sent two men whom he trusted.

> The next day, while they were on their way and nearing the city, Peter went up to the roof terrace to pray at about noontime. He was hungry and wished to eat, and while they were making preparations he fell into a trance. He saw heaven opened and something resembling a large sheet coming down, lowered to the ground by its four corners. In it were all the earth's four-legged animals and reptiles and the birds of the

sky. A voice said to him, "Get up, Peter. Slaughter and eat."
But Peter said, "Certainly not, sir. For never have I eaten
anything profane and unclean." The voice spoke to him
again, a second time, "What God has made clean, you are not
to call profane." This happened three times, and then the
object was taken up into the sky.

While Peter was in doubt about the meaning of the vision
he had seen, the men sent by Cornelius asked for Simon's
house and arrived at the entrance. They called out inquiring
whether Simon, who is called Peter, was staying there. (Acts
10:9-18)

Peter, directed by the Spirit, went with them to Cornelius in
Caesarea and there preached to him and baptized all his relatives, every one of them Gentiles. Throughout Judea, the word
spread and Peter was criticized for entering the house of Gentiles, eating with them, and baptizing them. Only on hearing
Peter's story of his vision did the objections begin to turn to
acceptance. Thus, the first giant step of Christianity into the
Western world came from Peter's being open to a vision. It is
the Child in us who allows us to attend to such irrational,
fantastic experiences.

It is our Child who knows the reality of the world of dreams,
imagination, and visions. Much of the life of the child is spent in
unconsciousness, since consciousness grows out of the unconscious. Symbols are the language of the unconscious; dreams
are built of symbols, the stuff of the unconscious world. Every
night, each of us returns to this unconscious world. Dream
researchers claim that we all dream at least five times a night.

In a phenomenological sense, a dream is an experience of life
that is recognized in retrospect, to have taken place in the
mind while asleep, although at the time it was experienced, it
carried the same sense of verisimilitude that we associate with
waking experiences; that is, it seemed to happen in a "real"
world that was only in retrospect acknowledged to be a
"dream" world. The phenomenology of dreams involves
events that are not experienced in the waking world: sudden
shifts of time and place, changes in age, the presence of
persons known to be deceased, or fantastic persons and animals that never existed. Perhaps, the most radical shift experienced in a dream is the shift of the ego-identity itself from

one character to another, or perhaps to no character at all, the dream ego seeming to observe events as if from an omniscient, floating position. (Hall, 1983:22)

In dreams then, we see ourselves playing many different roles, since the people and other characters almost always represent parts of our own personality. While characters sometimes play themselves and thus enact our relationship to the outside world, more often, in the Jungian view, they are intrapsychic realities. They are compensating to our conscious ego. That is, they most often show us what we need to know about ourselves to enlarge our present ego-consciousness. "Jung was struck by the superior intelligence of the dream which suggested a meaningful, new attitude toward life" (Von Franz, 1972:9).

Though not technically a dream but using the God-given kind of symbols from the unconscious, Peter's vision may be an example of compensation. The unclean animals and birds were rejected parts of Peter, his taboos. They included not only his attempts to practice dietary laws but also his desire to shun contact with Gentiles, in fidelity to his ego ideal as a good Jew. God wants to expand Peter's consciousness. There is something almost humorous in Peter's need to see and hear three times, "Take and eat." Three times he had denied and three times he had protested his love for Jesus. Significantly, three is a crucial number in many myths, fairy tales, religious symbols, and dreams. Three moves to four, or to wholeness, when Peter goes with the messengers. His consciousness has expanded, and with it the consciousness of the infant Christian community.

17

Dreams and Transformation

There are two ways in which a dream may be seen as compensatory. First, it directs one to a more comprehensive attitude or to more comprehensive actions, as did Peter's vision. Second, if one is deviating from one's own story, rejecting or failing to live out one's own story (that is, deviating from the right and true path of one's own individuation), a dream may warn of this. For example, as a feeling type in early mid-life, I was resisting the development of my thinking function and the assertiveness that I needed for real love of myself and others because I saw the highly thinking person (and so, my own thinking function) as cold and uncaring. I had a warning dream. In the dream there was a great conflict. I was most uncomfortable. (Feeling-type people dislike conflict.) The conflict was over procedures to be followed in launching a spacecraft. Finally, a person whom I know and admire and who in reality is an aerospace engineer and an extraverted thinker, slammed his hand on the table and shouted, "I don't care how they feel about it, whether they like it or not. I have one desire, to get that spaceship up safely and get it down safely!" I woke up. Very often, waking up in the middle of a dream, or at the very end, is a message from the unconscious: Wake up to this! This dream carried a powerful emotional impact and message: I was to see my thinking function as a way of loving, as real, if not more real, than my feeling function. The dream catapulted me out of my blocked process of individuation.

Although paying attention to dreams has seemed a weird waste of energy to many modern people, more and more serious study of dreams is going on. We know that deprivation of dream sleep can over a short time lead to serious psychosis.

186

More and more people have begun to look at their dreams as a source of great insight.

> Transformation takes place at that moment when, in dreams or fantasies themes appear whose source in consciousness cannot be shown. To the patient, it is nothing less than a revelation when from the hidden depths of the psyche, something arises to confront him [or her]—something strange that is not the "I" and is therefore beyond the reach of personal caprice. He has gained access to the source of psychic life and this marks the beginning of the cure. (Jung, *Modern Man in Search of a Soul:*242)

This turning to the inner world by paying attention to dreams is natural to the Child in us.

The Inner World

In our culture, where we automatically assume that only the outer world has real importance, it is hard for an adult to believe that our life patterns, almost everything we do in the outer world, every reaction to what's going on, and every relationship we form or fail to form, are the results of inner qualities and dynamics. It is to these inner patterns that dreams usually point. For so many of us the very real value of the external world is so all-consuming that only when we get into trouble with the inner world do we begin to pay attention to the fact that we have an inner world of meaning or lack of meaning, values or conflicting values, too many goals or no goals. We notice our inner world when it stops us in our tracks in some way, when we are caught by obsessions, moods, depressions, anxieties, insomnia, phobias, loneliness, periods of darkness, inexplicable physical symptoms, or clinically diagnosed emotional and mental suffering. Most of us work so hard developing our adaptation and correspondence with the visible world that our power of corresponding with the invisible world is left in a primitive condition.

> The risk of inner experience, the adventure of the spirit, is in any case alien to most human beings. (Jung, *Memories, Dreams, Reflections:*142)

In his book *Inner Works*, Robert Johnson puts it this way:

> It is fruitless to waste your time trying to understand an external situation unless you also identify the psychological patterns within that affect it. And it is toward those patterns that your dreams usually point. Still people often get confused over this issue, because the unconscious has a habit of "borrowing" images from the external situations and using those images to symbolize something that is going on inside the dreamer. Your dreams may borrow the image of your next door neighbor, your spouse, or your parent and use that image to refer to something inside you. (1986:68)

Even when one's dreams *are* making a comment on the external world, it is safe to assume that there is an inner dynamic involved. Because of our bias in favor of the external world it is often extremely tempting to see a dream image literally, and thus to miss its real point altogether. We want to use the dream to prove how right we are, for example, about the "bossy" neighbor who appears as "Hitler" in our dream, or when there is a house in a dream to see the dream as confirming our opinion that we must buy the house we looked at yesterday.

Every dream, however, paints a picture of the dreamer, not of the external world. Every dream is a mirror in which we may see our feelings, values, beliefs, and patterns of behavior.

> Whatever characteristics the dream figures have, whatever behaviors they engage in is also true of the dreamer in some way. By this I don't mean that the trait or behavior shown in the dream is "literally" true of the dreamer exactly as it is protrayed in the dream. Dreams often speak in extremes. They try to compensate for our lack of awareness of a quality by picturing it in extreme dramatic imagery. (Johnson, 1986:70)

Johnson goes on to point out that a thief in a dream does not literally mean that the dreamer is a thief. It may mean that one has been dishonest with oneself. It could signify some repressed good quality that needs to "steal" into or "break into" our lives.

What part of you will be hidden behind this symbol, the thief? Perhaps, a lively trickster, with all sorts of surprising talents; perhaps a juvenile delinquent in you who has never been allowed to grow up and put his heroic urge into something useful and mature. Perhaps it is Dionysius, who has to hide out in the unconscious because you have no natural place for his ecstatic and lyrical spirit in the midst of your purposive life. (Johnson, 1986:71)

Inner Work and Mid-life

We cannot go to a book for a ready-made dream interpretation. We must look at each symbol in the dream and brainstorm to determine every association we personally may have with each particular image in order to see which one "clicks." Then, we need to connect images to our inner qualities. Johnson suggests that we ask what traits we have in common with the image. Where do we find those same traits or qualities in ourselves? How are these characteristics mine? How is this behavior true of me too? What part of me is this? In regard to places in our dreams, we might ask, Who does this place belong to? Whose "turf" is it? Whose influence are we under?

An interpretation will come finally from the answer to these questions: What is the most important message? What is the dream advising me to do? What is the overall meaning of the dream for my life?

In many ways, working with dreams is similar to working with our projections. There we ask, What is an emotional overreaction to this person telling me about my Shadow? What in me, what trait in me, am I reacting to in the other with such overkill? So much of our own pain and so many of our external conflicts come from these unconscious, unlived, unintegrated parts of ourselves that *day* and *night* "bang us over the head" to get our attention. Our whole Self, if we but knew it, calls us to growth in consciousness.

Even at mid-life, so little of the vast energy field that each of us is has been assimilated into our conscious personality. There is so much potential that our Child is heir to and carrier of and that we have yet to bring to consciousness and incarnate in our life on this earth. Each of us adds to the consciousness of the human race and makes our consciousness incarnate in what we are and do in and with our lives. Each of us recapitulates the whole evolution of the race. From birth each of us relives the growth of primal unconsciousness over millennia to the consciousness of our own generation. Somehow, then, each one's personal consciousness makes an enormous difference in this labor of God and the universe. It is unconsciousness that keeps half of our world in hunger. It is unconsciousness that feeds greed and mindless squandering of the earth's resources. It is unconsciousness that causes holocausts. It is unconsciousness that could cause a nuclear holocaust. Jesus on the cross screamed out against unconsciousness and took all our unconsciousness into his heart when he cried, "Father, forgive them, they *know* not what they do" (Lk. 23:34).

> Mastery of the inner world with a relative contempt for the outer must inevitably lead to great catastrophe. Mastery of the outer world, to the exclusion of the inner, delivers us over to the demonic forces of the latter, and keeps us barbaric despite all outward forms of culture. (Jung, *The Secret of the Golden Flower*:viii)

The mystery of growing older without becoming old, the need to keep the Child alive in us and have an ongoing relationship to this inner Child, will keep us growing in consciousness since the whole thrust of the newborn is toward consciousness. The Child in us who moves toward consciousness "plays house," plays at being grown-up. "You be the mommy and I'll be the daddy." "I'll be the doctor." "I'll be the cop." "I'll be the teacher." In the healthy child the world of make-believe is used in the service of growing consciousness; the world of dreams, fantasies, fairy tales, myths, symbols, and imagination is at the service of expanding consciousness.

The archetypal Child can open the mid-life adult to greater consciousness through the same worlds of "make-believe"— playing and praying, fantasy, night dreams, daydreams, myths, fairy tales, literature, Scripture, dance, art, sound, music, and active imagination—as well as through the whole world of the Shadow: things valued and not valued, people liked and dis-

ISTP

liked, hates, loves, heroes and heroines, one's typology and its opposite, projections, conflicts, emotional overreactions and responses. If greater consciousness is what is at stake, it makes little difference whether I find myself attracted to Joan of Arc stories, which makes me conscious of my unlived heroine, or find myself despising alcoholics, which reveals to me my hidden addiction to needing always to be "high." Wherever there is increased consciousness, there is new energy released for the greater fullness of life. I need only open myself to letting the Child within me live contemplatively and open me to my inner world, which is a source of growth more vast than the outer universe.

In Jung's own mid-life crisis, in the midst of his feelings of disorientation, he went to the Child in him.

> Therefore, I twice went over the details of my entire life with particular attention to childhood memories; I thought there might be something in my past which I could not see and which might possibly be the cause of my disturbance. But this retrospection led to nothing but a fresh acknowledgement of my own ignorance. Thereupon I said to myself, "Since I know nothing at all, I shall simply do whatever occurs to me." Thus I consciously submitted myself to the impulses of the unconscious.

> The first thing that came to the surface was a childhood memory from perhaps my tenth or eleventh year. At that time I had a spell of playing passionately with building blocks. I distinctly recalled how I had built little houses and castles, using bottles to form the sides of gates and vaults. Somewhat later I had used ordinary stones, with mud for mortar. These structures had fascinated me for a long time. To my astonishment, this memory was accompanied by a good deal of emotion. "Aha" I said to myself, "there is still life in these things. The small boy is still around, and possesses a creative life which I lack. (Jung, *Memories, Dreams, Reflections:*173)

Jung knew that the surge of energy and emotion that he felt as he remembered was a revelation that somehow there was new life in this memory. He speaks of the seeming impossibility of bridging the gap. How was this grown man, an eminent doctor and psychiatrist, to reestablish contact with the Boy in him. One hears a struggle that any of us might experience in trying to let out the Child in us:

> I had no choice but to return to it and take up once more that child's life with his childish games. This moment was a turning point in my fate, but I gave in after endless resistances and with a sense of resignation. For it was a painfully humiliating experience that there was nothing to be done except play childish games. (Jung, *Memories, Dreams, Reflections:* 174)

It takes great humility to temporarily let go of the serious adult in us, who is so preoccupied with the world and important enterprises, in order to really play, and to really pray. Jung actually gathered his stones and began building a miniature village; he tried to work on it every day, after the noon meal and before his patients arrived.

> In the course of this activity my thoughts clarified, and I was able to grasp the fantasies whose presence in myself I dimly felt. Naturally, I thought about the significance of what I was doing, and asked myself, "Now really, what are you about? You are building a small town, and doing it as if it were a rite!" I had no answer to my question, only the inner certainty that I was on the way to discovering my own myth. For the building game was only a beginning. It released a stream of fantasies which I later carefully wrote down. (Jung, *Memories, Dreams, Reflections:* 174–75)

All his life after this Jung said that whenever he came up against a blank wall, he painted a picture or hewed a stone and each such experience became a rite of entrance for the ideas and works that followed.

18

Healing the Inner Child

Before Jung came in touch with the memory of his own childhood play, he evoked the Child archetype by owning his ignorance and saying to himself, "Since I know nothing at all, I shall simply do whatever occurs to me" (Jung, *Memories, Dreams, Reflections:*173). The Child archetype thus evoked is far more than our own childhood experiences. In *Seasons of a Man's Life* Levinson refers to this Child archetype when he reflects on the need of the mid-life man, and we would add, woman, to deal with the young/old polarity that comes into awareness at the mid-point of life.

> Ultimately, *Young* is an archetypal symbol with many meanings. It represents birth, growth, possibility, imitation, openness, energy, potential. It colors the meaning we give to many concrete images: the infant, sunrise, the new year, the seed, the blossoms and rites of spring, the newcomer, the promise, the vision of things to come. We are young at any age to the extent that these associations color our psychological, biological and social function. (Levinson:209–10)

Realizing all this, it is easier to see that our Child archetype may be the most crucial factor in the healing of our own painful childhood experiences. Since there is no such thing as a perfect parent or a perfect environment, all of us have some psychological scars from our early life. In order for us at mid-life to move into the future with newness, promise, openness, energy, and potential, it is necessary to spend some time and effort going back. Anyone who wants to leap forward needs to go backward to get a good running start. We need to come to faith in our past, find hope there, and even love our past. We need to own and make peace with and have some kind of closure on our past. We need to look at our past contemplatively, especially our experiences of being sinned against or any experiences of sickness, death, despair, or evil that marred our early life. We need to come to forgive our parents or others or the situations that brought us such deep hurt.

For some, this is a relatively easy task. For others it seems practically impossible. How can I forgive the brutal, selfish father who made me beg for the food money he was drinking or gambling away; the father who sexually abused me; the mother who locked me in the closet while she carried on with a series of abusive men; the mother who tore me down at every moment and tore up everything I ever made her or everything I ever valued? How can I forgive the brutal physical and psychological beatings I took at home, in school, in the neighborhood, in relationships, on my first job, in my marriage? How do I forgive those who abandoned me, starved me, cursed me, died and left me, trampled my innocence, pushed my wide-eyed wonder into the gutter? How do I forgive the alcoholism that robbed me of my childhood, the ignorance, the poverty, the rape, or the loveless couple who brought me unwanted into this world? I surely do not forgive, if forgiveness means denying or blinding myself to the real evil that victimized me. That would be unconsciousness, not growth in consciousness. I must truly grieve the evil that I experienced as a child and young person as I truly grieve the evil that I did. Grieving means feeling the pain and the anger, and finding healthy nondestructive ways to express it. However, forgiveness does not mean getting stuck in the anger, bitterness, or cynicism that may be a necessary stage in my process of forgiving. Forgiveness means trying to find the new life that was conceived and came to birth precisely *in the midst* of that painful situation. Even in the most evil of situations there is some transcendence, even transformation; there is some birth, growth possibility, initiation, energy, potential, sunrise, seed, spring, promise. There was resurrection somewhere in all my deaths, or I would not be alive. We need to find what great, strong, beautiful parts of ourselves, our personality, and our consciousness we owe *precisely* to our tragic experiences.

In *The Child,* Eric Neumann says:

The child psyche is so constituted as to assimilate instinctively the unpleasant factors of existence. The mechanisms of this assimilation or adaptation are embedded in the psyche from the start, merely waiting to be released as life provides the corresponding stimuli. (146)

Paul says something similar in Romans:

> But not only that—we even boast of our afflictions! We know
> that affliction makes for endurance and endurance for tested
> virtue and tested virtue for hope. And this hope will not leave
> us disappointed because the love of God has been poured out
> in our hearts through the Holy Spirit who has been given us.
> (Rom. 5:4–5)

love
virtue *an*
the access!

Being Born Again

"Birth is a supremely welcome mystery..."

The Child archetype incorporates our damaged child and transcends it. Each one of us must give birth to our child again. We must again and again be born of water and the Spirit—of the unconscious and the Love, the God, at life's origin. Nicodemus was a leader, a mid-life man who came secretly to Jesus at night probably because it would have been too humiliating for a member of the Sanhedrin to have been seen publicly with this itinerant teacher. Nicodemus's words echo in each of us who is too grown-up, rigid, or stuck in bitterness about the past.

> Nicodemus said to him, "How can a person once grown old be
> born again? Surely he cannot reenter his mother's womb and
> be born again, can he?" Jesus answered, "Amen, amen, I say
> to you, no one can enter the kingdom of God without being
> born of water and Spirit. What is born of flesh is flesh and
> what is born of spirit is spirit. (Jn. 3:4–6)

We are not locked into or determined by our past. In spirit we can go back; in memory and imagination, not only with the damaging cruelty that came to us from flesh and blood but with God's own Spirit, we can re-parent our own childhood. We can take the child that we were in our own arms and "kiss and make better." We can hold the sobbing child and receive her grief until the sobs give way to sleep and peace. We can even bring those who damaged us into this experience of God's Spirit and

New creature
⟹ :. new situation ...

in this light see them again. We can perhaps begin to understand now the victimization of those who made us their victims
and finally try to put an end to the cruelty passing from generation to generation.

Most of all we can nourish the Child in us now. We can see
where we can give her freedom now. We can let her escape
from the dark closet where we have been keeping her. We can
allow her laughter to ripple through us as we work and play at
what gives her joy.

A man on one of our retreats went out and climbed a tree. He
came back glowing and, in a voice filled with energy, said,

> That's the first time in my life I ever did that! When I was just
> six my dad died. I was the oldest of three and from that day
> on my mother called me "big brother" and demanded that I
> act the part.

Each of us could brainstorm to find what qualities of the child
we could most use in our lives just now for our personal and
spiritual growth. How would we live out those qualities? What
food would we need to give that child to keep it alive in us?
What kinds of activities? What changes in lifestyle would be the
daily bread for the vigor of those qualities? As we forgive those
who abused us in our childhood, we need to be sure that we are
not being even more abusive of our Child in the present.

19

The Child and the Persona

One common way in which mid-life persons can be guilty of abusing the Child within is by underidentifying or over-identifying with a role or roles, with a persona. Jung says that there are

> certain psychological experiences which show that certain phases of an individual's life can become autonomous, can personify themselves to the extent that they result in a vision of oneself—for instance one sees oneself as a child. Visionary experiences of this kind whether they occur in dreams or in the waking state are, as we know, conditional or a disassociation comes about because of various incompatibilities; for instance, a man's [or woman's] present state may have come into conflict with his childhood state or he may have violently sundered himself from his original character in the interest of some arbitrary persona more in keeping with his ambitions. He has thus become unchildlike and artificial and has lost his roots. All this presents a favorable opportunity for an equally vehement confrontation with the primary truth. (Jung, *The Psychology of the Child Archetype*: 162)

The Shadow can consume a person and bring about the collapse of the ego if one is in too tight an embrace with one aspect of the ego, with a persona, that has been blown out of all proportion. In such a case one has separated completely from the archetypal Child in one and so childishness may overtake one. A person to whom this happened was an extremely puritanical minister. He and everyone who knew him saw him as a fundamentalist, antisexual person. He was obsessed with the issue of sexuality and used every possible occasion to drive home the horror of sexual sin.

197

One night in his fifties, he had a dream that was extremely vivid and pornographic. He awoke from his dream, woke his wife, and shouted at her that he now knew that in truth he was a sex maniac. Within a month he had left his wife and his ministry and started to live out his dream and his new image of himself as a sex maniac. The puritan had lived the first half of his life, and especially his early adulthood, as an extremely disciplined man. Superficially, he would have seemed to have very good ego development, yet there was obviously something very unadapted about him that put him in great danger of the collapse of his insecure ego. He had virtually killed the Child in himself. The physical, sensual, emotional life that is the Child had been systematically destroyed in him. Any notion of sex as expressing several different dimensions of life within a relationship bond—from release and comfort to play, ecstatic union, and prayer—was unthinkable to him. He was as guilty of the dangerous separation of sex from erotic love and the rest of personality and life, as are the purveyors of depersonalized sex for casual entertainment.

A counselor in a seminary today would surely look at the women and men coming to her or him from the perspective of overall ego development to see how much structure had been internalized. The question that would need to be asked is: Which ones need to be loosened up and which ones need to be tightened up.

A young person (or any person) with such puritanical tendencies would need some prodding beyond his or her too rigid stance, some appropriate reintroduction to the body and to the Child within.

From Jung's perspective, a persona problem is an overidentification with a role, a relationship, a vice or virtue, a quality, or an aspect of one's personality. The puritan's overidentification with this image of himself, and his repression of the sensual and sexual Child within, set him up for the disaster of the complete collapse of his ego. All that he had become was totally overthrown as he began, after his dream, to live out his primitive, unadapted, infantile, unconscious side. In a way, he did not become "like a child," he became a child, a pseudo-child. His dream was symbolically informing him that human sexuality and sexual desire was part of every human person and that he had been totally condemning and repressing an important aspect of himself and everyone else. Had he been able to incorporate this new awareness, and not interpreted his dream literally and externally, he could have been transformed into a much more human and compassionate person and minister.

The Place of Persona in Ego Development

While every one of us always has some remedial personality work to do, mid-life integration cannot happen if ego development is very poor. Reducing the structure of the Child archetype to the status of a vestige of one's own childhood makes for very poor ego development. The engagement with the Shadow is a subtle and dangerous undertaking. One needs the childlike creativity of having played many roles well. One needs to know the grace of moving consciously from one role to the now appropriate one.

Jung took the word *persona* from the Greek word for the "mask" a player wore in acting each different role in a Greek comedy or tragedy. In much the same way, today's actors and actresses wear the costumes and personalities of the characters they play. Our several personas are not masks in the sense of being something false. Personas are real aspects of our personality; they are real vehicles of our personality. A healthy person has several personas, and moves automatically from one to another. In one day he may move from husband to accountant to daddy to son of an aging mother to Little League coach to eucharistic minister to volunteer fireman to handyman around the house to ballroom dancer to erotic lover.

The Persona is a complicated system of relations between the individual consciousness and society fittingly enough a kind of mask, designed on the one hand to make a definite impression upon others, and on the other, to conceal the true nature of the individual. That the latter function is superfluous, could be maintained only by one who is so identified with his Persona that he no longer knows himself; and that the former is unnecessary could only occur to one who is quite unconscious of the true nature of his fellows. (Jung, *Two Essays in Analytical Psychology:* 192)

A persona is an archetype of the collective unconscious. Society has different expectations of different social roles. How we are expected to play our different roles is very important to the collective and thus to our social functioning. If we cannot take on many appropriate roles and personas, we will be very poorly adapted and gauche. Like a child who says or does everything that comes to mind without regard for time or place, such a person has no discretion.

An early sign of the development of persona is when a child first keeps a secret from a parent. This is as crucial as the child's first no is to the movements of separation that need to take place as the child moves from total dependence through independence to interdependence.

A little girl named Ann Margaret showed a healthy emerging persona on the first day of school. Like most growth, this growth comes with some pain. She went rushing off to school like her three much older brothers. All summer she had talked of nothing else but this great event. She didn't even want Mommy to walk her to the bus stop on that first morning. Yet, on that first afternoon, arriving home, she was anything but the enthusiastic child of the morning. Her mother asked her about it. "Well," she said, "it was okay until after lunchtime. Then I began to feel very lonesome. I started to cry, but I 'scrunched up' my face so that the teacher wouldn't notice." That is a budding persona.

It takes a great deal of hard work and commitment to acquire an important role or aspect of personality. It takes a focusing of one's energies. It takes even a certain period of one-sidedness and dedication to make a team, become a dancer, earn a Ph.D. in engineering, maintain physical fitness, be a husband—in fact, to *be* anything.

A seventy-year-old woman told this story of her early marriage. It speaks of the difficulties anyone can have in taking on a new aspect of himself or herself, new relationships, new roles. At the time of their marriage, they were both in their midthirties. They had two children in the first three years. She was growing more and more uneasy about his pattern of eating quickly and rushing out five or six nights a week to be with his many longtime friends.

One night when she noticed him eating quickly she said,

"Wait a minute, Mike, I have plans tonight." She ate quickly, ran into the bedroom, threw on her good clothes and dashed out of the apartment, shouting some instructions to him about the babies. Since she had no place to go, she went down to the basement and stayed there for two hours. Then, she went upstairs and called as she opened the door, "Mike, I'm home!" He said, "Anne, let's sit down and talk about this." When they had finished talking, he said, "Anne, from now on, when I go out at night, we'll be going out together."

How hard it was, after all those years of freedom, for both of them to take on their new roles as husband and wife, mother and father to two babies. Some thirty-five years later, they went through a new role adjustment when he retired and both of them had to change roles and relationships again.

Persona Problems at Mid-Life

At mid-life, however, if one has overidentified oneself with a role, it will be impossible to engage one's Shadow fruitfully until the persona identification has been dissolved, and one has reconnected with the Child within.

A mid-life widow had one son. He graduated and went backpacking for a year. He came home and got a job. At the same time, Mother was invited by her friends to go on a cruise, all expenses paid. She was excited at first, but soon called her friends to decline. "Bobby is home," she said, "he has his first job and when he comes home he's tired and hungry. I just have to be here for him right now."

Now, Bob is the young man who made it on his own in Europe for one year. Why doesn't Mother know that he would be thrilled if she went on a cruise and left him the house? She has a persona problem. She identifies herself as Bobby's mother. She will not let it into her consciousness that Bob doesn't need her this way anymore. If she does, she will have to ask herself some potentially shattering questions about the meaning of her life and who she is now. Rather than do this, she could go on for forty years still identifying herself totally as Bobby's mother. He could be seventy and she could be ninety, still refusing to do anything because "Bobby needs me."

When the doctor or lawyer or police officer or minister

speaks to wife or husband and children and friends as though they were at work, they have a persona problem. If we father or mother or teach or entertain or coach or direct or organize everyone we meet, we have a persona problem.

Mid-life is a time when the changes in one's body and life and relationships tend to be dramatic, and thus many people begin to feel the sting of a persona problem and finally become aware of it. Diversification, newness, and rebirths are called for. Enter the Child: in this bind we will have to begin to apply energy in other new areas of life, in new parts of the personality. We will need to "learn to" walk and must be patient with the learning process of stumbling and falling and picking ourselves up. We need to take energy away from the all-encompassing persona and allow the Child within to find productive ways to invest that energy.

In extreme and long-standing cases of a persona problem, deflation of it is no small matter, for the personality has no real individuality but has been living out always and only those expectations that society has for a particular role.

The woman or man who has been only the pastor, the teacher, the doctor, or the general for twenty or thirty years and who has scrupulously adhered to society's expectations, will be a shell.

> When we analyze the Persona, we strip off the mask, and discover that what seemed individual is at bottom collective, in other words the Persona was only the mask of the collective psyche. (Jung, *Two Essays on Analytical Psychology*:193)

A woman told this story of a persona problem:

> I married an airline captain. After a few years I sensed something was wrong, but I couldn't put a finger on exactly what it was. Then one day he came home, after being away on flights for several days. He was in the house only a short time and I said to him, "Listen, Captain, this is not your plane, and I am not part of your crew, nor are your two sons."

She said she had a long struggle with him as he slowly came to see that he was being the captain in every situation in his life.

This persona of the captain had not had too many years in control before the man returned to other ways of being and relating. He was fortunate that his individuality did not get completely lost in his collective role.

Both

When such an identification goes on into mid-life, it can be a real source of neurosis. A person cannot submerge individuality in favor of an artificial personality without punishment.

> Even the attempt to do so brings on, in all ordinary cases, unconscious reactions in the form of bad moods, affects, phobias, obsessive ideas, backsliding vices, etc. . . . .an opposite forces its way up from the inside; it is exactly as though the unconscious suppressed the ego with the very same power which drew the ego into the Persona. The absence of resistance outwardly against the lure of the Persona means a similar weakness inwardly against the influence of the unconscious. (Jung, *Two Essays on Analytical Psychology:* 194)

Such was the fate of the puritanical minister whose years of stunted moral development and persona identification issued in a complete collapse of his way of being in favor of its exact opposite, or Shadow personality.

> The moment of irruption can be very sudden, so that consciousness is instantaneously flooded with extremely strange and apparently quite unsuspected contents. This is how it looks to the layman [or woman], and even the person concerned, but the experienced observer knows that psychological events are never sudden. In reality the irruption has been preparing for many years, often half a lifetime. (Jung, *Two Essays on Analytical Psychology:*175)

This kind of overthrow is by no means a rare phenomenon. There are all kinds of stories of "mid-life crazies." There are people who totally abandon their past roles and play out new relationships and roles in a completely childish way. Far from freedom this is a way of becoming stuck and atrophied in infantilism. These people have long since killed the true inner Child who could have moved them into newness, rebirth, resurrection, new parts of themselves, new meanings, values, and goals—moved them into living life to the full, living the spirituality of mid-life toward the Kingdom of the new heaven and the new earth.

> A characteristic of childhood is that thanks to its naiveté, unconsciousness, it sketches a more complete picture of the Self, of the whole man [or woman] in his pure individuality than adulthood. Consequently, the sight of a child . . . will arouse certain longings in adult civilized persons—longings which relate to the unfulfilled desires and needs of those parts of the personality which have been blotted out of the total picture in favor of the adopted persona. (Jung, *Memories, Dreams, Reflections:* 244)

We need constantly to take long, loving looks at the children of the world, so that their unconsciousness and naiveté will keep us open to the more complete picture of the Self we are always becoming, the more whole man or woman in pure individuality whom God has from eternity birthed us to be and dreamed that we would become.

> [Jesus] called a child over, placed it in their midst, and said, "Amen, I say to you, unless you turn and become like children, you will not enter the kingdom of heaven. Whoever humbles himself [or herself] like this child is the greatest in the kingdom. And whoever receives one child such as this in my name receives me." (Mt. 18: 2–5)

20

Reflective Exercises

1. Brainstorm about all the characteristics of a child. You may want to spend some time on this. Perhaps ask others to join you so that you can exhaust the characteristics.
   a) Choose the ten or twelve of these characteristics that you feel you most need.
   b) Narrow the chosen characteristics of a child down to the three or four you feel you most need.

2. Take out the photographs you have of yourself as a child. Put them around your room for a few days. Study them. Let these old photos bring you back to the mystery of being a child. Explore your childhood.

3. Recall the good things about your childhood, the blessings, and give thanks.
   Recall the hard things about your childhood. Do you need to be healed of childhood wounds?
   a) Share these wounds with a friend.
   b) Personify your wounds and write to them. Ask them how you can turn them into strengths.
   c) Let them write back to you.

4. Pay attention to your night dreams. Revere them.
   a) If you awake with a vivid dream get up and write it out.
   b) Take time in the morning to recall your dreams and write them out.
   c) Give each dream a name.

5. Choose a book on dream work and seriously engage your dreams. (The child wastes time in play and you must "waste time" in inner work.)

6. Ask yourself when, where, and in what circumstances you feel most alive.

7. Look at the history of your prayer life. How did you pray as a child, adolescent, and youth? How do you pray now? What can you do to enrich your life of prayer?

8. Plan a day of prayer for yourself once a month or twice a year. Where will you go? What will you do? Are you alone or with others?

9. If you could be a child for a day, what would you do? Write out your answer and read it to a good friend.

10. Make up a litany of thanksgiving for all you have to be grateful for. Pray it periodically.

11. Make a collage of what you would be like if your inner Child were born and became a leaven for the adult in you.

12. Do something you always wanted to do but never did because of fear.

13. Buy something you have always wanted but would not treat yourself to.

14. When was the last time you had fun? Give yourself some fun each day.

15. Make up a litany of all your needs. Pray it frequently.

16. Whom do you love? Have you told them? Imagine how you can tell each person you love that you love them in a special way and start to do so. Be as creative as possible.

17. Are you afraid to ask those you love for favors? Start now.

18. Are there complaints in your heart that you are afraid to verbalize to those you love? Pick one complaint and make it known to the one you love.

19. What can you do for at least one child in the world to make her feel loved and appreciated?

20. Is there something you can do for the children of the world? Take some action now.

PART IV

Emerging Wisdom and Full Life: Wisdom as Archetypal

by Janice Brewi

21

On the Road to Emmaus

As we look at the Gospels we find many sections addressing a person in the mid-life experience. Of these, the story of the disciples on the road to Emmaus (Lk. 13–35) is particularly poignant. It is a story about process, and the mid-life experience is about process. It is a story of death and resurrection, and mid-life is a time for deaths and resurrections. It is a story about human emotions, fears, heartbreaks, and the unexpected; so, too, is mid-life. It is a story about involvement and a call for full participation. Mid-life is also a call for personal involvement in growth and a call for full participation.

We find the story of two disciples on the road to Emmaus in the Gospel of Luke. In the course of this journey the disciples move from despair, disorientation, and alienation to hope, wisdom, and a new beginning. The two disciples are leaving Jerusalem because they have experienced the death of Jesus and not the resurrection. If, as Christian youngsters, we have grown up being catechized with, "He is risen from the dead, Alleluia!" it is difficult for us to imagine the two disciples and their state of being. They had left everything to follow him. They had believed in him and his cause and gave themselves to him and his work. Now he was dead and gone and they were in a state of disorientation. They would not stay around to discuss the meaning of what had happened to Jesus. They knew what had happened. He was dead. Gone. The kingdom they had hoped he had come to found was now a hopeless dream. All his efforts and all their efforts were futile, wasted time. Oh, we can imagine what they said to each other, "conversing about all the things that had occurred" (Lk. 24:14).

The mid-life experience is always initiated by some shock

209

received through the intervention of an unexpected inner or outer event in one's life. Both small and great events can be the cause of one's kingdom tumbling down. The infidelity of a spouse, one's own infidelity, the death of a spouse, a divorce, children leaving home, an empty nest, children not leaving home, a promotion, a demotion, young know-it-alls moving into the workplace, the death of a close peer, the sickness of aged and dependent parents, the death of parents, a child on drugs, an unwanted pregnancy, sexual problems, the inability to throw a ball as you used to or to swim or run with the same vigor, a first illness, putting on weight, forced retirement—any of these can be the cause of someone asking, Is this all there is? Is this what I spent myself for?

The two disciples on the road to Emmaus say, "We were hoping that he would be the one to redeem Israel" (Lk. 24:21). They had put all their hopes in him, had given up all to follow him, and now their hopes are shattered. He is dead now three days. There is no hope. Biblical scholars have often pointed out that verse 21, "We were hoping," appears to recapture precisely the actual historical mood of the disciples between Good Friday and the Easter revelation" (Fuller:105).

How much this reflects the person coming to the end of the first half of life. "I had such hopes," one cries internally. I had hoped our marriage, our children, our home, my career, my ministry, my church! I had hoped that by now, I, you, we, they! Great expectations and hopes are dashed to the ground as one realizes the time is over and things have not worked out as one had hoped or expected. One is in distress and dis-ease.

"While they were conversing and debating," Luke tells "Jesus himself drew near and walked with them, but their eyes were prevented from recognizing him" (Lk. 24:15–16). Our vision is always blurred when we are in the wake of a great shock. Emotionally stricken, in the grips of an unbearable disappointment, with no hope for the future, one surrenders oneself to the chaos of disillusionment.

All their hope is gone. He is dead three days. They had not the imagination to suspect that things were not as they appeared. He was discredited, this Jesus of Nazareth, they believed. They had no hope or expectation of his resurrection. And we? The mid-life person, too, has no expectation of new life, a third birth, a resurrection. The third day had a symbolic meaning in the Hebrew Scriptures. "The third day was traditionally the day of deliverance, or reversal, or victory snatched from the jaws of death and defeat" (Vawter, 1973:4).

In the wake of a broken relationship, shattered dreams, mental or physical collapse, lost joy and lost soul, painful betrayal, and a darkness never before imagined, one finds oneself without hope or expectation for new life, resurrection. One's vision is blurred, one cannot see clearly, one cannot see beyond this pain, one cannot dream that any of this has meaning.

The disciples on the road do not recognize Jesus. Mary Magdalene mistakes him for a gardener. Peter does not know who it is who is on the beach. Only the young John can still see: "It is the Lord!" (Jn. 21:7). Mid-life is going to be an invitation to a whole new way of seeing and believing. And the old way of seeing, so pure and idealistic—"no danger too great," "no mountain too large"—will fall into disarray before a new inner eye dawns in the center of one's being, before wisdom emerges.

Luke, the storyteller, goes on. The stranger engages them winning them over. They are vulnerable as they have never been before, and an intimate conversation is carried on. He encourages them to tell him the story because he knows that only in the telling of the story can healing come. Only in the telling of the story, pouring out their shattered hopes, dreams, and expectations can they come to know the truth about Jesus and about themselves. "We had hoped," they cry, and he receives it all.

Each of us needs to accept ourselves and our own wounds. We need to be heard by another and received in our state of disillusionment and brokenness. Above all we need to be received by the Other, just as we are, with all our feelings and emotions. Only after the telling, the sharing, and the receiving can we expect to be moved. In the telling and receiving newness occurs. Hope is resurrected when one is received in one's hopelessness. Hope is resurrected when one receives *oneself* in one's hopelessness.

"Was it not necessary that the Messiah should suffer these things and enter into his glory?" (Lk. 24:26). Handel's *Messiah* rings out the words, "I know that my redeemer liveth" (Jb. 19:25). Slowly, in the course of this living dialogue, the two disciples are moving into that new awareness. They are coming to know that he is not dead, "he has been raised" (Mk. 16:6b). Each of them is on the brink of experiencing new life.

Later they will reminisce about the conversation with Jesus and they will recall, "Were not our hearts burning within us while he spoke to us on the way and opened the scriptures to us?" (Lk. 24:32). Why were their hearts burning? They had only a short time ago been without hope, so downcast and shattered. It was not just that they had poured out the details of what had happened and how disillusioned they were. The stranger took the details of the story and put them in the context of the Bigger Story: the Scriptures are archetypal in essence; they proclaim the story of the human race. Each man and woman can find themselves there. The details of one's personal story are found in those sacred pages.

> At the core of our humanity there needs to be an ongoing creative tension between our personal stories and the Mytho-logical Stories of our Race, between our personal and culturally shared Myths. The Great Myths provide the com-mon images which the individual uniquely embodies in her own story. Such a truly personal appropriation is an act of self-transcendence rooted in one's psyche, in one's individu-ality and so an expanding horizon and a kind of integration which is personal, spiritual growth. (Brennan:444)

Luke's story tells us that the church read the personal life story of Jesus in the great living themes of life proclaimed in the Hebrew Scriptures. Jesus, in the story, enlightens the disciples by showing them the deeper meaning of what had occurred in the suffering and death of Jesus, as he "interpreted to them what referred to him in all the scriptures" (Lk. 24:27).

I know that in the course of my own mother's slow dying these same words of Scripture came to me regarding her. They lifted her sufferings and her death out of the purely personal realm and placed them in the story of Jesus Christ, in whose name she was baptized. Her story was the archetypal story of the human race, God's holy people. Again and again I pro-claimed in faith, "Was it not necessary that she should suffer these things and enter into her glory?"

Jesus told his story in the context of the archetypal stories and the disciples began to see in a new way. But the day was almost over and evening was coming. The disciples were going to go to the inn. Jesus would have gone on, it appears, putting an end to the exchange. He had come into their midst unexpected and uninvited. But now for him to stay, to linger on, continue the soul searching, they would have to express their desire, make known their wants. They begged him to stay. And each of us? We must be willing to ask, to beg. We must be willing to make known the fact that we are being touched. Each of us must fully participate in the encounter with the Lord. Jung understood Christ to be the archetype of the Self. Could this journey on the road not also represent an encounter with the ego and the Self? Must not one fully participate in the encounter of the ego with the Self, of the conscious with the unconscious?

Perhaps, only because he is invited does Jesus go inside. "So he went in to stay with them" (Lk. 24:29b). And supper comes. How often he had sat at table with them before. He had always mingled food for the body with food for the soul. Physical nourishment and spiritual enlightenment were not exclusive; in fact they are archetypal and go hand in hand. He had been condemned for this table fellowship with sinners and the unclean even as his table fellowship had won their hearts for him. He chose this familiar act to be the final awakening. "While he was with them at table, he took bread, said the blessing, broke it, and gave it to them. With that their eyes were opened and they recognized him" (Lk. 24:30–31).

Each of us will come to recognize the self at the "breaking of the bread." One finds one's story, one's calling, one's true vocation, in the midst of one's broken body, one's broken dreams, one's shattered hopes. Each one of us can come to know, at the mid-point of life, "that my redeemer liveth." Christ is the living waters within me. Christ is the beginning and the end of my journey.

> Psychologically, therefore, the Breaking of Bread is connected with the meals eaten with the risen Christ rather than with the memory of the Last Supper . . . . The confused sense they already had of being caught up in the mystery of Christ

(Luke 24:32) was sharpened and made clear during the meal:
by it they were introduced into the sphere of the risen Christ.
(Durwell:321)

The mid-life person rises up out of the ashes. The first
creation was that way. God breathed his living Spirit into the
creature made out of the dust of the earth. The third birth is
the breath of the living Spirit into the dead, dry bones of the
first half of life.

Luke goes on with his story. "They got up immediately and
returned to Jerusalem, where they found the Eleven and the
rest of the company assembled" (Lk. 24:33).

This is a time of great excitement. They had been dead, and
now they lived. He had been dead and now he was risen. They
had to follow him anew. It was an Alleluia time, as all new
beginnings are. As one lives out the mid-life years, with their
joys and sorrows, one encounters again and again the unexpected.

The disciples' joy turned into sorrow eventually. As Jews, they
continued the Jewish way of life. They went regularly to the
synagogue. "And all day long, both at the temple and in their
homes, they did not stop teaching and proclaiming the Messiah,
Jesus" (Acts 5:42).

> The church throughout all Judea, Galilee, and Samaria was at
> peace. It was being built up and walked in the fear of the
> Lord, and with the consolation of the holy Spirit it grew in
> numbers. (Acts 9:31)

We know the story. Time and time again this community was
challenged as to the meaning and significance of following
Christ. That one must be a Jew, circumcised and obey the law,
gave way to a new vision.

> Before faith came, we were held in custody under law, con-
> fined for the faith that was to be revealed. Consequently, the
> law was our disciplinarian for Christ, that we might be justi-
> fied by faith. But now that faith has come, we are no longer
> under a disciplinarian. For through faith you are all children
> of God in Christ Jesus. For all of you who were baptized into
> Christ have clothed yourselves with Christ. There is neither

Jew nor Greek, there is neither slave nor free person, there is not male and female; for you are all one in Christ Jesus. And if you belong to Christ, then you are Abraham's descendent, heirs according to the promise. (Gal. 3:23–29)

Living the life of the Spirit was turning things upside down as it always does. Continually they were being asked to break through cherished illusions, reverse the order of how things are, respond to the ongoing revelation of events and history, do violence to their expectations, and never settle in. All through the second half of life this is the pattern for us, too. Each of us is to be faithful to our story by responding to the ongoing revelation of events and history. Each of us can ask: "Lord how am I to be faithful to the Self, and therefore to you also, in and through what is happening and going on in and around me?

As time passed the Jerusalem community was ostracized from the synagogue. Perhaps a good deal of the anti-Semitism found in Christian Scripture dates back to this alienating turn of events. It certainly did not come from Jesus. It remains for us a witness to the shadow of the early church. It is a reminder to us that the church, the people of God, the body of Christ, has a human dimension and can both do evil and be the cause of evil even while being God's holy church. It reminds us that today, while we need to be aware of the dangerous shadows of the church, we must be careful not to *equate* the church with her present shadow.

After being put out of the synagogue this community of Christians was forced to ask the question: How can we follow the Lord now, in this situation? They came together in prayer, open to the Spirit showing them the way. In mid-life, we, too, do not know the way and we open ourselves to the Spirit leading. Times of peace, certainty, and clarity continually give way to their opposite. We look to the unconscious for a lead, for direction, for inspiration. In our personal life, and in the life of any institution, there is a rhythm: tension and conflict come again and again to do their work of evoking new developments and growth.

> . . . a numinous experience is no guarantee of inner peace, not in the long run anyway. So long as one continues to develop, inner peace even those whose life has been enriched

by an encounter with the unconscious, is only a breathing-space between the conflict solved and the conflict to come, between answers and questions that throw us into turmoil and suffering, until new insights or new transformations bring a fresh solution and the inner and outer opposites are once again reconciled. The experience of meaning which is what, ultimately, life is about—is by no means equivalent to non-suffering; yet the resilience of the self-aware and self-transforming consciousness can fortify us against the perils of the irrational and the rational, against the world within and the world without. (Jaffe:56)

Luke's story of the disciples on the road to Emmaus is our story. The story has a progression. Slowly the disciples through their honest interaction with Jesus grow in consciousness to see the meaning of the death of Jesus, the meaning of their own call and vocation, and the significance of the risen life of Jesus and their own new beginnings. In all of this, the disciples came to wisdom. Wisdom came to them. This is mid-life. This is mid-life spirituality: a call to growth in consciousness; a call to personal and spiritual growth; a call to the significance and meaning of our own suffering and pain, and of life itself; a call to intimate relationship with Christ the Beloved, with the Self, with Jew and non-Jew, male and female; a call to the transpersonal and to love and liberation of each other; a call to Wisdom.

Once again in this story, Christ can represent for us the larger personality, the Self. The disciples are leaving Jerusalem because he is dead, and with his death their own part with him and his cause dies. They equated themselves with the ego personalities that embraced him and his desire to bring the kingdom. They gave up everything to follow him and were even willing to die for him. True, in his hour of need they had saved their own skins. Only John and the three Marys had the courage to stand beneath the cross with him in his dying moment. For the most part, his followers disowned the whole thing; they had misunderstood: "We were hoping that he would be the one to redeem Israel" (Lk. 24:21), they cry out to the stranger. Their dreams are shattered. They are disillusioned. They will disown this tragic part of their lives.

But Christ has other things in mind. He knows how much he needs them. He knows his mission and work cannot go on without them. He can use, must use, all that they are, even their weakness—especially their weakness. Christ engages them in the most intimate conversation.

And the Self? Does not the Self know how it needs the ego? Without the ego one's work cannot be accomplished. One engages oneself in a most intimate conversation. The Self allows herself to pour out her disillusionment about how things have turned out. She freely participates in all the details of this crisis of feelings and negativity. Only in this participation can she ask, "Was it not necessary that the Messiah should suffer these things and enter into his glory?" (Lk. 24:26). The ego is in the process of moving out to let the Self be in the limelight and take the steering wheel. Like John the Baptist, the ego is learning that she was only to prepare the way for the Self: "one mightier than I is coming. I am not worthy to loosen the thongs of his sandals" (Lk. 3:16).

The wedding of the conscious and unconscious takes place. The Self waits for the invitation, "Stay with us, for it is nearly evening and the day is almost over" (Lk. 24:29). And then the great communion. The union acted out. "Take and eat. Take and drink." The eschatalogical meal marks the fullness of time. This holy meal is a sign of the kingdom realized and the kingdom to come. It is a sign of the most intimate union of ego and Self, conscious and unconscious, a divine intimacy that creation is all about. "Come aside and sup with me." The glorious work of individuation: being made in God's image and likeness, an acknowledgment of oneness.

Mid-life is a call to turn things upside down, not once, but again and again. It is a call to connect oneself to the archetypal psychic energy and source of living waters that belongs to the human family. It is a call to live the second half of life under the rhythm and the spell of the living experience, "I know that my redeemer liveth." The disciples on the road to Emmaus were at a fork in the road. Christ met them at this fork. The Self met each of them at this fork. In the mid-life experience each of us has the archetypal experience of being at the fork in the road. We, too, can encounter Christ at the fork. We can encounter the Self. Whichever way we turn, our lives will never be the same.

Mid-life and the mature years will be filled with the highs and lows, the peaks and valleys, of the journey on the road to

Emmaus. All suffering and death itself can be redemptive. Each of us is lifted into the bigger picture, the moaning and groaning of all creation as we await the coming together of all the fragments into the fullness of the Kingdom of God. "I consider that the sufferings of this present time are as nothing compared with the glory to be revealed for us" (Rom. 8:18). Living life and living through the mid-life experience, going through this "school of life," growing in consciousness, encountering the Self, and moving into and beyond one's personal experiences awakens transcendence and Wisdom in the human person.

22
The Archetype of Wisdom

The story of the disciples on the road to Emmaus illuminates for us the marks of the mid-life crisis and transition. The history of the infant church that follows the Emmaus event depicts for us the many movements in the period of mid-life itself. We are reminded again and again that all throughout the second half of life, both in the period of mid-life and in the period of the mature years, personality growth is going on.

Growth and development are as much the characteristics of the second half of life as they are of the first half of life. Mid-life is a beginning, not an end. The disciples came to see the death of Jesus as a beginning, not an end. In this century we have come to "acknowledge adulthood as a developmental and con-flictual phase in its own right, rather than merely the mature end of all development" (Erikson, 1982:9).

Growth does not cease. But the field of growth changes. Where outer life and achievements had been important, now one's inner life and psychic experiences become important. Where adaptation to the outer world was the necessity, adapta-tion to the inner world is now the necessity. Where one-sided-ness and exclusion were emphasized in the service of ego development, unity, integration of conflicting dualities, and inclusiveness are the cornerstones of the Wisdom of mid-life and the mature years. Where ego consciousness is the mark of the first half of life, the larger Self is the mark of the second half of life. Where ego consciousness comes to birth in child-hood, the first stage of the first half of life, and continues to grow through the second stage of youth, mid-life gives birth to the Self and it is the Self that continues to become in and through the stages of mid-life and the mature years.

219

As one comes to realize that the ego and the Self are not the same, as one is enlightened regarding the need for the diminishment of the ego and the gradual coming into prominence of the Self, one comes into contact with the archetype of Wisdom. Wisdom directs one to the right order of things. The mid-life conversion is a change in the order of things. Wisdom directs one to proper relationships with Self, others, world, and the greater reality of the universe and God.

Wisdom puts one in touch with the "deep down things" in one's own psyche and the psyche of others. Wisdom puts one in contact with "the underground stream" in oneself that connects and relates one to God, to all humanity, and to the ages past, present, and yet to come. Wisdom is at the heart of all healing, forgiveness, conversion, good relationships, right order, wholistic styles of life, praying, and playing. Wisdom allows one to deal with ambiguity and live with paradox. Wisdom brings the child out of the adult and the adult out of the child. Wisdom allows one to bring good out of evil and to discern life in death. Wisdom tutors one in a reality that includes possibilities.

I remember a young middle-aged couple sitting through one of our eight-week workshops. When I casually asked, "How are you doing with all of this," secretly wondering whether they were too young, they shared their story. They were trying to rebuild their life together after their experience of his infidelity. She was growing in the restoration of her faith, hope, and love in their relationship. His sorrow and his own struggle to forgive himself had helped her through her own anger and grief and into forgiveness. Both were terribly humbled; they were experiencing their own vulnerability. I was amazed at the Wisdom being lived out in this couple. They had the foresight and the courage not to equate themselves or their marriage with this infidelity of eleven months. They were both determined to grow from this experience.

Each of them was in pursuit of a greater self-knowledge. They both wanted a radical self-honesty to be at the foundation of the new relationship and style of life they were building. They both knew that the relationship would be only as good and as strong as their own individual selves. Wisdom allowed each of them to remember their beginnings as a couple and to know they still wanted that love to claim and name them.

Wisdom allowed each of them to know that this did not have to unmake them but could allow them to rebuild.

It is not always so. Another woman came to the workshop to help her through the first year of her divorce after a thirty-five-year marriage. She needed to contact her possibilities. She wanted to know she had something to live for. A retired school-teacher, she said:

> I used to be a daughter but my mother died. I used to be a mother but all my children are grown and gone. I used to be a teacher and then I retired. I was a wife but now I'm divorced. Am I anything now?

As she works through her anger, grief, loneliness, and despair, she may find her Self and the Wisdom within herself to affirm, direct, and guide her. I suspect she will come through, as she carried in her bag the words to the hymn we sang, "Be Not Afraid, I Go before You Always."

I remember reading Estée Lauder's account of her divorce in a magazine on one of the airlines. She told the story of her marriage and child and then her rapid rise in business. She was caught into it like a whirlwind, eating up the activity and celebrity. Some friends questioned her about her husband being a drag and holding her back. Those remarks led to their divorce. She remained friends with her husband primarily because of their child. Parenting kept them in contact and in relationship. Eventually, after their child's almost fatal illness, they remarried. Estée realized she had relinquished an essential part of herself. She now spends as much time as possible counseling people in similar circumstances. Helping them to contact their inner depths, the wisdom within. She knows that not everyone can have a second chance as she did.

Wisdom Literature

Every great religion and all great cultures had their wisdom traditions and wisdom literature. Such wisdom is often mundane and deals with the practical realities of life. Yet often wisdom literature points to the most profound mysteries of life itself and lifts one out of isolation and connects one to the great motifs of human existence and relationship.

The Book of Sirach (or Ecclesiasticus, as it is also called) is an example of wisdom literature that ranges from the practical to the inspirational. The author, a sage who lived in Jerusalem, wrote the book sometime shortly after 200 B.C. A sage is in contact with the deeper realities of life. A sage is in touch with the unconscious of individuals and the unconscious of the culture. The sage's wisdom grows out of deep, personal life experiences and reflection on them. At the same time the sage's ability to be wise is a charism, or gift. The sage is in touch with the psychic powers in himself or herself in an unusual way. Yet this power is in each of us: the archetype of Wisdom can be operative in each of us.

The Wisdom archetype is manifested in all the wisdom literature of the great religions. Wisdom is a quest inherent in the life journey of each individual. It allows one to find meaning and interpret one's own life journey. Wisdom puts one in contact with the unique significance of one's life story.

The Book of Sirach gives witness to the archetypal nature of Wisdom. Sirach has three major sections, each delineated by a hymn. The hymns are found in 1:1–10, 24:1–31, and 51:13–30 (Bergant:76). Each one of these hymns describes Wisdom as having existed even before time became a reality and as abiding in the depth of individuals even while in their mother's womb. Wisdom is thus being described as archetypal. It is a gift of the creator to humanity itself and part of the psychic equipment of each of us. It can be used or ignored or abused. It can be dormant or operative. It can be projected on other men and women as our gurus, and it can be owned as the ground of our own personal psychic reality.

All Wisdom comes from the Lord and with him it remains forever. . . . To whom has wisdom's root been revealed? Who knows her subtleties? . . . It is the Lord; he created her, has seen her and taken note of her. He has poured her forth upon all his works, upon every living thing according to his bounty; he has lavished her upon his friends. . . . The beginning of Wisdom is fear of the LORD, which is formed with the faithful in the womb. (Sir. 1:1, 5, 7–8, 12)

Wisdom sings her own praises. . . . "From the mouth of the Most High I came forth, and mistlike covered the earth. In the highest heavens did I dwell, my throne on a pillar of cloud. . . . Before all ages, in the beginning, he created me, and through all ages I shall not cease to be. . . . Come to me, all you that yearn for me, and be filled with my fruits. You will remember me as sweeter than honey, better to have than the honeycomb." . . .The first man [and woman] never finished comprehending wisdom, nor will the last succeed in fathoming her. For deeper than the sea are her thoughts; her counsels, than the great abyss. (Sir. 24:1a, 3–4, 9, 18–19, 26–27)

Come aside to me, you untutored, and take up lodging in the house of instruction; How long will you be deprived of wisdom's food, how long will you endure such bitter thirst? I open my mouth and speak of her: gain, at no cost, wisdom for yourselves. Submit your neck to her yoke, that your mind may accept her teaching. For she is close to those who seek her, and the one who is earnest finds her. (Sir. 51:23–26)

These passages can teach us much about the archetype of Wisdom and the archetype of Self, or "glory."

First, wisdom is initially manifested in creation. It is because of wisdom that creation is one, although this is a unity in duality. Sirach perceives reality as a harmony of opposites: good vis-à-vis evil, life vis-à-vis death, light vis-à-vis gloom, etc. The balance of opposites results in an order or harmony that Sirach calls "Glory." Creation reveals this glory which is also associated with the glory of God proclaimed again and again within the liturgical tradition of Israel. (Bergant:76)

Wisdom: The Art of Reflection and Integration

As the disciples dialogued with Jesus on the road to Emmaus they were about the most essential quality of the mid-life and the mature years: reflectiveness. It was the Christ who called them to this reflectiveness. They were to spend time contemplating all that had happened. He was the archetype of Wisdom for them calling them to touch the deep stream of Wisdom within. They had equated truth with consciousness. They had believed that Jesus was dead and gone because they quickly interpreted what they had seen and heard. His suffering, death, and burial contradicted all their expectations about his personal life and about what they were about and had committed themselves to. Yet, the journey to Emmaus puts each of them in contact with another reality. The mid-life person is put in contact with another reality, the unconscious. This introduction, this initiation into another reality, is Wisdom itself. Because of this reality, because of the Wisdom it brings, one has the means to reinterpret all of one's life.

Wisdom allows one to reinterpret the past, the present, and the future. Using the tools of unconscious as well as conscious realities, the true meaning of one's life journey emerges. One begins to sense the greater Self who has been at the heart and core of one's life since conception. The ego bows low to this Self that is to become the mistress of consciousness.

Once during a meditation from Progoff's *The Well and the Cathedral,* I was led down to the inner stream, to the deepest Self. I saw myself small and bowing low, kneeling on the ground before a huge golden monstrance holding the Blessed Sacrament. I was comfortable in my lowly position before Almighty God. I sensed that I was my ego bowing low before the greater Self. Since that time I have been attracted to the Magi. The Magi came with their gifts to the child. They bowed low in homage to one greater than they. They acknowledged the child as Messiah, the promised one. I felt that when I bowed low before the monstrance, I was like the Magi acknowledging the one greater than I, acknowledging the Self, the image of God in me as Messiah.

Because of Wisdom one comes to revere anew each minute detail of one's early life, one sees more in the personal events, joys, and sorrows of one's life than ever before. One reinterprets the adolescent phase, the struggle for independence and autonomy, the sexual awakening and search for intimacy, and one is moved to understanding and compassion, acceptance and forgiveness, for one's unique personal encounter with each of these archetypal motifs.

Wisdom at Mid-Life

Because of Wisdom one can look back at the period of ego development and know how necessary and therefore good it was. One realizes that the task of the first half of life has been foundational for the development of the self and plays an essential role in the development of this culture of ours and this universe. With Teilhard de Chardin, the person in whom the archetype of Wisdom has been evoked is able to say:

> Which is better for a Christian: activity or passivity? Life or death? Growth or diminishment? Development or curtailment? Possession or renunciation? Why separate and contrast the two natural phases of a single effort? Your essential duty and desire is to be with God. But in order to be united, you must first of all be—be yourself as completely as possible. And so you must develop yourself and take possession of the world in order to be. Once this has been accomplished then it is time to think about renunciation; then is the time to accept diminishment for the sake of being in another. (96)

The wise person knows the importance of the ego coming to autonomy and of outer achievements and knows the value in allowing that emphasis on ego to diminish in order to give birth to the Self. The person in whom wisdom has arisen knows that the vitality of future life will come from the inner recesses of the personality. A new attitude arises in the mid-life person. Wisdom erupts out of the chaos of mid-life. Wisdom is born out of the experience of living and life itself when one is brought to and through the reflective stage, giving witness to a larger reality in all of life and in the Self.

Jung comments on the third birth in *Psychological Types*. He understands the tension of the mid-life crisis as a necessary part of the coming new birth that is "likened in Isaiah to pregnancy" (262).

> As a woman about to give birth writhes and cries out in her pains, so were we in your presence, O Lord. We conceived and writhed in pain, giving birth to wind; Salvation we have not achieved for the earth, the inhabitants of the world cannot bring it forth. But your dead shall live, their corpses shall rise; awake and sing, you who lie in the dust. For your dew is a dew of light, and the land of shades gives birth. (Isaiah 26:17–19)

The birth of the Self signifies for the conscious personality not only that its place of prominence, at one time a necessity, has been usurped, but that the consequence of this reversal is "a completely new view of an attitude toward life, a 'transformation' in the fullest sense of the word" (Jacobi, 1973:127).

The birth of the Self allows one to see one's history or past in a new way and to expect from the present and the future a new creation; not the old stuff, ego, but the new, the Self, which incorporates the ego and the unconscious. We are a new creation.

Luke was an ordained minister pastoring a small country church that he deeply loved. He was sensitive to the fact that Peggy, his wife, was going through a hard time and looked for things he could do with their three children to give her more time to herself. Luke enjoyed the time he spent with the children and the time he spent with many of the church members: at the firehouse, at the town's funeral parlor, at the two local pubs, and so on. But all this backfired on Luke when Peggy asked for a divorce. She had been seeing another man and was in love.

Luke was devastated. Finally, although still in love with Peggy, Luke agreed to the divorce. This meant not only the loss of the woman he loved, but the loss of his children and of the church he loved and his ministry. He packed everything he owned into his little car and left.

Two years later, Luke found himself waking up in a jail, his face against a cold floor next to a urinal. He had been arrested for vagrancy. Next, he found himself in a hospital overhearing the nurses talking about him. "He doesn't have long to live," one said, "his insides are all gone." At the thought of his pending death Luke cried out, "My God, I can't die. I have three children I love who need me."

The day he left the hospital, Luke was penniless. Not knowing what to do or where to go he took a cab to his old seminary. He had one old professor in his mind. In his seminary days he looked up to and admired this man. Now he turned to him in need.

The old professor paid the cabby and listened to the story. He begged Luke to stay with them for the year. "Let us help to rehabilitate you. Go to classes. There is so much more to learn." The year passed. Unknown to Luke the old professor put his name in for a pastorate. Luke himself had not dared to think a church would want him, but a congregation filled with Wisdom chose Luke after hearing his story.

Luke had gone to the "nether world" and returned. He had died and now he lived. In the midst of his own despair, alcoholism, and degradation Luke found his true Self and Wisdom. The last time I spoke with Luke his three children were living with him and he was happily remarried. Please God, he is still abiding in Wisdom.

This transformation initiates one into a new journey, the journey of the Spirit, the journey of the Self, of the second half of life, the journey of the personality, the search for God, the appropriation of Wisdom. Is this what Robert Browning hinted at when he wrote, "Grow old along with me, the best is yet to be." In the first half of life the ego was formed from the hidden Self. Consciousness was formed out of the sea of the unconscious. Now, in the second half of life, the journey is not about the ego/Self separation but about the ego/Self reunion: a coming home to Self in a union of all the fragments of one's personality, known and unknown.

This new second journey, rooted in the Self, rooted in God, rooted in Wisdom itself, is about integration, a coming together of one's inner and outer life. One begins to pay attention to the inner movements, the inner voice. Listening to one's depths, to the heart of oneself, is the beginning and the end of wisdom. Speaking of this process Jolande Jacobi says:

> As between consciousness and the unconscious, so a dialectical relationship also exists between turning inwards and conscious participation in the inner happenings, and turning outwards and consolidation of what has been won in the outside world. (1967:99)

In mid-life one is in touch with and called to integrate the "two threads of one's life . . . the Within and the Without" (Teilhard:80). This is wisdom.

> To cleave to God hidden beneath the inward and outward forces which animate our being and sustain it in its development, is ultimately to open ourselves to, and put trust in, all the breaths of life. (Teilhard:80)

To be in touch with both one's inner and one's outer life is the heart of what the second half of life is all about. The spirituality of the mid-life years involves one in a continual correspondence with the inner self, the depths of oneself. If this openness ceases, or does not take primacy, one's inner and outer life will suffer; one will become sick and one's greatest contribution to the world will be denied.

At one workshop I met a woman who shared with me the story of her husband and herself. At a young age he became the head neurologist of a large metropolitan hospital. This position was the reward for his giftedness, dedication, intelligence, and industry. But the responsibilities mounted. He found himself always having to don the persona of chief neurologist in this prestigious hospital. He no longer was content with the fact that all his time and energy was being given to maintaining this demanding post.

His personal life was truncated. His wife gave him emotional suppport and maintained their home and their children beautifully, but he wanted more than that now. Now he wanted to be friends with her and to do things together. He was longing for intimacy. He wanted to be part of the lives of his children. He paid attention to his growing frustration and discontent. He asked the question: Is this really what I want and where I want to be?

When I met his wife they were living in a small village where they had moved ten years before. He had found the way to use his gifts and to be true to himself. He and two other doctors shared an office in a beautiful wooded area. He and his partners were making a genuine contribution to medical service in the area, but the performance level had totally changed. He had time now for the simple pleasures of life. He felt younger, healthier, and happier than he had since his college years.

Wisdom had called him to pay attention to essential parts of himself and give them life. He did not have to throw over his medical career, he just had to settle for less. Or was it more? Once he had realized what needed to change he had to summon the courage to do so. Once the courage came he needed to imagine and work out a suitable plan. Each of us has only one life to live and we are called to live it to the fullest. Each must find her own way and follow it. Wisdom knows the way.

Wisdom and the Self

The archetype of the Self is a paradoxical unity and incorporates other archetypes into a totality. It is here that we find the archetype of Wisdom to be distinct and yet inseparable from the archetype of the Self. Both are numinous. Both are larger than the ego and outside of time. Both have had manifestations in our life prior to mid-life. Both are the psychic reality inherited from humanity that we have been born with and into, even while we are in the process of becoming and creating.

It is in the mid-life crisis that one is given the opportunity to encounter the greater archetypal realities. The initial shock that thrusts one into mid-life crisis incorporates seeds for life that come from destruction and can only arise out of chaos.

> For when the outward-going of the life energy is checked, the unconscious is constellated, and the archetypes begin to manifest themselves in mythological images that portray the stage of development of the higher man [or woman], the twice born. A new kind of psychological development is initiated, leading to the discovery of the supreme value that Jung calls the Self. (Harding, 1965:129)

To be in touch with the Self is Wisdom. When the archetype of Wisdom emerges, the Self emerges. When the Self emerges, the archetype of Wisdom emerges. Each incorporates the other. Wisdom calls one to both inner and outer experience. Wisdom moves one toward wholeness. Wisdom calls one to a profound harmony between the world within and without. Wisdom proclaims greater realities than ever imagined. Wisdom acknowledges the profound necessity to contemplate what is: the reality within as well as the reality without. Wisdom acknowledges the Self.

If mid-life is an invitation into the inner life and the great reality of the Self, the mature years are an inundation in both. One's mature years could be twenty, ten, or five years of one's lifetime, or the hours preceding one's death, or the time of sickness leading to one's death. If a person has been introduced and schooled in the mid-life experience, has undergone the third birth, the mature years are a deepening of that process. They are a growth in wisdom.

In Jung's later life he received a request from a stranger, an admirer who requested time to share with Jung for their mutual enrichment. Jung's response was true to his primary function, thinking, but not without genuine signs of feeling: (he did take time to respond; he did not just say no but was intimate and shared his reasons.) His answer also reflects a great Wisdom. He had come to know himself. He knew his limitations. Long ago he had lost his heroic attitude (*Memories, Dreams, Reflections*: 181) and that gave way to the demands of the unconscious and the self. In his old age, because of a deeply religious attitude, he bowed to the reality of his own physical, emotional, and spiritual condition and gave a passionate, strong, but kindly no. He demonstrated Wisdom.

> I am now getting on to eighty-two and feel not only the weight of my years and the tiredness this brings, but, even more strongly, the need to live in harmony with the inner demands of my old age. Solitude is for me a fount of healing which makes my life worth living. Talking is often a torment for me, and I need many days of silence to recover from the futility of words. I have got my marching orders and only look back when there's nothing to do. This journey is a great adventure in itself, but not one that can be talked about at great length. What you think of as a few days of spiritual communion would be unendurable for me with anyone, even with my closest friends. The rest is silence! This realization becomes clearer as the need to communicate dwindles. (*Letters: 1951-61*: 363–64)

The Story of Patrick of Ireland

Chronological age does not ensure maturity or Wisdom or the becoming of the Self. Wisdom can be and often is operative in the child and the youth. We hear it said, "she has wisdom beyond her years" or "he expressed a wisdom unheard of in one so young" or "he was in touch with a wisdom that transcends his life experience and his age."

Those who work with terminally ill children speak of the Wisdom they gain in and through their experience of approaching death. Such children have been known to comfort their parents and prepare them for their coming departure and absence.

St. Patrick's *Confession* reveals a youth's early contact with an inner Wisdom that transcended his years. Wisdom arose in Patrick because of his life situation and the suffering inflicted on him as a young boy. One is reminded of the far more horrendous twentieth-century situation of Elie Wiesel and the tragic experience of his youth under Nazi Germany. The inhuman suffering that he and millions of other children and youths experienced served as the breaking point for many, and understandably so. Yet, for others like Elie, the same situation became and still is the most profound source of Wisdom.

Even today, Elie carries the memory of that evil in his psyche, even in his flesh. This is a necessary anamnesis if Wisdom is to predominate, if men and women are to learn from history and grow beyond and out of the demonic chaos of the experience of evil.

Patrick of Ireland also carried in his psyche the memory and the terror of his years in captivity. At the tender age of sixteen, Patrick, with thousands of others, was captured, taken into captivity, brought to Ireland, and sold as a slave (Duffy: 12). This terrifying experience amid total strangers and the deep loneliness of a young boy deprived of family, schooling, and youth itself, caused the young Patrick, no great respector of the spiritual, to turn to God. At the time Patrick's father was a deacon. His grandfather had been a priest and his family were third-generation Christians (Duffy: 41). Yet, Patrick had been up to this time "ungodly" and no more open to the spiritual than many boys of his age. The experience of captivity turned Patrick toward the God within, the God of all ages, the Christian God. With this God he found company, presence, consolation, comfort, courage, inspiration, and direction.

Patrick's slavery left a deep scar on his soul that never quite disappeared. He did come to realize that his slavery had served to purify and mature him spiritually in a remarkable way. This realization enabled him to accept this part of his story despite the fact that it terrified and pained him to the end (Duffy:8).

Patrick's *Confession* traces for us "his spiritual development, in other words he explores methodically his understanding of himself as a growing person coming to maturity of vision and practical wisdom" (Duffy:7).

The *Confession* reveals Patrick's deep appreciation of the

Scriptures and the fact that he interpreted the events of his own life in a biblical fashion, much as Jesus did with the events of his life, as shown in the discourse with the disciples on the road to Emmaus.

While in captivity, Patrick was overwhelmed with grace. The archetypes of God, Self, and Wisdom arose in him despite his youth. The Spirit of the Lord protected and counseled the young Patrick. The arena of the archetypal psyche served the Lord, as he himself ministered to the needy and totally open Patrick. "He showed concern for my weakness, and pity for my youth and ignorance, he watched over me before I got to know him and before I was able to distinguish good from evil. In fact he protected and comforted me as a father would his son" (Duffy:12).

> When I was young and innocent, I sought wisdom. She came to me in her beauty, and until the end I will cultivate her. As the blossoms yielded to ripening grapes, the heart's joy, my feet kept to the level path because from earliest youth I was familiar with her. In the short time I paid heed, I met with great instruction. Since in this way I have profited, I will give my teacher grateful praise. I became resolutely devoted to her—the good I persistently strove for. I burned with desire for her, never turning back. I became preoccupied with her, never weary of extolling her. My hand opened her gate and I came to know her secrets. For her I purified my hands; in cleanness I attained to her. At first acquaintance with her, I gained understanding such that I will never forsake her. My whole being was stirred as I learned about her; therefore I have made her my prize possession. The Lord has granted me my lips as a reward, and my tongue will declare his praises. (Sir. 51:13–22)

God's divine guidance came to Patrick in a series of psychic dreams that he recounts in his *Confession*. Patrick had been sold to a farmer. While in captivity Patrick had the task of tending the herds. It was while at this occupation that the terror and loneliness of his heart invited him to prayer. He prayed daily and God became his companion and guide. His first recorded pyschic experience was a dream he had one night after six years of captivity. In his sleep Patrick heard a voice, "It is well that you fast, soon you will go to your own country" (Duffy:18) and "Look, your ship is ready" (Duffy:19). Patrick did not doubt the counsel. He ran away and found a ship that he boarded. On that journey, before he finally came to safety, he suffered physically and spiritually; he bore temptations and severe depression.

Many years later Patrick had another vision that revealed his fate and yet another dimension of his story. A man he called Victor appeared. He was carrying many letters from Ireland. Victor handed the letters to Patrick. The opening words read, "The voice of the Irish." Even as he read the letter he heard voices cry out, "We ask you, boy, come and walk once more among us" (Duffy: 22). Still another night in sleep he heard the conclusion of a prayer. "He who has given up his life for you, he it is who speaks in you" (Duffy:23).

Joseph Duffy believes this to be Patrick's mid-life vocation. By then he would have been in his early thirties. Patrick was being called in these psychic experiences. Wisdom, learned in the harshness of life, had opened a space in Patrick's heart for the people of Ireland and his mission was erupting from this mingling of his mind and heart, as revealed in his dreams and visions. Again, Patrick experienced a person inside himself. She was at prayer and in great emotion and yet at peace. She revealed herself to be the Spirit. It took Patrick almost a decade before he could surmount all the disapproval of others and set out for Ireland to fulfill his unique call.

If Patrick had learned Wisdom in and through adversity while a young captive he was now to come to new dimensions of Wisdom through the adversity heaped on him by jealous, calculating, and relentless senior bishops. Evidence had come into their hands of Patrick's foolishness as a fifteen-year-old and they were using that to malign his character and prove him unfit for a mission to Ireland. It was a bishop who was considered to be Patrick's friend and ally who brought this evidence against Patrick. In this betrayal of confidence, Patrick was like Jesus, betrayed by his own. Once again Patrick was counseled through a vision. He was assured that God was concerned about his good name and knew his bewilderment and consternation. Patrick was rescued by God in his psychic experiences again and again. He was rescued from all kinds of dangers and conspir-

acies. "How did I come by this wisdom which was not my own?"
he asks (Duffy:27).

The Lord God, Patrick believed, was the source of his
Wisdom. Because of this Wisdom, Patrick had an everlasting
effect on the Irish people. He spent his days pouring himself
out on their behalf. He acknowledged his success in Ireland as a
gift of God.

According to Duffy, Patrick lived about eighty years; he died
circa 480 (58). Patrick had been schooled in the inner journey,
due to the shock of his early youth. He continued that inner
journey throughout his life. He grew in Wisdom, grace, and
nature in the years that followed and learned to listen to his
heart and respond totally. He became individuated. Individuation is becoming whole, reaching one's full potential, and sur-
rendering to the reasons for one's very existence, one's reason
for being, one's call. Patrick brought together his inner and
outer life. He found the way and lived it. He personified
Wisdom. The fullness of maturity is reached when one comes
home to oneself and moves outside of all projections.

23

Wisdom Rooted in Religious Experience

J ung tells us that the most powerful experience a man or a woman can have is a religious experience. The numinosity that accompanies a religious experience lifts one out of oneself and connects one to the deeper realities in oneself and outside of oneself, to Wisdom itself. We look to mystery, to the Other, to God, as the source of such transcendence. We know that such an experience is genuine and truthful when it overflows into acceptance; forgiveness; and love of self, other people, humanity, and the mystery of life, or God—in other words, wisdom.

At the heart of a religious experience is the meaning of one's life, one's essence and relatedness. This is Wisdom's bed and Wisdom's fruit. Because of this, a religious experience is memorable, the source of conscious and unconscious decisions and the source of integration (Baum:60). Because of such events one comes to know more about who one really is and who one is becoming.

I had one such experience recently. I was in a group and we were being led in a prayer of imagination. I had often participated in this prayer before, so as soon as the leader started to give instructions I found myself immediately engaged. "Imagine yourself on a beautiful summer day alone and enjoying yourself," we were directed. "Now, God appears to you as a tree" (Halpin:63). That was all I needed. From then on the leader and the group faded away and I was engaged by my unconscious. From the very start hot tears rolled down and continued to roll down my cheeks, a sacramental sign of the numinosity of what was occurring.

This experience occurred within a month of the first anniversary of my mother's death. The previous year had been a year of grieving. In fact, the grieving had started even a year and a half prior to her death. My mother, Grace, had been ill and aging and I participated in the pain of her diminishments. Then she suffered a stroke and spent the last eleven months of her life hospitalized and then in a nursing home mostly comatose until she died.

My brother and sisters and I had two years of grieving. We had all continually shared ourselves with our mother during that final year. Each one in his and her own way ministered to her and carried on a relationship with her. But consciously or unconsciously we each bore our own sorrow and the unfinished story of this woman who loved each of us to the end according to her gifts and limitations—as each of us did her.

Mother's funeral was beautiful in every way. I felt that all her children and grandchildren celebrated her birth into eternal life and the life she had shared with each of them. Grace died on June 15, and was buried on June 19, one day before the twentieth anniversary of my father's death. This appeared to me to be no small coincidence as I had had a strong experience of his presence during that year and felt he was involved in caring for her.

Nevertheless, I found myself often overwhelmed with grief during the months that followed. Often I would burst out crying at unexpected times and I frequently found myself in uncontrollable sobbing. The events of my mother's last years continued to be tragic to me and I grieved over all that had happened to her, as well as over my loss of her and all she had been to me.

In the midst of this grieving I had my experience. I found myself on the ground beside a beautiful lake. God appeared to me as a huge weeping willow tree. It was so big that it covered me, creating a wall-like curtain around me so that I could grieve and weep in total privacy. I did so and God received all my grief and all my sobs. My anguish ceased when I saw my father and mother coming out of the side of the tree. They appeared to be in their thirties, not young, not old. They came up to me and embraced me. After that my mother faded into the background. My father, looking well and vibrant (he had died after years combating Parkinson's disease), saw someone from afar and beckoned. My brother, the oldest, came in and my father shook his hand and hugged him enthusiastically. Following my brother was his wife and each of their children. Each one my father greeted with smiles, hugs, and hand clasps. I was amazed by it all. The ritual continued. Once again my father looked up and beckoned. In came my brother-in-law followed by my oldest sister, their two married girls, and families. My father greeted each one enthusiastically. Now, once again, he looked up and beckoned and the husband of the sister just a little younger than I came along, followed by my sister and all their children. Each one was clasped by the hand and hugged. And still to my astonishment my father beckoned once more and this time my youngest sister came along. Mother appeared at this time with the arrival of her youngest and both my father and mother embraced her. Immediately following the youngest came her husband and their two children. I was thoroughly amazed at all that took place. Then everyone disappeared, my parents faded away in the God-tree from whence they had come and the weeping willow tree itself disappeared. I was left alone under a huge blossoming cherry tree.

I cannot describe in words the effect this has had on me. Since then I have been at peace regarding my mother's death and all the events that preceded it. I am at a new place in my life since this experience. It will always be memorable. I know it was a turning point in my life. I have integrated her joys and sorrows and my own regarding her. Having gone through the grieving I am in this experience not only celebrating Grace's eternal life, but my father's and the eternal life that awaits each of us. I know experientially now the ongoing relationship we have with our living dead. Because of this experience I have let my parents go. They have let each of us go in peace and blessings.

I know that this experience of God as my weeping willow tree has implanted in me a greater wisdom about my own life and life in general. The weeping willow tree turned into a blossoming cherry tree. Alone under that blossoming cherry tree I am now expectant. I have memories of a significant cherry tree in my childhood and I feel now like a child set free to go forth and experience the beauty of life. Wisdom tells me that even the pain and suffering of life is redemptive, and this is freeing in itself. I know that in this experience I have become more who I am called to be.

I have no doubt that my God-tree experience was a movement away from a sense of responsibility regarding my parents and my family. The tears I shed so profusely were not only the final grieving but a sign of a much needed relinquishing of an ego stance of fifty years. "When tears accompany my depression it is often a sign that I am trying to let go of my perfectionist tendencies, my exclusionary self, or my need to be always in control" (Zullo:10). This kind of wisdom is personified in the prayer of St. Teresa that Alcoholics Anonymous has adopted:

> Lord, grant me the grace to change the things that can be changed, to accept the things that cannot be changed and the wisdom to know the difference.

Perhaps that was the symbolism in my father's prominence and taking charge. His illness had made him unable to take charge in real life. Was he not now freeing my siblings and me from a responsibility that always marked our ego. This psychic experience was a release from an identity that needed to be broken. Like Jung I can say, "This identity and my heroic idealism had to be abandoned, for there are higher things than the ego's will, and to these one must bow (*Memories, Dreams, Reflections:*181).

Yet in my vision, the feminine God, the weeping willow, received me where I was, gave me the privacy to grieve uncontrollably, and took me in. Now I was ready to be fathered. My father moved me out of the situation of grief into the reality of life. Each of us is alive and that is good. My parents' feelings about each of us are loving and hopeful, filled with friendliness and blessing. Integration in my parents has occurred. My mother does not have to be the one acting. She can step back and my father can take command. I can relinquish all responsibility for what was. Jung's words are true "Man [or woman] is never helped in his sufferings by what he thinks for himself, but only by revelation of a wisdom greater than his own. It is this which lifts him out of his distress" (*Modern Man in Search of a Soul:*241).

This religious experience of mine brings together in a gestalt a multiplicity of forms of religious experience. There was a sense of God as the Holy One, but it was a maternal presence, all-knowing and all-caring and all-receiving. It was not a presence that lifted me out of my grief and caused me to transcend it. It was a presence that received me and created for me the privacy I needed to express fully the depths of my sorrow. It was a new experience of contingency insofar as I know that my life and my well-being is in the hands of this God of ours. I could not consciously bring an end to my grieving. I could not will a happy conclusion. I was and am totally dependent on forces outside myself. Paradoxically this did not mean that I did not have my part to play, my homework to do. But in the end I was given a grace. This healing is gift, and more than I could have ever expected.

Experience of the Holy

Many religious experiences fall into the category of an experience of the Holy as presence and as contingency. All the classic world religions have the experience of the Holy as their primal roots. We see the experience of the Holy as presence in the story of Moses and the burning bush. While Moses was tending the flock, God appeared to him as a fire flaming out of a bush. To his surprise the burning bush was not being consumed. Intrigued, Moses surrendered to his curiosity and went to examine the remarkable sight to see why the bush was not burning. Obviously, the Lord was counting on such a reaction from Moses. Moses, it seems, surrendered to the Child in himself.

> When the Lord saw him coming over to look at it more closely, God called out to him from the bush, "Moses! Moses!" He answered, "Here I am." God said, "Come no nearer! Remove the sandals from your feet, for the place where you stand is holy ground. I am the God of your father" (Ex. 3:4–6)

Moses' senses took in a remarkable scene and he responded. He responded to the call of his name in this strange fashion. This place was holy not only because the Lord chose to make himself known to Moses on this spot but because on this spot the Lord made known to Moses his call: "Come now! I will send you to Pharaoh to lead my people, the Israelites, out of Egypt." Moses is having an intense encounter with his own roots: "I am the God of your *father* . . . the God of Abraham, the God of Isaac, the God of Jacob" (Ex. 3:6). He is having a lesson on mission and call, and on heroism and protest. But Moses is not to be left on his own. He has the lasting memory of the burning bush and his encounter with the Holy as well as the promise of God, "I will be with you," and the gift of the divine name, "tell the Israelites, I AM sent me to you" (Ex. 3:12, 14).

Moses' experience of the Holy, evoked by his own disposition of curiosity and wonder, was the occasion for his profound call and mission and the assurance of God's presence and power at his disposal.

Jesus had a similar experience at his baptism. He, too, responded to the situation at hand. Jesus was involved in this religious ritual of purification. He would go down and participate. What proceeded was a profound experience of the Holy, the presence of God, God's claim on him, and an affirmation that clearly from all that followed implied a call and a vocation.

> After Jesus was baptized, he came up from the water and behold, the heavens were opened for him, and he saw the Spirit of God descending like a dove and coming upon him. And a voice came from the heavens, saying, "This is my beloved Son, with whom I am well pleased." (Mt. 3:16–17)

Bill Wilson, Founder of Alcoholics Anonymous

A more modern and contemporary experience of the Holy is the experience of Bill Wilson at the midpoint of his life. His profound experience of the Holy was also in a sense a commission because it was the basis of his founding Alcoholics Anonymous.

Bill had a history of alcoholism. It was the cause of his physical and emotional deterioration. He had gone through many periods of recovery and new intense vigor but always fell again, a victim of his own obsession. In the course of his many battles against drink he had the good fortune to come into contact with one of the first doctors to acknowledge alcohol as a disease and not the result of a lack of willpower or a moral defect (Alcoholic Anonymous World Services:102). But even with his help Bill Wilson could not persevere in his abstinence. The doctor finally gave Bill only a year before drink would cause him to be either dead or insane. Bill had looked into "religion" as a way to sobriety. He had tried everything. Finally, consumed by the cancer of alcohol, facing the abyss of death or insanity, helpless and desperate, he once again signed himself into a hospital.

In a state of poverty and deflation, Bill Wilson sat on his hospital cot and cried out from his depths, "If there is a God, let him show himself!"

> What happened next was electric. Suddenly, my room blazed with an indescribable white light. I was seized with an ecstasy beyond description. Every joy I had known was pale by comparison. The light, the ecstasy—I was conscious of nothing else for a time. Then, seen in the mind's eye, there was a mountain. I stood upon its summit, where a great wind blew. A wind, not of air, but of spirit. In great, clean strength, it blew right through me. Then came the blazing thought "You are a free man." (Alcoholic Anonymous World Services:121)

Bill remained enraptured for a while and when he finally came again into contact with the walls of his own room, the "here and now," he found himself in a strange state of quiet, peace, and calm. He felt himself to be in a "presence" and he knew himself to be on the "shores of a new world." This was the turning point of Bill Wilson's life. This was his conversion.

> Savoring my new world, I remained in this state for a long time. I seemed to be possessed by the absolute, and the curious conviction deepened that no matter how wrong things seemed to be, there could be no question of the ultimate rightness of God's universe. For the first time, I felt that I was loved and could love in return. I thanked my God, who had given me a glimpse of His absolute self. Even though a pilgrim upon an uncertain highway, I need be concerned no more, for I had glimpsed the great beyond. (Alcoholic Anonymous World Services:121)

At the time of this experience Bill had just completed his thirty-ninth year and he had another thirty-nine years to live. This experience of the holy was more than memorable. It changed his life. It gave him life. After that experience he never doubted the existence of God and he never took another drink. For Bill Wilson, this religious experience was the source of decisions consummated in the depths of his psyche and he became through it the whole person and the generative person he was meant to be.

A Child's Experience of the Holy

Not all our experiences of the Holy are as profound as Bill Wilson's. But every true experience of the Holy as the three characteristics of religious experience mentioned: it is memorable, it is a source of decision, and it is a cause of integration. As a nine-year-old I remember trying to learn to float. Because I am an intuitive type, many physical things came hard to me. I had difficulty pronouncing words and was delayed in talking. Skating, bicycle riding, and floating on water took much effort. Of course, to float you must "let go"; it takes a form of trust and faith. After days of attempting to float only to sink, one day I made my usual attempt and to my utter amazement I was indeed floating on top of the water. I looked up at the sky from that position of being buoyed by the ocean and I said, "Oh! This is what they mean by prayer." That little nine-year-old girl experienced the Holy and connected it to what people had been calling prayer. Although I had received sacraments and said "prayers," I believe that that was the first time I prayed. And my prayer was an attitude, a state of being created by the Holy inviting and calling me in that situation. Because of that experience of the presence of God I became a prayer, and I became more myself, more the one I was uniquely called to be. The experience of the Holy always opens one to a dimension of oneself and invites one to participate in the Other.

As one gets in touch with the deepest parts of the Self in religious experience and is oriented toward the mystery of God and life, one is in the grips of Wisdom itself. In personal psychic experiences one comes to a personal faith or to a new dimension of faith. As Jung tells us,

The seat of faith . . . is not consciousness but spontaneous religious experience, which brings the individual's faith into immediate relation with God." (*The Undiscovered Self*:100)

Such experiences give a person a sense of identity, relatedness, uniqueness, and meaning. Because of religious experience a person comes to know a depth and a breadth that tells them that they are. Religious experience gives one a face and a name so that one is not a stranger, one is no longer unknown, dispossessed, unrelated, going nowhere.

At mid-life it becomes essential that we allow the remembering and the recollecting of our religious experiences to renew, reawaken, and reenergize us. At the heart of our religious experiences we find our true Self and true Wisdom. Here we discover and reconnect to the mysteries of life and to our personal story and myth.

Secular Religious Experiences

It is possible that someone at mid-life has had no experience of the Holy, of God's presence, or of one's own contingency. Such a person can open herself to the religious experiences, or the "peak moments," that have marked her journey, are memorable, were the source of decisions, and were integrating. Gregory Baum tells us that many of the truly religious experiences of life are the so-called secular ones such as friendship, conscience, truth, love, encounter, birth, death, solidarity, and protest (63–81). He further names for us the religious experiences embedded in the deep questions that arise in our experiences of sin, evil, and despair (81–86).

It is essential that we acknowledge the moments of our life that have helped us to become the unique person each of us is. Just as we celebrate the Exodus or Passover; the birth, death, and resurrection of Jesus; the birth of our nation; and the heroes and heroines of our land, we must learn to name, revere, and celebrate the religious experiences that make us.

But past religious experiences are not enough. We must be open to the numinous in the present. At the midpoint in one's life, as at no other time, each of us must ask, "Have I any religious experience and immediate relation to God, and hence that certainty which will keep me, as an individual, from dissolving in the crowd?" (Jung, *The Undiscovered Self:*100).

As one looks back to the peak moments of one's life (those that are memorable, were the source of decisions, and caused a greater integration), one must be willing to acknowledge the divine touch that was present. Strange though it may seem, Jung assures us that

> experience shows that many neuroses are caused by the fact that people blind themselves to their own religious promptings because of a childhood passion for rational enlightenment." (*Modern Man in Search of a Soul:*69)

Has someone ever come into your life and made a profound difference? It could have been a teacher, counselor, therapist, the author of a book you read, a lecturer, or a chance encounter that lasted only a few minutes. Looking back you can say that because you met that person you did this or changed that, met so and so, discovered what you like to do or are best at, and so on. Wisdom came to you through that encounter. You made certain decisions and came to be more yourself. Can you not see that in this encounter your ongoing creation took place in a remarkable way? Was not such an encounter a grace and a gift?

I am calling an encounter like this a secular religious experience. But in reality there is no such thing. All is holy: "By virtue of the creation and, still more, of the incarnation, nothing here below is profane for those who know how to see. On the contrary everything is sacred" (Teilhard:66).

Friendship can be a profound experience that puts one in touch with one's own goodness as well as giving one the joy of intimate sharing with another. Spending time with a friend is a consolation. It lightens our burdens and increases our pleasures. Being with a friend or friends gives one something to look forward to. Having a friend to talk with, share our values, and challenge us can be a genuine source of Wisdom. Husbands and wives can be friends. Often friends are found in our immediate family. Friendships outside the family are important for our self-esteem and the broadening of our horizon. Deep friendships can be found between men as well as between

women. In the Hebrew Scriptures we have the classic friendships of David and Jonathan and of Ruth and Naomi.

One must be willing to put time and energy into friendship.
In order to have a good friend, one must be a good friend.
There is a mystery present in every genuine friendship. It is the
mystery of mutuality. Every friendship calls for both giving and
receiving. Often one must be willing to spend oneself for one's
friend.

Genuine love is a religious experience. It can be the romantic
love of a man and woman, the love of friends, parental love, the
love of a child for a parent, or familial love. As Robert Johnson
tells us,

> Love is an archetype. To love is a preformed tendency in
> humans, part of the primordial blueprint for our human way
> of feeling, relating, and acting toward others. It finds its way
> into every person and every culture. (1986:31)

Love of another or others gives meaning to our lives. "Love
makes the world go round." The power to love is ingrained in
the human psyche. Romantic love, erotic love, marital love,
parental love, familial love, love of nation, love of God, love of
Christ, love of beauty, love of the world, love of one's profession
or life's work, love of neighbor, love of nature, love of the
universe—whenever our heart opens to receive another with
graciousness and receptivity, whenever we look kindly on and
wish well toward another or others, we are loving. Love connects us to others. Love expands our horizon. Love is behind
the decisions we make. Love makes us more real and whole.
Love humbles us to open ourselves. Love calls us to spend
ourselves for another.

Erotic Love as Religious Experience

There are many pros and cons to the sexual revolution. One
grace has been the attention given to the human ability to
experience erotic love. The Book of Hosea began the tradition
of describing the relation between Yahweh and Israel in terms
of erotic lovers and marriage. Later, in the Christian Scriptures,
both John and Paul use the same imagery to express the union

between Christ and the church. In times past, consecrated virgins in the Christian tradition were called "brides of Christ."

There is much mystery about the prophet Hosea but we do know that his own painful experience with his unfaithful wife, Gomer, deepened his prophetic message and call. Gomer came to symbolize faithless Israel. Hosea remained faithful to Gomer despite her acts of adultery and he longed to bring her back to the days of their first love, days that were fresh, pure, and ecstatic. Hosea knew that if constant love could come from his heart Yahweh's love must also be constant for Israel, who was playing the harlot and being unfaithful to Yahweh. Israel's infidelity took the form of idolatry, materialism, triumphalism, and ruthless oppression of the poor. Yahweh longed to seduce Israel and call her back to the joy of her first love.

> So I will allure her; I will lead her into the desert and speak to her heart. . . . She shall respond there as in the days of her youth." (Hos. 2:16, 17b)

The Song of Songs is another revelation in the Hebrew Scriptures of the sacredness and meaning of erotic love and of the depth of the marriage union. As a portrayal of ideal human love it is a poetic masterpiece, proclaiming the glory of the human body in its greatest act of lovemaking. Like all great poems, it has a wealth of symbolic meanings and so it also portrays the love of God for his people. The Lord is the lover and we are the beloved.

This "Greatest of Songs" begins:

> Let him kiss me with kisses of his mouth!
> More delightful is your love than wine!
> Your name spoken is a spreading perfume—
> that is why the maidens love you. Draw me!

The Song goes on. The Lover sees his Beloved as an "enclosed garden. . . . a garden fountain, a well of water flowing fresh from Lebanon" (4:12, 15). She answers:

> Arise, north wind! Come south wind!
> blow upon my garden that its perfumes may spread abroad.
> Let my lover come to his garden and eat its choice fruits. (4:16)

I have come to my garden, my sister, my bride;
I gather my myrrh and my spices,
I eat my honey and my sweetmeats,
I drink my wine and my milk.
Eat, friends; drink! Drink freely of love! (5:1)

How beautiful you are, how pleasing,
my love, my delight!
Your very figure is like a palm tree,
your breasts are like clusters.
I said: I will climb the palm tree,
I will take hold of its branches,
Now let your breasts be like clusters of the vine
and the fragrance of your breath like apples,
And your mouth like an excellent wine—(7:7–10)

God's gifts to humanity are numerous. We are made in God's
image and likeness. We are filled with God's Spirit. Our intricate
bodies are made for ecstasy and erotic lovemaking. This greatest of transcendent moments creates in the heart of the lovers a
love for life, an affirmation of the goodness of one's own being,
and a willingness to give intense pleasure to the beloved as well
as to receive. How beautiful when the fruit of new life, a child,
can originate in this love. How the child of this love must be
blessed in her psyche! In the mid-life years the child born out
of erotic love can be the Child in each of us.

This may all seem unreal, too idealistic. And that is a pity. We
must open ourselves to the fullness of life. The man and
woman gifted with such a love can overcome all difficulties,
transcend all limitations. Such a love is an expression of God.
Such a love brings together the conscious and unconscious and
is an expression of Self, an experience of the Holy.

During orgasm, in fact, some people fall into complete unconsciousness, which may last a matter of seconds or even minutes—"la petite mort," the little death. Perhaps it is precisely
to this condition that all our passion has drawn us, to the place
of no-place, the time of no-time. Having arrived at this point
of sublime nothingness, we return to the world of ordinary
consciousness, realizing only that what we have most desired
we can least recall. (Leonard:22)

Attitude is everything. A wrong attitude can deprive us of great joys and blessings. I recall watching a television show called "Birth of a Child" with my mother. We both sat enthralled, I who had never given birth and she who had borne five children. Afterward, in amazement and consternation, she said, "I never experienced any of that. Even though I had five children I was made unconscious for all five deliveries. I never experienced the birth of a child." There was sorrow in her voice. She had experienced that film as an awakening. It was for her, as it was for me, a religious experience. The birth of a child can be that for someone. Birth is archetypal and it can release in you an overwhelming gratitude for life. For many a person it can lift them out of their own egocentricity into the wonder of another tiny new being. The human person is willing to die in order to make room in the heart, style of life, very flesh, for this one filled with promise. Wisdom is present in this experience of Self, in this experience of another.

We are looking at the built-in religious experiences of human life. The thought of a nuclear holocaust is particularly terrifying for those who have had the religious experience of the Holy, or who have come to know the gift that life is. A nuclear holocaust is unthinkable to those who have experienced the religious event of friendship, erotic love, or the birth of a child. Religious experience gives meaning to our personal life and makes the mystery of life, with its joys and sorrows, a divine encounter.

Religious experience engages us in life consciously and unconsciously. We come to appreciate the many sides of self and others. Life becomes a choice wine and we come to desire to drink it to the full because of religious experience.

Work as Religious Experience

One's life work can be a religious experience. When our whole being is involved in and dedicated to our work we are lifted out of ourselves and into the joy of dedication and creativity. Work, too, is archetypal. Teilhard reminds us that the

> closeness of our union with him [God] is in fact determined by the exact fulfillment of the least of our tasks . . . God . . . awaits us every instant in our action, in the work of the

moment. There is a sense in which he is at the tip of my pen, my spade, my brush, my needle—of my heart and of my thought. (64)

I recall that in the midst of my own mid-life crisis one of the memorable moments that lifted me into prayer occurred while I was preparing stringbeans for a meal. I had been doing spiritual reading during the day. As I handled the beans I was drawn to feel their texture; to look at their color, size, and shape; to examine the ends as I clipped them off. An overwhelming feeling of graciousness came to me. I felt enveloped in goodness and love, all emanating from the beans in my hands. I touched a bean to my face and lips in amazement. The bean signified for me my life, all of life, God's life. In those few instants, I knew that all was holy. All would work out for the good.

> Why should there not be men [or women] vowed to the task of exemplifying, by their lives, the general sanctification of human endeavor?—men [or women] whose common religious ideal would be to give a full and conscious explanation of the divine possibilities or demands which any worldly occupation implies, men [or women] in a word who would devote themselves, in the fields of thought, art, industry, commerce and politics, etc. to carrying out in the sublime spirit these demands—the basic tasks which form the very bonework of human society." (Teilhard:67)

Teilhard calls us to experience fully the spur of the intoxication of advancing God's kingdom in every domain of human life (69). He himself dedicated "body and soul to the sacred duty of research" and he urges us to "test every barrier, try every path, plumb every abyss . . . God wills it" (69–70).

All the effort we put into life—into our stewardship of the earth, our chosen careers, and our life's work—can be the source of spiritual growth and our greatest religious experience.

> Of its very nature, work is a manifold instrument of detachment, provided a man [or woman] gives himself to it faithfully and without rebellion. In the first place it implies

effort and a victory over inertia. And then, however interesting and intellectual it may be . . . work is always accompanied by the painful pangs of birth. . . . An honest workman [or woman] not only surrenders his calm and peace once and for all, but must learn continually to jettison the form which this labor or art or thought first took, and go in search of new forms. . . . Over and over again he must go beyond himself, tear himself away from himself, leaving behind him his most cherished beginnings. . . . Those who spread their sails in the right way to the winds of the earth will always find themselves borne by a current towards the open sea. The more nobly a man [or woman] wills and acts, the more avid he becomes for great and sublime aims to pursue.

He will no longer be content with family, country and the renumerative aspects of his work. He will want wider organizations to create, new paths to blaze, causes to uphold, truths to discover, an ideal to cherish and defend. So gradually, the worker no longer belongs to himself. Little by little the great breath of the universe has insinuated itself into him through the fissure of his humble but faithful action, has broadened aim, raised him up, borne him on. (Teilhard:71–72)

One's work can be experienced even as the central core of one's being. Jung himself discovered his life myth to be involved in the pursuit of the relationship of the inner and outer world. He dedicated himself to the service of the psyche and to gaining knowledge of the secret of the human personality and the "cure of souls."

There are two volumes of his letters. In the second volume, we find the letters he wrote during the last ten years of his life (1951–1961). They tell us how he carried on his work from his seventy-sixth to his eighty-sixth year. Laurence Van der Post tells us that he visited Jung shortly before his death and found him researching the passage over his door, "Called or not called, God shall be there." Surely God is at the heart of the careers and life's work of all of us. Wisdom is found in the human need to work, in the adventure of work, in the tasks of caring for the earth and carrying on the commerce of human life. Work itself is archetypal, a pattern built into each of us.

In the course of our own work, Anne Brennan and I once visited a woman in her sixties who was dying of cancer. The nurses told us that she was in the last stages of cancer and that her pain was great. When we went in we found her alive with her work, her cause. She had been watching us talk on the video intercom and so she knew what we were about. We had been talking abut the life cycle and its four births and four deaths. "I don't know," she said, "whether I even want to go to heaven. I'm sure when I get there I'll find two floors, one for men and one for women. The men will have the upper floor and it will be better equipped as usual."

We were delighted and inspired. Our dying woman was filled with protest. She had been involved in the women's movement and it still occupied her mind and heart. She would carry her work with her into eternity. Her cause was doing a better job than any painkiller. Like Jesus on the cross carrying on his work with the "good thief" even in the midst of his own dying, she was involved in her call even to the end. Like Jesus, I believe, she must even now be about it. "But after I am raised to life, I will go to Galilee ahead of you" (Mk. 14:28).

Philemon

Philemon was the name that Carl Jung gave one of the archetypal images of Wisdom within himself. In his autobiography, *Memories, Dreams, Reflections,* he tells us

> Psychologically, Philemon represented superior insight. He was a mysterious figure to me. At times he seemed to me quite real, as if he were a living personality. I went walking up and down the garden with him, and to me he was what the Indians call a guru. (183)

He first encountered the archetypal image of Philemon in a dream. He seemed in some way to evolve out of an image of Elijah, who appeared in his dreams with Salome. Many years later he recognized Elijah and Salome as personifications of logos and eros. When Jung first encountered Philemon in his dream he did not understand the significance of the dream image. He painted a picture of the wise old man as he had seen him.

We can follow Jung's example regarding the images that come to us in dreams, daydreams, imaginings, fantasies, and visions. We can give a name to a particular image. If it is a

Wisdom figure, it could appear as a biblical image, as one of the saints, as an historic figure, or, like the case of Philemon, as a strange and fascinating old man. In the case of a Wisdom figure, the image is usually an old man or old woman or a representative of ancient times or of the past because the Wisdom within us is a legacy of generations. Wisdom is timeless. Wisdom knew us before we were born. Wisdom knows all about life and death. Wisdom knows the intricacies of our bodies and our souls. The archetype of wisdom is part of the collective unconscious of each of us and connects us to past, present, and future.

> Our souls as well as our bodies are composed of individual elements which were already present in the ranks of our ancestors. The "newness" in the individual psyche is an end-lessly varied recombination of age-old components. (Jung, *Memories, Dreams, Reflections*:235)

After naming our image of Wisdom we, too, can paint or draw it. Like Jung, we can engage our Wisdom image in conversations. This kind of "inner work" is part of the care of soul we must engage in, especially in the second half of life. Honoring our Wisdom figure in this way may very likely cause us to have further dreams or fantasies where the wise old man or the wise old woman in us is schooling us about our own life situations as well as about the greater mysteries of life.

For Saint Paul the image of Christ was the archetypal image of Wisdom who directed his inner and outer life, from the moment of his first encounter with him on the road to Damascus throughout the whole second half of his life. The conversion of Paul as we know it came from his encounter with the risen Christ. He had been empowered "that, if he should find any men or women who belonged to the Way, he might bring them back to Jerusalem in chains" (Acts 9:2) While he was traveling, a light flashed from the sky and Paul fell to the ground. He heard a voice, "Saul, Saul, why are you persecuting me?" "Who are you, sir?" he asked. The voice answered, "I am Jesus, whom you are persecuting. Now get up and go into the city and you will be told what you must do" (Acts 9:4–6).

Wisdom: Gift of the Spirit

At mid-life each of us wants to be opened up to the store and treasure of wisdom within us. We long to encounter Christ or the Wisdom figure within us as the disciples did on the road to Emmaus and as Paul did on the road to Damascus. We, too, are looking for the way. This way for each of us is embedded within us. The hidden Self has the key to the spiritual growth we are being called to and the good that we are to accomplish. Mid-life spirituality demands of us a conversion to the way for us and to loving fidelity to that way. Wisdom allows us to find the way, the inner blueprint for our days, nights, and years, that will allow us to become the self we are called to be.

Wisdom is the gift of the Spirit. It is integral to human life and the human spirit, both gifts of God to us. Wisdom can and often does arise in us at unexpected moments. Wisdom also comes slowly and cumulatively as we gain in years and experience, both gifts of God. We can ask for Wisdom, Wisdom to interpret our life and our own life situations, our particular way and direction, our relationships and engagements. Every person can ask for and expect the Wisdom of the Spirit, a gift of God to each of us. Wisdom is our birthright by reason of our humanity. Jesus calls us to experience this even as he did:

> Ask and you will receive; seek and you will find; knock and the door will be opened to you. For everyone who asks, receives; and the one who seeks, finds; and to the one who knocks, the door will be opened. (Lk. 11:9–10)

Let each one of us continue to ask for this experience:

> In the stillness of my expectant heart let Wisdom arise, O Lord. In the midst of turmoil, conflict, and suffering, let Wisdom arise, O Lord. In joy and ecstasy, let Wisdom arise, O Lord. In the fullness of life and in each diminishment, let Wisdom arise, O Lord. As this life draws to an end and the new life approaches, let Wisdom arise, O Lord.
> Spirit of Wisdom, when I am in the midst of experiencing my own sin and evil give me the Wisdom to know my own goodness. When I am inflated and identify with my goodness,

blinded to my own evil and sin, give me the Wisdom to know the truth. Great Wisdom abiding in me, create me anew, bring me to my own fullness and the fullness of time. Wisdom, let me be the source of bringing others and this world of ours to your fullness of time.

24

Reflective Exercises

1. Scripture encourages us to have dreams and see visions. Contact your wishes and dreams for your life now. Make a list of them. Circle the four or five that you most want to become realities. Now, choose the one you want most of all. Sit back and make yourself as relaxed as possible. Listen to the sounds in and around you. Pay attention to your breathing. Imagine that your dream has come true. Imagine how you feel with this new reality. Now, imagine how it came about. What brought your dream to completion?

   Now, if you choose, write down:
   a) your dream or wish
   b) how you experienced yourself when your dream or wish became a reality
   c) the steps or process you went through to make the dream or wish a reality
   d) a prayer to God or your Wisdom figure (Ask the Lord to help you to realize your dream if it is an expression of your inner Wisdom.)

2. Follow the same procedure as above for the dreams you have for friends and relatives and the world. Locate one dream for each and visualize the dream come true. Visualize how it became a reality. Visualize your part, if any, in making the dream a reality. (If your dream is the fruit of your inner wisdom perhaps it would help if you shared this experience with the person.)

3. Look back over your decades and ask yourself what, if any, experiences of the Holy you have had?
   a) In prayer take the time to recall each experience as it

was. See how it has influenced your life and made you who you are today.

b) Share this part of your life with a friend.

c) See whether you can put your experience into an art form: painting, sculpture, poem, song, or prose.

d) Compose a prayer of thanksgiving for your own personal experience of the Holy.

4. Recollect the secular experiences of your life that were religious: experiences that were memorable, were a source of decision, and were integrating.

a) Recall each experience. See how each one caused you to know yourself, make important decisions, and become more who you really are. Understand how each experience has made you who you are today.

b) Put each experience into some art form.

c) Make up a litany of prayer for each of your experiences.

d) Share this important part of yourself with a friend.

5. Look back now on all your peak moments, all your religious experiences, and find a myth or symbol that represents these key moments in your life. (It may be a Scripture passage, a symbol from nature, or a religious symbol.) Let each religious experience with its myth and symbol occupy your mind and heart in prayer. Take days or weeks to do this as needed.

6. Recall now your own mid-life crisis and transition, be it past or present. Allow yourself to feel the range of emotions it involved or involves. Take colored pencils or crayon and draw a picture of your mid-life crisis and transition.

7. Be still and quiet. Allow yourself to sink into your inner depths where your Wisdom abides. Rest in that Wisdom. Rest in the Spirit of God.

8. Think about how old you are now and what age you would like to live to.

a) Imagine now all the days of the rest of your life. See yourself living to conclusion this life you have been given.

b) See yourself living all the days left to you as you would like to live them.

c) Imagine your final days and your death. See yourself being born into eternal life.

9. Think about what you believe about eternal life. What parts of Scripture, if any, speak to you about your fourth death and your fourth rebirth?

10. Think about the many needs of the world today. What evils need to be overcome? Scripture tells us that all the world is groaning to be born anew. What are the groanings and cries of our cultures? How can you respond in prayer and action?

11. Wisdom dwells within you. Wisdom is in your house.
    a) Write or dance your own prayer to Wisdom.
    b) Acknowledge your own personal experience of Wisdom.
    c) Call on Wisdom as you experience your need for her in your own life now.

12. Draw up a list of people you admire for their Wisdom. What wisdom did each express? Ask these people living or dead to help you to contact the same Wisdom.

Appendix

Theological and Psychological
Background of This Book

In this book we have relied on those theologies that take the contemporary secular world very seriously, not as an "enemy" but as an arena of God's activity. These theologies have gone beyond naive optimism about modern human progress and modern secularism. They are profoundly indebted to biblical historical criticism and to the extension of its hermeneutical approaches to doctrines and dogmas. In this attempt to begin to sketch a Judeo-Christian mid-life spirituality, we have relied on theologies that are fiercely committed to the Judeo-Christian revelation, but just as fiercely committed to the world's present and future. With them, we see Judeo-Christian truth and the symbols, myths, and rituals of Christianity as rooted in the historical Jesus, and simultaneously as eschatological, as an authentic interpretation, motivation, celebration, and critique of the whole human enterprise. These theologies, while truly committed, are not exclusivist. While seeing a universal validity for the Christian message, they are in open, mutually enriching dialogue with all the sciences, with all other religions, and with agnosticism and atheism. Further, they focus not only on the contents of revelation but on the human subject of revelation.

For example, underpinning this study is a theologically reinterpreted doctrine of creation and incarnation. The historical criticism of the Genesis account, the theory of evolution, the scientific explorations of the universe, and so on, have called into question the vision of creation as complete and perfect "in

258

the beginning," as well as the whole fall redemption version of the meaning of history.

Creation theology reinterpreted becomes radically historical. It attempts to reunite creation and redemption, nature and supernature, the division between the first and second creations. Resurrection and eschatology are integral to such a new theology of creation.

Incarnation, in this same kind of dynamic worldview is not seen as a kind of miraculous intrusion of a wholly other divine being at a certain point in human history. Incarnation *is* creation, as epiphany, manifestation, and embodiment of God. A new moment in the history of incarnation is the emergence of self-reflective human persons, embodied spirits who are conscious of themselves. The history of this growing self-awareness is, at the same time, a history of the notions of the immanence and transcendence of God. Jesus, as the incarnate Word is a wholly new yet, at the same time, continuous development from within humanity as open to transcendence. (We have treated this further in *Mid-Life: Psychological and Spiritual Perspectives,* pp. 66–83.)

Christian spirituality flows from this core of the faith-content of Christianity: God living humanly in Christ and therefore in all humanity. Looking to the history of spirituality for the Christian spiritual giants, one gets a sense of the anthropology and theology they were living out. One sees that they were true to their own historical situations and at the same time to their own life experience and their own uniqueness. They lived the Gospels, avoiding dangerous extremes or inhuman deviations.

Today we have a heightened awareness that aging and stages are constitutive of human life and human experience; an authentic spirituality always flows from how a person lives out his or her theology throughout the whole life cycle. It involves expanding horizons and ongoing conversion in effective love of God, self, and all of creation.

In the individual's living out a kind of incarnational theology and spirituality, psychology (and especially Jungian psychology) has much to say to the mid-life Christian today. We have seen the need to find a middle course between a spiritual theology so jealous of its prerogatives, so supernatural and otherworldly as to be closed to the insights of psychology, and a too facile identification of elements of Jung's psychology with elements of the Christian mysteries.

Jungian psychology has often been described as not just a theory and practice of transformation but as an alternative to the traditional religious paths of both the West and the East. He has thus been accused by theologically informed critics of attempting to undermine Judaism and Christianity. At the other end of the spectrum, Jung has been defended by other theologically informed Jungian students who have praised his insights on Christian themes and doctrines and see in his work not only a valuable resource for Christian theology but a challenge and help to the development of doctrine and the revitalization of the tasks of Christian living and pastoring souls.

Was Jung a Christian apologist? Or, was he mounting a hidden and devastating attack on Christian doctrine under the guise of empirical psychology? Was he a heretical Gnostic or a modern agnostic? Or, was he a Christian healer of modern souls and of Christianity itself?

No less a respected theological giant than Martin Buber warned that Jung's relationship to all religions, including Christianity, was infected by a kind of new religion of psychological reductionism. Because Jung emphasized "knowledge" over "faith," Buber believed that he thereby denied the transcendence of the Godhead. He warned that behind Jung's stance as an empirical psychologist he had the hidden agenda of proclaiming a new religion. Many of the other theological critics of Jung voice similar concerns.

Victor White, a Roman Catholic theologian, was extremely sympathetic to Jung's work. He and Jung had a warm and fruitful exchange of ideas from 1945, when White was forty, until their intellectual and emotional falling out in 1955. Victor White died in 1960, on the eve of the Second Vatican Council. White is among the first theologians who attempted to show that Jung's work precisely as empirical psychology would give scientific evidence for the existence of psychological structures and dynamics that correspond in striking ways to Christian teachings. When Father White sent Jung copies of his first publications (1945) about this, Jung wrote back,

> You are the only theologian I know who has really understood something of what the problem of psychology in our present

world means. You have seen its enormous implications. I cannot tell you how glad I am that I know a man, a theologian, who is conscientious enough to weigh my opinions on the basis of a careful study of my writings! . . . I envy you and all those enjoying full possession of Scholastic philosophy and I would be the first to welcome an explicit attempt to integrate the findings of psychology into the ecclesiastical doctrine. (*Letters* 1:383, 385)

Through the years of their collaboration, White explored the correlations and parallels between nature and grace, human experience and divine revelation, knowledge and faith, and concluded that Jung's psychology supported the idea that Christianity completes rather than contradicts human nature.

Thus, unlike Buber who saw Jung's work as undermining religion, White saw it as strengthening religion. Yet, White's break with Jung came when he, too, questioned whether Jung's relationship to Christianity was solely that of empirical scientist. White struggled with Jung's need to critique and revise certain Christian doctrines (for example, *privatio boni* definition of evil, and the Trinity). In *Answer to Job,* Jung seemed to White to have gone too far beyond presenting psychic facts to put his science at the service of religion.

Jung saw himself as empirical scientist, not as a philosopher or theologian. While he protested this again and again when he was accused of making metaphysical or theological statements, he also saw himself as reconnecting modern people to their ancestral religions. He saw himself reinterpreting Christian dogmas and symbols to those who had lost touch with the religious experience that underlies them. Miguel Serrano quotes Jung as saying, about five months before his death:

What I have tried to do is show the Christian what the Redeemer really is and what the resurrection is. Nobody today seems to know, or to remember, but the idea still exists in dreams. (Stein, 1985: 10, 11)

Jung was above all a doctor of souls concerned on the one hand with negative psychological effects of loss of faith and religious experience and on the other hand with the negative effects of the practice of some unhealthy kinds of religion.

Jung was the son of a Christian pastor whose own doubts and

struggles with religious belief came, Jung felt, because of a divorce of that belief from any religious experience. Jung thought this to be a cause for his father's mental breakdown and premature death. All his life, Jung was passionately concerned with knowing God, with a kind of immediate intuitive awareness of God. He believed that the religion of many Christians, like his father's, was belief divorced from any experience of the realities believed in, and he saw this as defective. In 1945 he wrote,

> It is of the highest importance that the educated and "enlightened" should know religious truth as a thing living in the human soul and not as an abstruse and unreasonable relic of the past. (*Letters* 1:387)

Theology today surely has recognized that faith is much more than intellectual belief and must involve a profound commitment and include at least some intuition of God. Experience is central to much current theological discussion. Karl Rahner's transcendental theology rests on an analysis of the individual human subject as displaying an openness and tendency toward an ultimate horizon of unconditional being in every experience of a particular being.

Jung's relationship to religion, and to Christianity in particular, was intense and extremely complex. He was aware over fifty years ago of an emerging interest in subjective reality and saw in the psyches of modern people a wave of curiosity concerning the occult and the *irrational* that was sweeping over the modern world. While in the 1940s, theologians were laboring to demonstrate the reasonableness of the Christian faith, he saw many people already taking an interest in astrology, spiritualism, and black magic. Jung recognized here possibilities for much superstition and moral and intellectual perversity.

Jung had a passionate interest in the damage certain religious ideas and kinds of piety could do to the human psyche.

> A strong case could be made that Jung's recommendations for abandoning the *privatio boni* definition of evil and for expanding the trinitarian into a quaternitarian doctrine of God were put forward because of his concern for the psychological well-being of practicing Christians. (Stein, 1985:13)

Jung was afraid that if evil was looked at as nonbeing (nothing but the absence of good) people would not take their own shadows seriously and that the future of humanity was dependent on this. For him, evil psychologically speaking was terribly real and it was a fatal mistake to diminish its power and reality metaphysically.

While Jung's doctrinal deviations were certainly related to his own psychology, it is a mistake to see them as merely narcissistic and reflective of his personal struggle for self-coherence (Homans, 1979). It is likewise a mistake to see them as merely a projection of a troubled father-son relationship. Jung was concerned about the healing not only of Christians but of Christianity per se, as Stein (1985) has so brilliantly argued. His relationship to Christianity was that of a psychotherapist who was applying his therapy to an ailing Christianity and Western culture as to a patient. Stein argues that the therapeutic relationship, with its central concern for transformation and the patient's health and wholeness, and with its highly complex internal psychodynamics, best describes the nature of Jung's relationship to Christianity, as expressed in his late writings on Christian themes. Jung himself never completely clarified the nature or the full meaning of his writings on Christianity. Yet, this strong urge toward healing possibly led him to the very heart of the culture's and the tradition's ailments and demanded that he at least try to offer some help.

In the recent attempts at dialogue among the various Christian branches and of Christians with other religions, with science, and even with atheists, the participants have learned that they cannot enter into true dialogue and expect to change others and remain unchanged themselves. In the process both partners are challenged and transformed.

Victor White—and any of us who enter into dialogue with Jungian psychology—cannot expect this science, any more than any other science, to be merely a handmaiden to our theology. While White attempted to hold fast to a long-standing Thomistic metaphysical and theological tradition, the analytical psychologist was subjecting that very tradition to the corrosive effects of psychological interpretation, as physics, biology, and geology had done before. Yet out of that very critique, Christian theology can rise phoenixlike with new vitality. The development of doctrine has always occurred in just this kind of struggle. For while the psyche cannot be identified with the transcendent Other, nor the evil in the psyche be attributed to evil in the transcendent Other, nor the mystery beyond be reduced to "pure psychic immanence," neither can doctrines and dogmas be identified with the mystery and transcendence to which they point. They are historically influenced expressions of unfathomable and inexpressible mystery.

At this point, the paternalistic cast of the trinitarian image of God is being subjected to a mounting theological critique from the feminine half of the human race. Jung's proposals for a quaternitarian doctrine and his celebration of the proclamation in 1950 of the dogma of Mary's assumption as the assimilation of the image of the feminine into the image of the Godhead may not be sound theology but it surely is a sound identification of one of the core areas in need of theological discussion and revision.

These theological issues and theological critiques of Jung's psychology lie behind this work, although they are not explicitly discussed. We have simply attempted to get on with the work of giving some direction for the spiritual growth of people in the second half of life, especially those who are Christian or who have been formed in and influenced by Western civilization. We obviously do not share the fears of those who think Jung has undermined Christianity but we do share the concern of those who feel that Jung is "dangerous" to Christian theology in the sense that his findings might bring some presuppositions into question. We share the caution of those who have not simply swallowed Jung's "theological" speculations whole (Brennan and Brewi, 1985:52–109). We share the belief of those who feel Jung's work must be wrestled with, admired, and disseminated.

In this book we have wrestled with Jung's thought and used his hermeneutical method to reinterpret various Christian doctrines and symbols in order to make them more accessible to the modern mid-life person who is turning to the spiritual with a thirst for meaning and for the inner life. Jung is one guide who has gone before who can show us how to clear away the debris that blocks the ancient streams from which our ancestors drew the waters of life. With Jung we need not reject the discoveries of modern science nor the riches of our own tradition, but with him we can claim the wisdom within to help us use the power that science and technology have placed in our hands.

Jung was convinced that the meaning of the second half of life was to be found in each of us serving culture in the broadest sense. Culture is everything that expands the mind and uplifts the spirit and gives transcendent meaning to life.

> In primitive tribes, we observe that old people are almost always the guardians of the mysteries and the laws and it is in these that the cultural heritage of the tribe is expressed. (*Modern Man in Search of a Soul:*110)

In the spiritual growth of the person in the second half of life is the growth and transformation of the culture. The spiritual growth and transformation of Christians will lead to the growth and transformation of Christianity.

These reflections on mid-life spirituality reflect the importance of each mid-life person's confrontation with certain archetypes or human patterns of being and relating on the way to her or his individuation or wholeness. The important mid-life confrontation with what Jung identified as the archetypes of contrasexuality (the animus, or masculine principle in women; the anima, or feminine principle in men) has not been dealt with in this work. Because of the significant developments in the culture since Jung and the magnitude of the issues involved, this area would require a separate study at least as long as this one. It is a study that we hope to undertake in a future work.

In every way this book is only a beginning. Yet, it is our hope that in the reader's participation in and dialogue with the text, and especially with the exercises that follow each chapter, this beginning will be deepened.

Bibliography

Because of the number of quotes from Jung and to familiarize the reader with the works of Jung, his works are referred to in the text by title rather than by date of publication.

Biblical quotations are from *The New American Bible,* including the Revised New Testament (New York: Catholic Book Publishing Company, 1987), except where noted JB, *Jerusalem Bible* (New York: Doubleday, 1985).

Alcoholic Anonymous World Services
1984   *Pass It On.* New York: Alcoholic Anonymous World Services.

Allman, Lawrence, R., and Dennis T. Jaffe, eds.
1977   *Readings in Adult Psychology: Contemporary Perspective.* New York: Harper and Row.

Allport, Gordon
1950   *The Individual and His Religion.* New York: Macmillan.

Barron, Mary Catherine
1981   *Unveiled Faces: Men and Women of the Bible.* Collegeville, Minn.: Liturgical Press.

Baum, Gregory
1969   *Faith and Doctrine.* New York: Paulist Press.

Becker, Ernest
1973   *The Denial of Death.* New York: Free Press.

Beesing, Maria, O.P., Robert J.
Nogosek, C.S.C., and Patrick H.
O'Leary, S.J.
1984   *The Enneagram: A Journey of Self Discovery.* Denville, N.J.: Dimension Books.

Bergant, Diane
1984   *What Are They Saying About Wisdom Literature?* New York: Paulist Press

Bianchi, Eugene C.
1982   *Aging as a Spiritual Journey.* New York: Crossroad.

1985   *On Growing Older: A Personal Guide to Life After 35.* New York: Crossroad.

Bolen, Jean Shinoda

1979   *The Tao of Psychology: Sunchronicity and the Self.* San Francisco: Harper and Row.

1984   *Goddesses in Every Woman.* San Francisco: Harper and Row.

Bolles, Richard
1972   *What Color Is Your Parachute? A Practical Manual for Job Hunters and Career Changers.* Berkeley, Calif.: Ten Speed Press.

1978   *The Three Boxes of Life and How to Get Out of Them.* Berkeley, Calif.: Ten Speed Press.

Bornkamm, Gunther
1960   *Jesus of Nazareth.* Translated by Irene and Fraser McLuskey with James M. Robinson. New York: Harper and Row.

Botwinick, Jack
1973   *Aging and Behavior.* New York: Springer.

Brennan, Anne
1980   Myth in Personal Spirituality. *Religious Education* 75 (July, Aug.): 441–51.

Brennan, Anne, and Janice Brewi
1981   Mid-Life Transition: Finding the Way. *Review for Religious* 40 (Sept., Oct.):773–79.

1983   Mid-Life Transition: A Conversion. *Review for Religious.* 42(Mar., Apr.):272–77.

1985   *Mid-Life Directions: Praying and Playing Sources of New Dynamism.* New York: Paulist Press.

1986   The Mystery of Dying and Rising in Mid-Life. *Spiritual Life* 32(Spring):26–30.

Brewi, Janice, and Anne Brennan
1982   *Mid-Life: Psychological and Sprirtual Perspectives.* New York: Crossroad.

Brown, Raymond E.
1967   *Jesus, God and Man.* Milwaukee: Bruce.

1970   *Priest and Bishop.* New York: Paulist Press.

1977   *The Birth of the Messiah: A Commentary on the Infancy Narratives in Matthew and Luke.* New York: Doubleday.

1979   *The Community of the Beloved Disciple.* New York: Paulist Press.

1984   *The Churches the Apostles Left Behind.* New York: Paulist Press.

Brown, Raymond E., Karl P. Donfried and John Reumann, eds.

1973

Peter in the New Testament. New York: Paulist Press.

Brueggemann, Walter
1977

The Bible Makes Sense. Winona, Minn: Saint Mary's Press.

1982

Praying the Psalms. Winona, Minn: Saint Mary's Press.

Bryant, Christopher
1983

Jung and the Christian Way. New York: Seabury.

Buber, Martin
1957

Eclipse of God. New York: Harper and Brothers.

Burghardt, Walter J.
1983

Seasons That Laugh or Weep. New York: Paulist Press.

Campbell, Joseph
1973

Myths to Live By. New York: Bantam.

Campbell, Joseph, ed.
1971

The Portable Jung. Translated by R. F. C. Hull. New York: Viking.

Campbell, Peter A., and Edwin M. McMahon
1985

Bio-Spirituality: Focusing as a Way to Grow. Chicago: Loyola University Press.

Canale, Andrew
1985

Understanding the Human Jesus: A Journey in Scripture and Imagination. New York: Paulist Press.

Capps, Walter H., ed.
1970

The Future of Hope. Piladelphia: Fortress.

1976

Hope Against Hope: Moltmann to Merton in One Theological Decade Philadelphia: Fortess.

Carroll, Lewis
1962   *Alice's Adventures in Wonderland.* New York: Macmillan.

Chester, Michael P., and Marie C. Norrisey
1974   *Prayer and Temperament: Different Prayer Forms For Different Personality Types.* Charlottesville, Va. Open-Door.

Clift, Wallace B.
1983   *Jung and Christianity: The Challenge of Reconciliation.* New York: Crossroad.

Clinebell, Howard J.
1977   *Growth Counseling for Mid-Years Couples.* Philadelphia: Fortress.

1979   *Growth Counseling.* Nashville: Abingdon.

Coll, Regina, C.S.J., ed.
1982   *Women and Religion: A Reader for the Clergy.* New York: Paulist Press.

Collins, Paul
1985   The Ministry of Hope. *Review for Religious* 44(Jan., Feb.):85–95.

Conn, Walter E., ed.
1978   *Conversion.* New York: Alba House.

1981   *Conscience: Development and Self-Transcendence.* Birmingham, Ala: Religious Education Press.

Davitz, Joel, and Lois Davitz
1976   *Making It from 40 to 50.* New York: Random House.

deBeauvoir, Simone
1973   *The Coming of Age.* New York: Putnam

deLaszlo, Violet, S., ed.
1958

Psyche and Symbol: A Selection of the Writings of C. G. Jung. New York: Doubleday.

deMello, Anthony, S. J.
1978

Sadhana a Way to God: Christian Exercises in Eastern Form. St. Louis: Institute of Jesuit Sources.

1985

Wellsprings: A Book of Spritual Exercises. New York: Doubleday.

DeRosa, Peter
1974

Jesus Who Became Christ. Denville, N.J.: Dimension Books.

Dodd, C. H.
1970

The Founder of Christianity. New York: Macmillan.

Donnelly, Dody H.
1984

Radical Love: An Approach to Sexual Sprituality. Minneapolis: Winston Press.

Donohugh, Donald. L., M.D.
1983

The Middle Years. New York: Berkeley.

Downing, Christine
1984

The Goddess: Mythological Images of the Feminine. New York: Crossroad.

Downs, Tom
1977

A Journey to Self Through Dialogue. Mystic, Conn.: Twenty-Third Publications.

Duffy, Joseph
1975

Patrick: In His Own Words. Dublin: Veritas Publications.

Dunne, John S.
1973

Time and Myth: A Meditation on Storytelling as an Exploration of Life and Death. Notre Dame, Ind.: University of Notre Dame Press.

1985   *The House of Wisdom.* San Francisco: Harper and Row.

Durka, Gloria, and Joanmarie Smith
1976   *Modeling God: Religious Education for Tomorrow.* New York: Paulist Press.

Dupre, Louis
1976   *Transcendent Selfhood the Rediscovery of the Inner Life.* New York: Seabury.

Durwell, F. K.
1960   *The Resurrection: A Biblical Study.* Translated by Rosemary Sheed. New York: Sheed and Ward.

Edinger, Edward F.
1968   "An Outline of Analytical Psychology." *Quadrant.* Spring, issue no. 1. Jung Foundation for Analytical Psychology.

1972   *Ego and Archetype: Individuation and the Religious Function of the Psyche.* New York: Putnam.

Edwards, Tilden
1977   *Living Simply Through the Day: Spritual Survival in a Complex Age.* New York: Paulist Press.

1982   *Sabbath Times: Understanding and Practice for Contemporary Christians.* New York: Seabury.

Eliade, Mircea
1963   *Myth and Reality.* Translated by Willard R. Trask. New York: Harper and Row.

1969   *The Quest History and Meaning in Religion.* Chicago: University of Chicago Press.

English, John
1978
    Choosing Life, Significance of Personal History in Decision Making. New York: Paulist Press.

Erikson, Erik H.
1982
    The Life Cycle Completed: A Review. New York: Norton.

Erikson, Erik H., ed.
1978
    Adulthood. New York: Norton.

Evans, Richard I.
1976
    Jung on Elementary Psychology: A Discussion between C. G. Jung and Richard I. Evans. New York: Dutton.

Fadiman, James, and Robert Frager
1976
    Personality and Personal Growth. New York: Harper and Row.

Fairchild, Roy W.
1980
    Finding Hope Again: A Pastor's Guide to Counseling Depressed Persons. San Francisco: Harper and Row.

Fisher, Kathleen R.
1983
    The Inner Rainbow: The Imagination in Christian Life. New York: Paulist Press.

Fiske, Marjorie
1979
    Middle Age: The Prime of Life. San Francisco: Harper and Row.

Fonda, Jane, with Mignon McCarthy
1984
    Women Coming of Age. New York: Simon and Schuster.

Fordham, Freida
1981
    An Introduction to Jung's Psychology. New York: Penguin.

Fowler, James
1981
Stages of Faith: The Psychology of Human Development and the Quest for Meaning. San Francisco: Harper and Row.

1984
Becoming Adult, Becoming Christian; Adult Development and Christian Faith. San Francisco: Harper and Row.

Fox, Matthew
1972
On Becoming a Musical Mystical Bear. New York: Paulist Press.

1976
Whee! We, Wee All the Way Home. . . . Wilmington: N.C.: Consortium.

1980
Breakthrough: Meister Eckhardt's Creation Spirituality in New Translation. New York: Image Books.

Freud, Sigmund
1943
A General Introduction to Psychoanalysis. Translated by Joan Riviere. New York: Garden City Publishing.

Fried, Barbara
1976
The Middle Age Crisis. New York: Harper and Row.

Fuller, Reginald H.
1971
The Formation of the Resurrection Narrative. New York: Macmillan.

Gelpi, Donald L.
1978
Experiencing God: A Theology of Human Emergence. New York: Paulist Press.

Gendlin, Eugene T.
1978
Focusing. New York: Everest House.

Gill, Jean
1982
Images of My Self. New York: Paulist Press.

276　　　　　　　　　BIBLIOGRAPHY

1985

Unless You Become Like a Little Child. New York: Paulist Press.

Gilligan, Carol
1982

In A Different Voice: Psychological Theory and Women's Development. Cambridge, Mass.: Harvard University Press.

Girzaitis, Loretta
1981

Your Life: More Radiant Than Noonday. Mystic, Conn.: Twenty-Third Publications.

Gould, Roger
1978

Transformations: Growth and Change in Adult Life. New York: Simon and Schuster.

Grant, W. Harold, Magdala
Thompson, and Thomas E.
Clarke
1983

From Image to Likeness: a Jungian Path in the Gospel Journey. New York: Paulist Press.

Greeley, Andrew
1975

Sexual Intimacy. New York: Seabury.

1977

Love and Play. New York: Seabury.

1979

Ecstacy: A Way of Knowing. Englewood Cliffs, N.J.: Prentice-Hall.

1982

Religion: A Secular Theory. New York: Free Press.

Groeschel, Benedict J.
1984

Spiritual Passages: The Psychology of Spiritual Development. New York: Crossroad.

Hall, James A., M.D.
1983

Jungian Dream Interpretation: A Handbook of Theory and Practice Toronto: Inner City Books.

Halpin, Marlene
1982   *Imagine That! Using Phantasy in Spiritual Direction.* Dubuque, Iowa: Wm. C. Brown.

Hannah, Barbara
1971   *Striving Toward Wholeness.* New York: Putnam.

1981   *Encounters with the Soul.* Boston: Sigo Press.

Happold, F. C.
1968   *The Journey Inwards.* Atlanta: John Knox.

Harding, M. Esther
1956   *Journey Into Self.* New York: David McKay.

1973   *The I and the I Not: A Study in the Development of Consciousness.* Princeton: Princeton University Press.

Hart, Ray L.
1979   *Unfinished Man and the Imagination Toward an Ontology and a Rhetoric of Revelation.* New York: Crossroad.

Hassel, David J., S. J.
1983   *Radical Prayer: Creating a Welcome for God, Ourselves, Other People and the World.* New York: Paulist Press.

Haughton, Rosemary
1967   *The Transformation of Man: A Study of Conversion and Community.* New York: Paulist Press.

1983   The Emerging Church. *The Way* 23, no. 1 (Jan.):27–39.

Hayes, Helen
1983   *A Gathering of Hope.* Philadelphia: Fortress.

278   BIBLIOGRAPHY

Heaney, John J.
1973   *Psyche and Spirit.* New York: Paulist Press.

Hillman, James
1983   *Archetypal Psychology: A Brief Account.* Dallas: Spring Publications.

Homans, Peter
1979   *Jung in Context: Modernity and the Making of a Psychology.* Chicago: University of Chicago Press.

Howells, John G., ed.
1981   *Modern Perspectives in the Psychiatry of Middle Age.* New York: Brunner, Mazel Publishers.

Hulme, William E.
1980   *Mid-Life Crisis.* Philadelphia: Westminster.

Jacobi, Jolande
1959   *Complex, Archetype Symbol in the Psychology of C. G. Jung.* Princeton: Princeton University Press.

1967   *The Way of Individuation.* Translated by R. F. C. Hull. New York: Harcourt, Brace and World.

1973   *The Psychology of C. G. Jung.* New Haven: Yale University Press.

Jacques, Elliott
1965   Death and the Mid-Life Crisis: *Journal of Psychoanalysis* 46: 502–14.

Jaffe, Aniela
1971   *The Myth of Meaning: Jung and the Expansion of Consciousness.* Translated by R. F. C. Hull. New York: Putnam.

James, William
1961   *The Varieties of Religious Experience.* New York: Collier.

Saint John of the Cross
1959

Dark Night of the Soul. Translated and Edited by E. Allison Peers. New York: Image Books.

John XXIII
1965

Journal of a Soul. Translated by Dorothy White. New York: McGraw-Hill.

Johnson, Paul E.
1945

Psychology of Religion. Nashville: Abington.

Johnson, Robert A.
1974

He: Understanding Masculine Psychology. San Francisco: Harper and Row.

1976

She: Understanding Feminine Psychology. San Francisco: Harper and Row.

1986

Inner Work: Dream Work and Active Imagination. San Francisco: Harper and Row.

Johnston, William
1978

The Inner Eye of Love. New York: Harper and Row.

1981

The Mirror Mind: Spirituality and Transformation. San Francisco: Harper and Row.

Johnston, William, ed.
1973

The Cloud of Unknowing. New York: Doubleday.

Jones, Earnest
1955

The Life and Work of Sigmund Freud. New York: Basic Books.

Jung, C. G.
1931

The Secret of the Golden Flower: A Chinese Book of Life. Translated and explained by Richard Wilhelm. London: Routledge & Kegan Paul.

1933   *Modern Man In Search of a Soul.* Translated by W. S. Dell and Cary F. Baynes. New York: Harcourt, Brace and World.

1938   *Psychology and Religion.* New Haven: Yale University Press.

1939   *The Integration of the Personality.* Translated by Stanley Dell. New York: Farrar and Rinehart.

1953a   *Psychology and Alchemy.* Translated by R. F. C. Hull. Vol. 12 of *Collected Works.* Princeton: Princeton University Press.

1953b   *Two Essays on Analytical Psychology.* Translated by R. F. C. Hull. Vol. 7 of *Collected Works.* Princeton: Princeton University Press.

1954   *The Development of Personality.* Translated by R. F. C. Hull. Vol. 17 of *Collected Works.* Princeton: Princeton University Press.

1956   *Symbols of Transformation.* Translated by R. F. C. Hull. Vol. 5 of *Collected Works.* Princeton: Princeton University Press.

1957   *The Undiscovered Self.* Translated by R. F. C. Hull. New York: New American Library.

1958a   *Psychology and Religion: West and East.* Translated by R. F. C. Hull. Vol. 11 of *Collected Works.* Princeton: Princeton University Press.

1958b   *Symbol and Psyche.* Edited by Violet de Laszlo. New York: Doubleday.

1959a   *Aion.* Translated by R. F. C. Hull. Vol. 9, Pt. 2 of *Collected Works.* Princeton: Princeton University Press.

1959b   *The Archetypes and the Collective Unconscious.* Translated by R. F. C. Hull. Vol. 9, Pt. 1 of *Collected Works.* Princeton: Princeton University Press.

1960   *The Structure and Dynamics of the Psyche.* Translated by R. F. C. Hull. Vol. 8 of *Collected Works.* Princeton: Princeton University Press.

1963   *Mysterium Coniunctionis.* Translated by R. F. C. Hull. Vol. 14 of *Collected Works.* Princeton: Princeton University Press.

1964   *Man and His Symbols.* New York: Doubleday.

1965   *Memories, Dreams, Reflections.* Edited by Aniela Jaffe. Translated by Richard and Clara Winston. New York: Vintage Books.

1968a   *Alchemical Studies.* Translated by R. F. C. Hull. Vol. 13 of *Collected Works.* Princeton: Princeton University Press.

1968b   *Analytical Psychology: Its Theory and Practice.* New York: Vintage Books.

1971   *Psychological Types.* Translated by H. G. Baynes, revised by R. F. C. Hull. Vol. 6 of *Collected Works.* Princeton: Princeton University Press.

1973   *Letters.* Vol. 1, *1906–1950.* Princeton: Princeton University Press.

1975   *Letters.* Vol. 2, *1951–1961.* Princeton: Princeton University Press.

282 BIBLIOGRAPHY

Kasemann, Ernst
1968
Jesus Means Freedom. Translated by Frank Clarke. Philadelphia: Fortress.

Kasper, Walter
1976
Jesus The Christ. London: Burns & Oates.

Keen, Sam
1977
Beginnings Without End. New York: Harper and Row.

Kelsey, Morton
1976
The Other Side of Silence: A Guide to Christian Meditation. New York: Paulist Press.

1978
Discernment a Study in Ecstasy and Evil. New York: Paulist Press.

1981
Transcend: A Guide to the Spiritual Quest. New York: Crossroad.

Kennedy, Eugene
1977
Believing. New York: Doubleday.

Kiersey, David, and Marilyn Bates
1978
Please Understand Me: An Essay on Temperament Styles. Del Mar, Calif. Prometheus Nemesis Books.

Kopp, Sheldon
1982
Mirror, Mask and Shadow. New York: Bantam.

Kosnik, Anthony, et al.
1977
Human Sexuality New Directions in American Catholic Thought. New York: Paulist Press.

Kubler-Ross, Elizabeth
1969
On Death and Dying. New York: Macmillan.

Küng, Hans
1967
The Church. Translated by Ray and Rosaleen Ockenden. New York: Sheed and Ward.

1976   *On Being a Christian.* Translated by Edward Quinn. New York: Doubleday.

1978   *The Signposts For The Future.* New York: Doubleday.

1979   *Freud and the Problem of God.* Translated by Edward Quinn. New Haven: Yale University Press.

1982   *The Church Maintained in Truth.* Translated by Edward Quinn. New York: Vintage Books.

1984   *Eternal Life? Life After Death as a Medical, Philosophical, and Theological Problem.* New York: Doubleday.

Kushner, Harold S.
1981   *When Bad Things Happen to Good People.* New York: Avon.

Kysar, Robert
1976   *John: The Maverick Gospel.* Atlanta: John Knox.

Lane, Dermot A.
1975   *The Reality of Jesus.* New York: Paulist Press.

1981   *The Experience of God.* New York: Paulist Press.

Lawler, Michael G.
1980   *Raid on the Inarticulate: An Invitation to Adult Religion.* Lanham, Md.: University Press of America.

Lawrence, Gordon
1979   *People Types and Tiger Stripes: A Practical Guide to Learning Styles.* Gainesville, Fla.: Center for Application of Psychological Type.

284   BIBLIOGRAPHY

Lee, Bernard
1974   *The Becoming of the Church.* New
                                        York: Paulist Press.

Leech, Kenneth
1977   *Soul Friend: The Practice of Chris-
                                        tian Spirituality.* San Francisco:
                                        Harper and Row.

1980   *True Prayer: An Invitation to Chris-
                                        tian Spirituality.* San Francisco:
                                        Harper and Row.

1985   *Experiencing God: Theology as Spir-
                                        ituality.* San Francisco: Harper
                                        and Row.

Leonard, George
1984   *The End of Sex: Erotic Love After the
                                        Sexual Revolution.* New York:
                                        Bantam.

Le Shan, Eda J.
1973   *The Wonderful Crisis of Middle Age.*
                                        New York: David McKay.

Levinson, Daniel J., et. al.
1978   *The Seasons of a Man's Life.* New
                                        York: Knopf.

Linn, Dennis, and Matthew
Lynn
1978   *Healing Life's Hurts: Healing Mem-
                                        ories Through the Five Stages of
                                        Forgiveness.* New York: Paulist
                                        Press.

Lockhart, Russell A.
1980   Psyche in Hiding. *Quadrant* 13,
                                        no. 1 (Spring): 76–105.

Loder, James E.
1981   *The Transforming Moment Under-
                                        standing Convictional Experiences.*
                                        San Francisco: Harper and Row.

London, Perry
1984   *The Modes and Morals of Psychol-
                                        ogy.* New York: Hemisphere.

Lonergan, Bernard
1972   *Method in Theology.* New York: Herder and Herder.

Luce, Hay Gaer
1979   *Your Second Life.* New York: Delacorte.

Luke, Helen M.
1975   *Dark Wood to White Rose: A Study of Meanings in Dante's Divine Comedy.* Pecos, N.M.: Dove Publications.

1980   *The Life of the Spirit in Women: A Jungian Approach.* Wallingford, Penn.: Pendle Hill.

1982   *The Inner Story: Myth and Symbol in the Bible and Literature.* New York: Crossroad.

1984   *The Voice Within: Love and Virtue in the Age of the Spirit.* New York: Crossroad.

Lynch, William F.
1973   *Images of Faith: An Explanation of the Ironic Imagination.* Notre Dame Ind.: University of Notre Dame Press.

1974   *Images of Hope.* Notre Dame, Ind.: University of Notre Dame Press.

Macquarrie, John
1975   *Thinking About God.* New York: Harper and Row.

1978   *Christian Hope.* New York: Seabury.

Maitland, David J.
1985   *Looking Both Ways: A Theology for Mid-Life.* Atlanta: John Knox.

Mandell, Arnold J., M.D.
1977   *Coming of Middle Age: A Journey.* New York: Summit Books.

Marsh, John
1968   *The Gospel of Saint John.* New York: Penguin.

Maslow, Abraham H.
1970   *Religion, Values and Peak-Experiences.* New York: Viking.

Masters, William, and Virginia Johnson
1970   *The Pleasure Bond.* New York: Bantam.

May, Rollo
1936   *The Art of Counseling.* Nashville: Abingdon.

1953   *Man's Search for Himself.* New York: New American Library.

1975   *The Courage to Create.* New York: Bantam.

Mayer, Nancy
1978   *The Male Mid-Life Crisis.* New York: Doubleday.

McDonnell, Thomas P., ed.
1974   *A Thomas Merton Reader.* New York: Image Books.

McGarry, Michael, B., C.S.P.
1977.   *Christology After Auschwitz.* New York: Paulist Press.

McGill, Michael E.
1980   *The 40 to 60 Year Old Male.* New York: Simon and Schuster.

McKenzie, John L.
1965   *Dictionary of the Bible.* Milwaukee: Bruce.

Meister, Eckhart
1981   *Meister Eckhart: The Essential Sermons, Commentaries, Treatises, and Defense.* Translated with Introduction by Edmund Colledge

and Bernard McGinn. New York: Paulist Press.

Merton, Thomas
1948   *The Seven Storey Mountain.* New York: Harcourt, Brace.

1953   *The Sign of Jonas.* New York: Harcourt, Brace.

Michael, Chester P., and Marie C. Norrisey
1984   *Prayer and Temperament Different Prayer Forms for Different Personality Types.* Charlottesville, Va.: Open-Door.

Miller, William A.
1973   *Why Do Christians Break Down?* Minneapolis: Augsburg.

1981   *Make Friends With Your Shadow.* Minneapolis: Augsburg.

Mott, Michael
1984   *The Seven Mountains of Thomas Merton.* Boston: Houghton Mifflin.

Moulton, H. K.
1972   *John, Johannine Epistles, and Revelation.* Denville, N.J.: Dimension Books.

Murphy, Sheila M.
1983   *Midlife Wanderer: The Woman Religious in Midlife Transition.* Whitinsville, Mass: Affirmation Books.

Myers, Isabel Briggs, and Mary H. McCaulley
1985   *A Guide to the Development and Use of the Myers-Briggs Type Indicator.* Palo Alto, Calif.: Consulting Psychologist Press.

Myers, Isabel Briggs and Peter
B. Myers
1980   *Gifts Differing.* Palo Alto, Calif.: Consulting Psychologist Press.

Navone, John
1977   *Toward a Theology of Story.* Slough, England: Saint Paul Publications.

1985   Christian Conversion: Suffering Out of Love. *Review for Religious.* 44(Jan., Feb.):33–38.

Neugarten, Bernice
1968   *Middle Age and Aging.* Chicago: University of Chicago Press.

Neumann, Eric H.
1969   *Depth Psychology and a New Ethic.* Translated by Eugene Rolfe. New York: Putnam.

1970   *The Origins and History of Consciousness.* Translated by R. F. C. Hull. Princeton: Princeton University Press.

1973   *The Child.* New York: Putnam.

Oates, Wayne
1976   *Pastoral Care and Counseling in Grief and Separation.* Philadelphia: Fortress.

O'Collins, Gerald
1978   *The Second Journey.* New York: Paulist Press.

Olson, Richard P.
1980   *Mid-Life, A Time to Discover A Time to Decide: A Christian Perspective on Middle Age.* Valley Forge, Pa.: Judson Press.

Ornstein, Robert E.
1972   *The Psychology of Consciousness.* New York: Penguin.

Otto, Rudolf
1923

The Idea of the Holy. Translated by John W. Harvey. London: Oxford University Press.

Padovano, Anthony Q.
1984

The Human Journey: Thomas Merton Symbol of a Century. New York: Image Books.

Peck, M. Scott, M.D.
1978

The Road Less Traveled: A New Psychology of Love, Traditional Values and Spiritual Growth. New York: Simon and Schuster.

Powell, John, S.J.
1976

Fully Human, Fully Alive. Niles, Ill.: Argus Communications.

1984

The Christian Vision: The Truth That Sets Us Free. Allen, Tex.: Argus Communications.

Powell, John, and Loretta Brady
1985

Will The Real Me Please Stand Up? Allen, Tex.: Texas: Argus Communications.

Progoff, Ira
1963

The Symbolic and the Real. New York: McGraw-Hill.

1973a

Depth Psychology and Modern Man. New York: Doubleday.

1973b

Jung, Synchronicity, and Human Destiny. New York: Dell.

1975

At a Journal Workshop. New York: Dialogue House.

1977

The Well and the Cathedral. New York: Dialogue House.

1980

The Practice of Process Meditation, The Intensive Journal Way for Spiritual Experience. New York: Dialogue House.

1983   *Life-Study: Experiencing Creative Lives by the Intensive Journal Method.* New York: Dialogue House.

Rahner, Karl
1978   *Foundations of Christian Faith.* Translated by William V. Dyck. New York: Seabury.

Raines, Robert A.
1978   *Going Home.* San Francisco: Harper and Row.

Reumann, John
1968   *Jesus in the Church's Gospels.* Philadelphia: Fortress.

Sanford, John A.
1970   *The Kingdom Within.* New York: Lippincott.

1974   *The Man Who Wrestled with God: Light from the Old Testament on the Psychology of Individuation.* New York: Paulist Press.

1978   *Dreams and Healing: A Succinct and Lively Interpretation of Dreams.* New York: Paulist Press.

1980   *The Invisible Partners.* New York: Paulist Press.

1981   *Evil: the Shadow Side of Reality.* New York: Crossroad.

1982   *Between People: Communicating One-to-One.* New York: Paulist Press.

1985   *King Saul, The Tragic Hero: A Study in Individuation.* New York: Paulist Press.

Savary, Louis M., and Patricia H. Berne
1980   *Prayerways.* San Francisco: Harper and Row.

Savary, Louis M., Patricia H.
Berne, and Williams Stephan
Kaplan
1984

Dreams and Spiritual Growth: A Christian Approach to Dreamwork. New York: Paulist Press.

Savary, Louis, and Margaret
Ehlen-Miller
1979

Mindways: A Guide for Exploring Your Mind. New York: Harper and Row.

Scarf, Maggie
1980

Unfinished Business. New York: Doubleday.

Schillebeeckx, Edward
1969

God and Man. Translated by Edward Fitzgerald and Peter Tomlinson. New York: Sheed and Ward.

1979

Jesus: An Experiment in Christology. Translated by Hubert Hoskins. New York: Seabury.

Schoonenberg, Piet, S.J.
1965

Man and Sin. Translated by Joseph Donceel, S.J. Notre Dame, Ind.: University of Notre Dame Press.

Schultz, Duane
1976

Theories of Personality. Monterey, Calif.: Brooks/Cole.

Schultz, Hans Jurden, ed.
1971

Jesus in His Time. Translated by Brian Watchorn. Philadelphia: Fortress.

Segundo, Juan Luis, S.J.
1973

Grace And the Human Condition. Translated by John Drury. Maryknoll, N.Y.: Orbis.

1974

The Sacraments Today. Maryknoll, N.Y.: Orbis.

Senior, Donald
1975

Jesus: A Gospel Portrait. Cincinatti: Pflaum Standard.

Serbin, David
1984

In Conversation with Joseph B. Wheelwright. *Psychological Perspectives* 15:149–67.

Shea, John
1978

Stories of God: An Unauthorized Biography. Chicago: Thomas More Press.

1983

An Experience Named Spirit. Chicago: Thomas More Press.

Sheehy, Gail
1976

Passages. New York: Dutton.

1981

Pathfinders: Overcoming the Crisis of Adult Life and Finding Your Own Path to Well-Being. New York: William Morrow.

Singer, June
1972

Boundaries of the Soul. New York: Doubleday.

1976

Androgyny: Toward a New Theory of Sexuality. New York: Doubleday.

Spencer, Anita
1982

Seasons: Women's Search for Self Through Life's Stages. New York: Paulist Press.

Staude-John, Raphael
1981

The Adult Development of C. G. Jung. Boston: Routledge & Kegan Paul.

Stein, Murray
1983

In Mid-Life: A Jungian Perspective. Dallas: Spring Publications.

1985   *Jung's Treatment of Christianity.* Wilmette, Ill.: Chiron.

Steindl-Rast, David, Br.
1984   *Gratefulness, the Heart of Prayer.* New York: Paulist Press.

Stevens, Anthony
1983   *Archetypes: A Natural History of the Self.* New York: Quill.

Studzinski, Raymond, O.S.B.
1985   *Spiritual Direction and Mid-Life Development.* Chicago: Loyola University Press.

Taylor, Jeremy
1983   *Dream Work: Techniques for Discovering the Creative Power in Dreams.* New York: Paulist Press.

Teilhard de Chardin, Pierre
1960   *The Divine Milieu.* New York: Harper and Row.

Tillich, Paul
1952   *The Courage to Be.* New Haven: Yale University Press.

1957   *Dynamics of Faith.* New York: Harper and Row.

Tournier, Paul
1976   *The Season of Life.* Translated by John S. Gilmour. Atlanta, Ga.: John Knox.

Tracy, David
1979   *Blessed Rage for Order: A New Pluralism in Theology.* New York: Crossroad.

Ulanov, Ann Belford
1971   *The Feminine in Jungian Psychology and in Christian Theology.* Evanston, Ill.: Northwestern University Press.

1981 | *Receiving Woman: Studies in the Psychology and Theology of the Feminine.* Philadelphia: Westminster.

1985 | A Shared Space. *Quadrant* 18, no. 1 (Spring):65–80.

Ulanov, Ann and Barry
1975 | *Religion and the Unconscious.* Philadelphia: Westminster.

1982 | *Primary Speech: A Psychology of Prayer.* Philadelphia: John Knox.

United Church of Christ Board for Homeland Ministries
1977 | *Human Sexuality A Preliminary Study.* New York: United Church Press.

Van Kaam, Adrian
1979 | *The Transcendant Self.* Denville, N.J.: Dimension Books.

Vaughan, Frances E.
1979 | *Awakening Intuition.* New York: Anchor Books.

Vawter, Bruce
1973 | *This Man Jesus: An Essay Toward a New Testament Christology.* New York: Doubleday.

1983 | *Job and Jonah: Questioning the Hidden God.* New York: Paulist Press.

Viorst, Judith
1973 | *How Did I Get to Be 40 and Other Atrocities.* New York: Simon and Schuster.

Von Franz, Marie-Louise
1974 | *Shadow and Evil in Fairy Tales.* New York: Spring Publications.

1975 | *C. G. Jung: His Myth In Our Time.* Translated by William H. Kennedy. New York: Putnam.

1978a
Interpretation of Fairytales: An Introduction to the Psychology of Fairytales. Dallas: Spring Publications.

1978b
Time: Rhythm and Repose. New York: Thames and Hudson.

Von Franz, Marie-Louise, and James Hillman
1971
Lecture on Jung's Typology. Zurich: Spring Publications.

Welch, John, O. Carm.
1982
Spiritual Pilgrims: Carl Jung and Teresa of Avila. New York: Paulist Press.

Westman, Heinz
1983
The Structure of Biblical Myths: The Ontogenesis of the Psyche. Dallas: Spring Publications.

Wheelwright, Jane H.
1978
Women and Men. San Francisco: C. G. Jung Institute of San Francisco.

1984
For Women Growing Older: The Animus. Houston: The C. G. Jung Educational Center.

Wheelwright, Joseph B., ed.
1968
The Reality of the Psyche. New York: Putnam.

White, Victor
1952
God and the Unconscious. Cleveland: World Publishing.

1960
Soul and Psyche: An Enquiry into the Relationship of Psychology and Religion. London: Collins.

Whitehead, Evelyn, and James D. Whitehead
1979
Christian Life Patterns: The Psychological Challenges and Religious

Invitation of Adult Life. New York: Doubleday.

1984   *Seasons of Strength: New Visions of Adult Christian Maturing.* New York: Doubleday.

Whitman, Walt
1975   *Walt Whitman: The Complete Poems.* Edited by Francis Murphy. New York: Penguin.

Whitmont, Edward C.
1969   *The Symbolic Quest.* Princeton: Princeton University Press.

Williams, Stephan Kaplan
1980   *Jungian-Senoi Dreamwork Manual.* Berkeley, Calif: Journey Press.

Wink, Walter
1980   *Transforming Bible Study.* Nashville: Abingdon.

Wolff, Toni
1956   "Structural Forms of the Feminine Psyche." Zurich: privately printed.

Woods, Richard, ed.
1980   *Understanding Mysticism.* New York: Doubleday.

Zullo, James R.
1982   The Crisis of Limits: Midlife Beginnings. *Human Development.* 3(Spring): 6–14.